Michael Waddle

POLYGAMY RECONSIDERED

African plural marriage
and the Christian Churches

Eugene Hillman, C.S.SP.

ORBIS BOOKS
Maryknoll, New York

ACKNOWLEDGMENTS

*For the help and encouragement given by each of
them, during the preparation of this work, an expression
of gratitude is due to Hans Hoekendijk and Roger Shinn
of Union Theological Seminary in New York, to Jean-Guy
LeMarier of St. Paul University in Ottawa, and to
Bernard Häring of the Academia Alfonsiana in Rome.*

Copyright © 1975 ORBIS BOOKS, Maryknoll, New York 10545

Library of Congress Catalog Card Number: 74-19967

ISBN: 0-88344-391-0

Printed in the United States of America

CONTENTS

Foreword   v

Preface   ix

Introduction   3

I. The Problem in Historical Perspective   17

II. Culture and Christianity   47

III. The Occurrence of Polygamy   87

IV. Polygamy in Society   109

V. Polygamy and the Bible   139

VI. The Reasoning of Theologians   179

Appendix: Polygamy and the Council
    of Trent   217

Bibliography   241

Index   261

ABBREVIATIONS

AG   *Ad gentes.* Vatican II. Decree on the Missionary Activity of the Church, December 7, 1965.

CT   *Concilium Tridentinum: Diariorum, Actorum, Epistolarum, Tractatum Nova Collectio,* ed. Societas Goerresiana. Freiburg: Herder, 1901.

GS   *Gaudium et spes. Vatican II.* Pastoral Constitution on the Church in the Modern World, December 7, 1965.

LG   *Lumen gentium.* Vatican II. Dogmatic Constitution on the Church, November 21, 1964.

PL   *Patrologia latina,* ed. J.P. Migne. Paris, 1844.

UR   *Unitatis redintegratio.* Vatican II. Decree on Ecumenism, November 21, 1964.

Citations from conciliar documents are taken from Walter M. Abbott, S.J., ed. *The Documents of Vatican II* (New York, Guild-America-Association, 1966).

FOREWORD

Pluralism of expression in theology and in liturgy is generally accepted in the Church today. Pluralism, when it is extended to moral problems of basic relevance, is apt to yield some acutely disturbing questions. The faith of Christians in one God and one Redeemer, who has opened the way of salvation for all men, provides a great unity in the most fundamental orientations of human life. This unity must not be jeopardized. So there are limits to pluralism in the realm of Christian morality.

Christians have commonly considered both indissolubility and monogamy to be basic expressions of the sacramentality of marriage. The equality of man and woman before God, the liberation from attitudes of dominance by one partner over another, and the vocation to signify in Christian marriage the indissoluble covenant between Christ and his Church, all point in this direction. By strenuously promoting fidelity to the ideal of indissoluble and monogamous marriage, the Church has surely contributed to the growth of mankind's moral energy. None of this, however, has hindered the development of an evident pluralism in the pastoral approaches to marriage problems in the West and in the East.

The Latin Church has tried to help those whose first marriage had failed. A solution was sought by carefully scrutinizing the quality of the first bond to see whether it was not truly invalid from its very inception. The Eastern Churches, while first doing everything possible to save an existing marriage, took a very different approach once the marriage was hopelessly destroyed, provided there was no reasonable hope of the partners living as celibates. The solution was not sought in a retrospective legal examination but in a compassionate *oikonomia:* a pastoral choice of the lesser evil, which was at the same time seen as the best possible choice under the circumstances. This kind of pluralism, as the Council of Florence acknowledged in 1438, does not contradict the unity of faith, nor does it hinder the reunion of separated Christian Churches.

Should not the same kind of pluralism be generally acceptable, or even more acceptable, with respect to the problem of achieving the ideal of monogamy? Our traditional theology usually assumed that all the biblical texts against divorce could be used also as proof-texts against any toleration of polygamy. But this way of theologizing produces a moral short-circuit when Western Christians demand, as a condition for baptism, that a polygamist of another culture, although previously married in good faith, should divorce one or more of his wives. Such an insistence on monogamy works against the stability of marriage, against the concept of fidelity, and against the most vital covenants established between families and clans in societies which normally expect their leading and most respected members to be the heads of polygamous households. In such a cultural context, divorce, for no reason other than a man's wish to be baptized, can be as much a social shock as the introduction of an arbitrary divorce law in some Western cultures.

What sort of public image of the Christian God is projected by this application of moral principles in societies which traditionally regard polygamy as a preferential form of marriage? Is the proclamation of the gospel supposed to threaten family stability, disrupt social covenants, and even separate mothers from their children? Where, in this approach, is the patient pedagogy of Yahweh, the God of the Old Testament, who is the Father of our Lord Jesus Christ? Is it not possible, at the very least, for the Church to permit the baptism of a holy polygamist and his wives, if the gospel has reached them in this situation? Did not the Jewish levirate marriage in the time of Jesus amount to a form of compulsory polygamy, and is this not still a normal practice in the Coptic Church of Ethiopia?

These questions, and many others, are being asked today, especially in parts of Africa where the gospel is presented to peoples for whom polygamy is a socially approved, honored, and preferential system with deep cultural roots. These questions involve the credibility of the Church's evangelizing mission which has been, and still is, all too frequently encumbered by rigid conditions that are far from the spirit of the gospel and far from the missionary spirit of the Church in the first eight centuries.

Eugene Hillman has not created new problems for us. He has simply articulated for us some very urgent problems which he himself witnessed during his many years of service in East Africa. The very same problems were presented to me repeatedly during the past few years when I gave some forty courses and numerous lectures to the missionary and pastoral servants of the Church in fourteen different African countries. Now all of us owe a debt of gratitude to Father Hillman for his careful research on this topic and for his courage in putting all of this together in such a clear and challenging book. We may agree or disagree with him in many details, or even in his overall perspective; but we cannot simply dismiss his efforts and his proposals. Indeed, he deserves our careful attention.

There is no suggestion here that polygamy should be introduced into the Western world. What is posed, however, is a fundamental question of conscience for Western Christians: whether we are not guilty of unethical colonialism if we refuse now to make a serious effort to distinguish between abiding orientations of life and culturally conditioned applications, between normative ideals and pastoral or pedagogical approaches.

I personally read Father Hillman's study in the light of the message of Bethlehem: "Peace on earth to all men of good will." So I ask myself whether our way of proposing, and eventually imposing, our norms on the peoples of totally different cultures does not contradict our basic message. We ourselves can live in hope and abound in peace only because the morality of the gospel allows us adequate time for growth and for conversion. We must manifest our gratitude for God's enduring patience with us. We can do this by learning to be more patient with the different ways of other peoples and by allowing them also the time required for the leaven of the gospel to become gradually more active within their varied cultures. If we truly convey to them the gospel of salvation, and they accept it with joy, not hampered by any legalism, the dynamism of the faith will produce an infinitely greater harvest than what might be produced through the abrupt imposition of all our rules and regulations. Besides, it is no longer possible today for people in certain cultural situations to accept, with a sincere conscience, such impositions—even though it may be foreseen that the faith will eventually lead them in the same direction intended by our rules and regulations.

Bernard Häring, C.Ss.R.

PREFACE

While it may not be possible in six chapters and one appendix to say everything that could, or perhaps should, be said on the topic of polygamy and Christianity in Africa, the following pages are nevertheless presented with the conviction that any serious theological discussion of the topic must take account of the data, the considerations, and the questions offered here. As a way of organizing a vast amount of material, the chapters are grouped under three general categories: historical, anthropological, and biblical-theological.

The general principles and method used in this study are outlined in the Introduction. Here also—to avoid any misunderstanding from the very start—the precise meaning of African polygamy is explained and distinguished from other forms of plural marriage and mating.

The missionary and pastoral problem of African polygamy is presented historically in Chapter 1. This brief historical overview, without pretending to be exhaustive, should suffice to show how and where this particular problem fits into the more general history of Christian marriage. With a view to situating the problem in its much wider human context, as one of many similar problems arising from mankind's cultural diversity and the Church's unifying significance, Chapter 2 proffers some wide-ranging reflections on the perennial tension between culture and Christianity. It is here that some fundamental questions are raised concerning the cultural presuppositions and attitudes which have profoundly influenced the whole Western Christian approach to the peoples of the much larger world elsewhere.

The relevant demographic and anthropological aspects of African polygamy are treated in Chapters 3 and 4. An effort is made in this section to see the extent to which polygamy is still practiced in sub-Saharan Africa, to ascertain what the prevailing attitude is today with regard to this custom, and to reach some understanding of polygamy's social significance in terms of African social structures and cultural values.

In Chapter 5 the biblical texts, which are usually used in support of the traditional position, are reexamined; and their traditional interpretation is questioned. The theological rationale of the traditional position is critically examined in Chapter 6, and some different theological opinions are presented. Here also a new solution is proposed for deliberation by the appropriate Church leaders; and another, more radical, solution is suggested for further consideration by competent theologians.

Finally, an Appendix focuses upon one particular period of European history for the benefit of those who might still argue, with Denzinger in hand, that all questions concerning polygamy and Christianity (in its Roman Catholic version) were settled once and for all by the Council of Trent.

POLYGAMY RECONSIDERED

INTRODUCTION

"Experience shows that, because of circumstances, it is some-times difficult to harmonize culture with Christian teaching" (GS 62). This one sentence might well be regarded, at least by those who serve the Church in non-Western world, as the most notable understatement of the Vatican Council II. For all its bare simplic-ity, however, this sentence really contains the major challenge facing Christian churchmen and theologians everywhere in the world today. The missionary and pastoral problem of customary plural marriage in sub-Saharan Africa is merely one of many similar problems embraced by this central question: How is Western Christendom's traditional understanding and practice of the faith to be reconciled harmoniously with an entirely new awareness of the intrinsic value and validity of the diverse human cultures through which Christianity is supposed to become in-carnate, contemporary, relevant, and catholic?

GUIDING PRINCIPLES

Here again is the perennial question of Christianity's cultural catholicity. This issue was first raised, and settled in principle, at the Jerusalem meeting of "the apostles and elders" in the year 49 A.D. (cf. Acts 15:1–30; Gal. 2:1–10). Just as the peoples of the world need the sign of a servant savior who does not quench the wick already burning among them (cf. Isa. 43:3; Matt. 5:17), so also the Church—for the fulfillment of her catholic vocation —needs the cultural "riches of the nations" and the "hidden wealth of the peoples" (cf. Isa. 10:13–14; 45:3,14; 60:3–16). This "wonderful exchange," as the fathers of Vatican II expressed it, is to be accomplished "in imitation of the plan of the Incarnation" (AG 22; cf. LG 13). Hence the Church is not constitutionally bound to the limited world view, the ephemeral forms and ethnic conventions, the local laws, customs, and practices of any particular segment of humanity. In the words of Vatican II:

> The Church, sent to all peoples of every time and place, is not bound exclusively and indissolubly to any race or nation, nor to any particular way of life or customary pattern of living, ancient or recent. Faithful to her own tradition and at the same time conscious of her universal mission, she can enter into communion with various cultural modes, to her own enrichment and theirs too (GS 58; see also LG 17 and AG 21).

So it is, also, that missionaries are bound always and everywhere to take a positive, respectful, and sympathetic approach to the ways of the peoples to whom they are sent. This guiding principle, often repeated in the official missionary directives of the Roman Catholic Church, is succinctly set forth by Albert Perbal, paraphrasing the words of Pope Pius XII:

> Native custom has the privilege of "*melior condicio possidentis.*" Before in effect decreeing the eventual suppression of a custom, the missionary must prove that it is indissolubly linked with error or immorality or absurb superstition. Insofar as this proof is not conclusive, the custom holds. It has the force of law. It possesses legal right.[1]

However, as every missionary knows, it is one thing for ecclesiastical functionaries to verbalize the principle of cultural catholicity and it is quite another thing for them to permit its application in the real world. Indeed, the practical application of his principle has been a matter of debate ever since that day in Antioch when Paul withstood Cephas to his face (cf. Gal. 2:11). As a result of the Church's missionary encounter with one new people after another during the past nineteen hundred years, the same debate, in countless different historical contexts, has been an ever recurring source of anguish, of schism, and even of renewal. But each generation of Christians must face, in its own time and place, the same central question: How are we to harmonize culture and Christianity?

Far from undermining the faith and practice of the Church, it is now widely recognized that the very difficulties presented by this question can, as the fathers of Vatican II tell us, "stimulate the mind to a more accurate and penetrating grasp of the faith" (GS 62). And this, after all, is what the whole theological enterprise is seeking: "a more accurate and penetrating grasp of the faith." As "recent studies and findings raise new questions which influence life and demand new theological investigations," it becomes both appropriate and necessary to make use "not only of theological principles, but also of the findings of the secular sciences" (GS 62). In view of the Church's universal mission and her need to be fully at home among all peoples, the Council fathers offered the following clear directives:

> Theological investigation must necessarily be stirred up in each major socio-cultural area . . . In this way, under the light of the tradition of the universal Church, a fresh scrutiny will be brought to bear on the deeds and words which God has made known, which have been consigned to sacred Scripture, and which have been unfolded by the Church Fathers and the teaching authority of the Church.
>
> Thus it will be more clearly seen in what ways faith can seek for understanding in the philosophy and wisdom of these peoples. A better view will be gained of how their customs, outlook on life, and social order can be reconciled with the manner of living taught by divine revelation. As a result, avenues will be opened for a more profound adaptation in the whole area of Christian life (AG 22).

What is envisaged by the Council is obviously much more than an intellectual exercise for theologians. What is expected is that the way should be opened for "a more profound adaptation of the whole area of Christian life," not only in the outward practices of religion and ecclesiastical organization, but also in the realm of "morality and doctrine" (GS 62). Even in this realm the pilgrim Church is summoned "to that continual reformation of which she always has need, in so far as she is an institution of men here on earth" (UR 6). So another guiding principle is provided by Vatican II:

> Therefore, if the influence of events or of the times has led to deficiencies in conduct, in Church discipline, or even in the formulation of doctrine (which must be carefully distinguished from the

deposit itself of faith), these should be appropriately rectified at the proper moment (UR 6).

It is in this spirit of Vatican II, and with this understanding of theological inquiry, that the following pages are offered as an evaluation of the traditional Christian approach to the socio-economic and culturally integrated institution of plural marriage in Africa south of the Sahara.

AIM AND METHOD

In his earlier writings on marriage, Bernard Häring simply and uncritically repeated the usual arguments in support of the traditional ecclesiastical discipline respecting customary polygamy in a missionary situation.[2] After an extensive visit to the Christian communities of Africa, however, he has since come to express some serious reservations about the adequacy of the traditional position. Now Häring asks this question: "Have the moral theologians really made a serious attempt to distinguish in marriage ethics and marriage law the specifically Christian elements from those elements which were more or less a successful accommodation to European culture?"[3] Bishops and priests, both local and foreign in various parts of Africa, have reproached theologians "for their failure to pay sufficient attention to the question of evangelizing polygamous peoples and for providing ready-made answers before they had really studied the situation."[4] Thus, according to Häring, "the urgent question for the moralists is not whether they can offer a ready-made solution," but "whether they have ever really seriously thought about this and other similar questions which are of such decisive importance in many missionary situations."[5]

Häring is not the only one to have recently recognized the need for a fresh examination of this whole polygamy problem. Josef Fuchs is also among those who have given a sympathetic hearing to the question being asked more and more frequently these days by missionaries and pastors in Africa. "Their question," as Fuchs understands it, "is whether perhaps the marriage institution we [in the Western world] have discovered belongs in fact only to our given culture," and is not therefore consonant with the conception and the realities of marriage elsewhere.[6] "To raise the question," says John L. McKenzie "does not imply an encouragement of polygamy."[7] For McKenzie, after his visit to parts of Africa, the basic question is "whether we made a cultural change a condition of faith and baptism." He, therefore, requests "simply that moral theologians examine the question anew without prejudice and with some attention to the study of culture."[8] It is just such an examination that is undertaken in the following chapters.

The aim of the present study is to fully set forth this polygamy question in all of its anthropological and theological dimensions, and thus to provide a sound basis for discussing anew the problem of missionary evangelization and pastoral care in areas where simultaneous polygamy is both an immemorial custom and a contemporary reality. If the traditional ecclesiastical discipline were entirely compatible with all the demands of Christian love and justice, if it were quite adequate from the viewpoint of modern anthropology, and if it were obviously based on sound biblical exegesis and compelling theological reasons, there would of course be no need for an inquiry of this kind. However, the anthropological perspectives of the European Middle Ages are just no longer adequate, nor are the exegetical methods and the theological arguments of Pope Innocent III. A "fresh scrutiny" is long overdue.

Theology, because it is the work of men at a particular time in history and within limited cultural horizons, is always dated and never entirely free of ethnocentrism. Medieval scholasticism, with its passion for objective knowledge in the form of abstract principles, and with its emphasis on perfect certitude in the form of propostions deduced from general principles, was particularly wanting in historical and cultural consciousness.[9] The limitations imposed by time and place were not sufficiently appreciated. The tendency, therefore, was for theologians to read a text or comprehend a fact only within the historico-cultural perspective of the European Middle Ages. Little account was taken of the perspective within which the given text or fact was historically and culturally embedded, while less thought was given to the possibility that the human experience at some later period and in some other part of the world might be vastly different from what was known and defined in the Middle Ages. According to Yves Congar, "the absence of a historic sense many times has pushed the medieval Masters into interpreting the terms and statements of the Bible not as part of the Bible itself but as ideas of their time and their milieu or again as theoretic ideas sometimes foreign to the literal and historic sense of the text."[10]

So, in the present study it is not assumed *a priori* that the traditional Christian position regarding African polygamy is so firmly established that theologians today can do no more than repeat exactly what was said the last time this matter came up for discussion. Nor is it simply taken for granted that the traditional approach to this question is the only possible way of reaching a correct understanding and a right judgment. In the past, emphasis has been placed upon logical inferences made from abstract ethical norms and from supporting biblical texts. Much more attention is here given to information that was not available to theologians and churchmen in the past, to viewpoints that were generally inaccessible to them, and to questions that seldom arose among them. Indeed, the present study does not even start off by presenting the traditional position with its numerous supporting arguments taken from the Bible, the Fathers of the Church, the theologians, and the magisterium. To repeat all of this once again would be superfluous, especially as each aspect of the traditional position will be duly considered in the course of the present inquiry. Moreover, the traditional positon is already very well known; it is fully presented and amply defended, with practically no variations, in almost any manual of moral theology or canon law, or in any comprehensive work on Christian marriage.[11]

An increasing number of Christian scholars today recognize with Josef Fuchs that "moral questions will not be solved by logical inferences but by insight and understanding."[12] Much more emphasis must now be placed upon man himself in the complexity, diversity, mutability, and ambiguity of his historico-cultural experience. If varied estimations of the man-woman relationship are reflected in the different and changing conditions of mankind, then "different principles have to be applied," as Fuchs says.[13] For human nature is not a fixed philosophical abstraction but an historically living reality that is real only in this or that concrete socio-cultural situation, in this or that particular period of time. Christian solutions to moral problems are not reached simply by imposing in a cold and impersonal manner what Fuchs calls "pre-printed principles," but rather by looking at "the complete concrete reality in all its living proportions and Christian humanness."[14] While abstract norms of human conduct are indeed very helpful, they are also apt to yield erroneous judgments when they are used without sufficient regard for the way human nature actually exists. However, as Daniel Maguire points out, the historical understanding of human nature and of moral experience, although insufficiently emphasized in the past, was not entirely overlooked:

> Clearly Thomas [Aquinas] does not support the attempt to do ethics by the deductive use of principles conceived as static derivatives of an immutable nature . . . Almost anticipating the modern realization of the difficulty of teaching morality transculturally, Thomas wrote that law is not everywhere the same, "because of the mutability of the nature of man and the diverse conditions of men and of things, according to the diversity of places and of times" (De Malo, 2, 4, and 13).[15]

In accord, therefore, with a "more historically conscious methodology,"[16] the present inquiry takes as its point of departure the human phenomenon itself of customary polygamy, as it occurs in the real world of moral experience, as it is understood by anthropologists, and as it is observed by perceptive missionaries and local pastors. The human reality itself of this kind of marriage—not the parody of it that is found in some textbooks of moral theology and canon law—must first be appreciated for the meaning and value it has in its own historico-cultural context before it can be properly evaluated in the light of Christian revelation; moreover, this revelation itself must be carefully distinguished from its historically and culturally conditioned interpretations.[17]

By way of evaluation some questions must necessarily be raised regarding the traditional position, and some doubt, at least, may be cast upon the authenticity, validity, and correctness of the various answers already given by the Christian Churches to the perplexing questions raised by customary plural marriage in Africa. Some proposals also will be made with a view to finding a more fully Christian solution to the problem under discussion: a solution, that is, which is more apt in the here and now to promote human dignity, love, and justice because it is more in accord with what man really is, with all of his bodily and social implications.[18]

Nevertheless, the aim here is not immediately to answer all or any of the practical missionary and pastoral questions that necessarily arise from the encounter of Christianity with polygamy in its real-life context. The aim—to put it very briefly—is to show both the urgency and the possibility of fully reconsidering this whole matter in the light of contemporary anthropology, biblical exegesis, and theological reflection. If some "deficiencies in Church discipline or even in the formulation of doctrine" (UR 6), should become manifest through this evaluation, or as a result of further studies that might eventually be undertaken along the lines indicated here, then it would be for the appropriate ecclesiastical authorities to modify the Church discipline and reformulate the doctrine. This, after all, is a course of action proposed by the fathers of Vatican II.

AFRICAN POLYGAMY

Plural marriage, or polygamy, is found throughout the world in a variety of forms that are culturally determined. The familiar form among Western peoples is *consecutive* polygamy: one spouse after another in a sequence involving divorce and remarriage. What this amounts to is a kind of serial monogamy: one spouse engaged consecutively in discrete monogamous unions. This is called consecutive polygyny when a man has one wife after another, or consecutive polyandry when a woman has one husband after another. Elsewhere in the world plural marriage usually means *simultaneous* (or contemporaneous) polygamy: more than one spouse at the same time. This is called simultaneous polygyny when a man has more than one wife at the same time, or simultaneous polyandry when a woman has more than one husband at the same time.

Most anthropologists would surely agree with Bronislaw Malinowski that every real marriage, whether monogamous or polygamous, is "based on an individual legal contract between one man and one woman, though these contracts may be repeated."[19] Marriage would, moreover, be almost universally understood in connection with the legitimacy of children; and it would be generally regarded as a means of providing that "no child should be brought into the world without a man—and one man at that—assuming the role of sociological father, that is, guardian and protector, the male link with the child and the rest of the community."[20] The so-called "group marriage," mentioned by some of the early anthropologists, really does not exist as an authentic form of marriage in any known society.[21] Concubinage is another arrangement which does not involve marriage and so should not be confused with polygamy in any of its forms. In other words, plural mating, a custom found in many different forms throughout the world, should not be confused with plural marriage. "Sexual," as Malinowski reminds us, "is not synonymous with conjugal."[22]

Plural marriage in Africa almost always means that a man has more than one wife at the same time; and it is a matter of some importance to note that this form of plural marriage, unlike consecutive polygamy, does not alsways and necessarily imply divorce and remarriage. So there is a profound sociological and moral difference between the types of plural marriage found in Africa and in the Western world. In popular usage, moreover, the words *polygamy* and *polygyny* tend to be interchangeable with reference to the African system of plural marriage. Thus, in speaking of polygamy or polygyny throughout this study, what we have in mind always is a culturally determined, socially accepted, and legally recognized form of permanent marriage in which a husband may have more than one wife at the same time. Following popular usage, the term *polygamy* will be generally used, although the word *polygyny* will be employed wherever it may seem helpful for the sake of clarity.

Polygamy is a widely recognized and socially valid form of marriage in many regions of the world: for example, in parts of India, New Guinea, Papua, Indonesia, and, of course, in most of the Islamic world. But the precise focus of attention in the present study is upon sub-Saharan Africa; for it is in this vast region that polygamy is socially accepted among most of the peoples; a sufficient amount of data is available on the subject; and many African Christians are now asking some searching questions about the negative attitude of their churches toward this traditional African conception of marriage. In some areas of Africa, moreover, the practice of polygamy has given rise to missionary and pastoral problems which churchmen and theologians can no longer ignore with impunity. Nevertheless, it may be found that the reflections presented here have also some relevance for those who are faced with missionary or pastoral problems arising from the various forms of plural marriage in other parts of the world.

At the present time simultaneous polygyny may be regarded as a problem peculiar to parts of the non-Western world. It is not fantastic, however, to suppose that in the future this could also become an acute problem among Western peoples. Considering their traditional methods of settling international disputes and the sinister potentials of modern warfare (nuclear, biological, chemical), it is quite conceivable that these genicidal techniques, failing to achieve a "final solution," could produce so drastic an imbalance among the sexes that plural marriage would become a necessary means of survival for this or that particular people in the West.[23] Then, contrary to previous custom and law, an overriding natural and moral inclination might arise in favor of polygamy. In such a situation, we may be sure, theologians and church leaders would quickly enough produce weighty reasons and biblical texts to justify a new conception of marriage among their own people. How weighty must the reasons be? How many biblical texts are needed? Indeed, it might even be asked just how much of our moral theologizing ever really goes beyond the rationalization of the accepted behavior in the historico-cultural evironment of our theologians?[24]

NOTES

1. Albert Perbal, "L'ethnologie et les missionaires," *Rythmes du Monde* 5 (1950) 3–4. See Pius XII, "Summi pontificatus" (October 20, 1939), in *Acta Apostolicae Sedis* 31 (1939) 429.

2. Bernard Häring, *Marriage in the Western World* (Westminster, Md.: Newman Press, 1965), pp. 258–266.

3. Bernard Häring, *A Theology of Protest* (New York: Farrar, Straus, and Giroux, 1970), p. 144.

4. *Ibid.*, p. 145.

5. *Ibid.*, p. 146.

6. Josef Fuchs, "Theology of the Meaning of Marriage Today," in *Marriage in the Light of Vatican II*, ed. James T. McHugh (Washington: Family Life Bureau, U.S.C.C., 1968), p. 20. See also Josef Fuchs, "The Absoluteness of Moral Terms," *Gregorianum* 52 (1971) 437–438.

7. John L. McKenzie, "Q.E.D." *The Critic* 29 (November-December 1970) 95.

8. *Ibid.* For other examples of this kind of questioning, see Hermann Ringeling, "Die biblische Begrundung der Monogamie," *Zeitschrift für Evangelishe Ethik* 10 (January 1966) 81–102; Robert Holst, "Polygamy and the Bible," *International Review of Mission* 56 (April 1967) 205–213; Harold W. Turner, "Monogamy: A Mark of the Church?" *International Review of Mission* 55 (July 1966) 313–321; Lesslie Newbigin, *Honest Religion for Secular Man* (London: SCM Press, 1966), pp. 72–74; Eugene Hillman, "Polygyny Reconsidered," in *The Renewal of Preaching*, ed. Karl Rahner, Concilium 33 (New York: Paulist Press, 1968) pp. 173–192; Eugene Hillman, "The Development of Christian Marriage Structures," in *The Future of Marriage as Institution*, ed. Franz Bökle, Concilium 55 (New York: Herder and Herder, 1970), pp. 25–38; Donald A. McGavran, ed. "Polygamy and Church Growth," *Church Growth Bulletin* 5 (March 1969) 59–60, 66–68; Harry Boer, "Polygamy," *Frontier* 11 (Spring 1968) 24–27. See also *Africa Theological Journal* 2 (February 1969), especially the articles by Judah B. M. Kowovele, "Polygyny as a Problem to the Church in Africa," pp. 7–26; and Manas Buthelizi, "Polygyny in the Light of the New Testament," pp. 58–70.

9. See Yves Congar, *A History of Theology*, trans. Hunter Guthrie (Garden City, N.Y.: Doubleday, 1968), p. 139: "The great weakness of Scholastic theology is its lack of a historical sense. This consists of being able to read a text or comprehend a fact not in one's personal intellectual perspective but according to the persepective in which the given text or fact is really found. This means to seek out the proper context of each

fact. The absence of a historic sense consists in locating everything in one's present personal context. Only rarely did the Middle Ages have this historic sense. It was interested in objectivity, the absolute character of the object, the equating of the intellect to a kind of knowing endowed with perfect certitude."

10. Congar, *History of Theology*, p. 139. Although Congar does not accuse the Scholastics of doctrinal deviations, he shows examples of their misleading methodology; and he affirms (p. 140) "that we have here all the elements of a false method, the danger of developing theology in a purely dialectical and deductive manner simply for decorative purposes."

11. See Timothy L. Bouscaren and A.C. Ellis, *Canon Law: A Text and Commentary* (Milwaukee: Bruce, 1957), pp. 447–449: George Hayward Joyce, *Christian Marriage: An Historical and Doctrinal Study* (London and New York: Sheed and Ward, 1933), pp. 560–572; Jacques Leclercq, *Marriage and the Family: A Study in Social Philosophy*, trans. Thomas R. Hanley, 4th ed., rev. (New York and Cincinnati: Pustet, 1949), pp. 66–81; and Charles A. Schleck, *The Sacrament of Matrimony: A Dogmatic Study* (Milwaukee: Bruce, 1964), pp. 57–65, 130–150.

12. Josef Fuchs, "Is There a Specifically Christian Morality?" *Theology Digest* 19 (Spring 1971) 44. See also Enda McDonagh, "Towards a Christian Theology of Morality," *Irish Theological Quarterly* 37 (July 1970) 188–189; Edward Schillebeeckx, *God the Future of Man*, trans. N.D. Smith (New York: Sheed and Ward, 1968), pp. 149–153; Charles E. Curran, "Absolute Norms and Medical Ethics," in *Absolutes in Moral Theology?* ed. Charles E. Curran (Washington and Cleveland: Corpus Books, 1968), pp. 132–149.

13. Fuchs, "Theology of the Meaning of Marriage Today," p. 17.

14. Josef Fuchs, *Human Values and Christian Morality*, trans. M.H. Heelan, Maeve McRedmond, Erika Young, and Gerard Watson (Dublin: Gill and Macmillan, 1970), p. 72.

15. Daniel Maguire, *Moral Absolutes and the Magisterium* (Washington and Cleveland: Corpus Papers, 1970), p. 20. See also Liam Ryan, "The Indissolubility of Marriage in Natural Law," *Irish Theological Quarterly* 31 (January 1970) 77; and Denis O'Callaghan, "Theology and Divorce," *Irish Theological Quarterly* 37 (July 1970), 216: "Even though St. Thomas did use on a number of occasions the axiom *natura humana mutabilis est*, this did not mean that he had worked out very explicitly the notion of variability. . . . The principles based on metaphysical nature are the primary principles of natural law; they never vary and can never be

dispensed. The principles which take account of man's historical nature, which depends on how man realizes himself in space and time, are the secondary principles of natural law; these hold true in the majority of cases but they may cease to bind or they may be dispensed. . . . All I wish to state here is that Thomistic tradition does allow for actual variability in some natural law precepts, and that this is applied to the precepts of monogamy and indissolubility."

16. On this "historically conscious methodology," see Charles E. Curran, "Absolute Norms and Medical Ethics," pp. 138–139; and C.E. Curran, "Methodological and Ecclesiological Questions in Moral Theology," *Chicago Studies* 9 (1970) 60, 62: "We need a more historically conscious methodological approach. . . . The fact that it is easier to point out the deficiencies in the older approaches without being able to elaborate any systematic newer methodology remains symptomatic of the problems facing Catholic ethical reflection today."

17. See Fuchs, *Human Values and Christian Morality*, p. 73: "Possibly certain moral values are formulated only for very definitive conditions which, however, were not expressed in the original formulation, since in other times men could not even imagine different situations. Moreover, it would be rash to believe that humanly formulated principles are always absolutely correct and exact."

18. See Schillebeeckx, *God the Future of Man*, pp. 150–151; and Fuchs, *Human Values and Christian Morality*, pp. 120–121.

19. Bronislaw Malinowski, "Parenthood, the Basis of Social Structures," in *The Family: Its Structure and Functions*, ed. Rose L. Coser (New York; St. Martin's 1964), p. 10, footnote 2.

20. *Ibid.*, p. 13.

21. See Malinowski, "Parenthood," pp. 9–10; Keith F. Otterbein, "Marquesan Polyandry," in *Marriage, Family, and Residence*, ed. Paul Bohannan and John Middleton (Garden City, N.Y.: Natural History Press, 1968), p. 293; and George P. Murdock, *Social Structure* (New York: Macmillan, 1949), pp. 24–25.

22. Malinowski, "Parenthood," p. 18.

23. See J. Hajnal, "European Marriage Patterns in Perspective," in *Population in History: Essays in Historical Demography*, ed. D.V. Glass and D.E.C. Eversley (Chicago: Aldine and Edward Arnold Ltd., 1965), p. 126, footnote 40: "An interesting study might, perhaps, be made of the way in which societies which take the universal marriage of women for granted deal with the grave shortage of men due to war losses. In ancient Athens, after the disastrous Sicilian expedition of 413 B.C., a law was

passed permitting double marriage. Among those who availed themselves of it was Socrates. (See Alfred Zimmern, *The Greek Commonwealth*,
5th ed. Oxford, Clarendon Press, 1931, p. 340)."

   24. See Yves Congar, *This Church That I Love*, trans. Lucien Delafuente
(Denville, N.J.: Dimension Books, 1969), pp. 81–82; "Have theologians
ever done anything but rationalize the status quo, with a few exceptions,
among which we must acclaim the figure of Las Casas?"

CHAPTER I

THE PROBLEM
IN HISTORICAL PERSPECTIVE

> *Now indeed in our time, and in keeping*
> *with Roman custom, it is no longer allowed*
> *to take another wife, so as to have more*
> *than one wife living.*
> SAINT AUGUSTINE

Every socio-cultural and religious institution has a history. Christian marriage, as it is now canonized, did not just come down from the sky; it is the result of historical development that is still in process. All such institutions are shaped by culturally conditioned human judgments, which dictate this way of development rather than that way, thus also precluding development in several other directions that might have been possible in different historico-cultural situations. Hence the development of the theology and the structures of Christian marriage in the Western world, although periodically arrested, is discernible; and this ongoing process has been outlined by scholars in our time.[1]

However, it is still difficult to say very much about such a development under the influence of non-Western cultures during the past few hundred years of the Church's missionary history. Practically speaking there has been none. At least there has been no ostensible movement of a positive kind. Certainly there has been nothing comparable to the evangelical-cultural symbiosis that occurred during the period of the Church's missionary engagement with the peoples of Europe. The reasons for this later rigidity will be seen in the chapter following this one, where the general relationship between culture and Christianity is considered in depth. The aim of the present chapter is simply to locate the missionary and pastoral problem of African polygamy within the more general history of Christian marriage, and thus to present the problem in its proper historical perspective.

Polygamy was never a widespread practice in the cultural areas where Christianity took root and developed during most of the past nineteen hundred years; so it is really an alien custom to the peoples who make up the vast majority of the Christian population in the world today. Church history, therefore, has relatively little to say directly and explicitly about this custom. Still, for the sake of perspective, the contemporary questions now being asked concerning African polygamy and Christianity should be seen against the background of historical change, such as it was, in the Christian understanding of marriage. With a view to dramatizing in a concise manner the general situation regarding both the development of Christian marriage structures and the lack of such development, a number of selected historical observations are here offered.

IN THE WESTERN WORLD

An incarnational, or accommodating, approach was common enough in former times, especially during the period of the Church's missionary expansion among the peoples of the Mediterranean basin, and even to some notable extent among those living on the northern and western frontiers of the Roman Empire. It could not have been otherwise in the beginning. Thanks to Saint Paul, the ethnocentric approach of the Judaizers was discredited both on theological and on pragmatic grounds. Given the impossibility of inventing original socio-religious institutions and ethical patterns, the apostles quite sensibly expressed their message in the cultural terms and patterns of the peoples to whom they were sent; so it was in these terms that Christianity was accepted into daily life. Through a gradual process, which was sometimes fully incarnational and sometimes merely symbiotic, Greco-Roman attitudes, practices, and conceptions shaped the understanding and the structures of Christian marriage, even as these very attitudes and practices and conceptions were themselves being influenced by the Christian message. The central notion, for example, that Christian marriage is constituted by consent comes directly from Roman law and the particular historico-cultural practices and conceptions that gave rise to that law.[2]

Until the end of the fifth century in the West the customary pagan forms characterized both the conception and the celebration of Christian marriage; and the ninth-century nuptial rite, prescribed by Pope Nicholas I, differed from the imperial Roman rite only in that the Mass was substituted for the traditional pagan sacrifice.[3] The use of the ring, for example, as a symbol of betrothal and later as a sign of the contract, comes directly from pre-Christian Roman practice.[4] The Christian understanding of betrothal itself, regarded as the beginning of the marital relationship and almost as difficult to dissolve, was simply taken over from early Roman custom.[5] Indeed, even more than the pagans themselves, the officials of the Church insisted upon the strict observance of the betrothal regulations, so much so that parents who broke off the engagements, which they themselves had arranged for their own sons or daughters, were excluded from communion for three years.[6] Concessions in this matter came only gradually. It was eventually allowed, thanks to Pope Alexander III in the mid-twelfth century, that the betrothal would be binding only after the prospective mates had reached the age of seven and then assented to the engagement. After this, however, the pledge could be broken only by "an episcopal sentence of dissolution," which also prevented any subsequent marriages between the formerly betrothed and the members of each other's families.[7]

Pre-Christian Rome also provided the Church with a readymade formulation of the purpose of marriage: "in order to bring forth children."[8] Moreover, it was the traditional pagan "religion of the hearth" that directly inspired the original Greco-Roman view that marriage is both indissoluble and monogamous.[9] From this same socio-religious source came also the various norms, still used by the Church today in all parts of the world, for determining the validity of Christian marriage; for example, the impediments arising from impotence, consanguinity, affinity, and disparity of cult.[10] The comprehensive character of this early historico-cultural influence on the Christian understanding of marriage is indicated by Edward Schillebeeckx:

> According to the evidence of a contemporary letter, the *Epistula ad Diognetem*, Christian marriage was much the same as that of pagans. As a general rule, Christians were bound to conform in this and in similar matters to the pattern of life of their own environment. The synod of Elvira, held around the year 306 . . . also accepted as its point of departure that the marriages of baptized Christians were celebrated like those of unbaptized pagans. The church simply accepted the subjection of her members to the Roman legislature . . . . In Catholic communities, marriages concluded according to the prevailing social customs were considered to be valid; only clandestine marriages were forbidden . . . . As far as pagan ceremonies were concerned, the clergy was only intent to point out that Christians should refrain from sacrifices, and, although they might rejoice in their celebrations, they were bound to avoid all pagan excesses.[11]

It is not surprising therefore that "Canon Law's basic principles and obligation of the marriage contract seem to be similar to, if not identical with, Roman Law."[12] For our purpose it is particularly interesting to note that Christianity did not introduce monogamy into the Greco-Roman world.[13] As a result of the pagan religio-ethical conception of marriage and family life, monogamy was already present as the only legal form of marriage; and polygamy was already proscribed for Roman citizens when Christianity was just coming to life in the forms of that culture.

In the Jewish communities of that time, however, polygamy was still practiced.[14] Josephus, the Jewish historical writer of the first century, mentions in two places that this custom still existed among his people. Justin Martyr, in his *Dialogue with Trypho* (c. 165 A.D.), also gives witness to the existence of simultaneous polygamy among the Jews of that time. In 212 A.D. the *lex Antoniana de civitate*, while reaffirming the law of monogamy for

Roman marriage, tolerated polygamy among the citizens who were Jews. This toleration was rescinded in 285 by Diocletian and Maximian, but the continuation of polygamy among the Jews later gave rise to a special law, issued in 393 by Theodosius, against the custom. Still, the practice survived until the eleventh century among the Jews of northern Europe.

If the influence of the Judaizing Christians had waxed rather than waned during this initial stage of the Church's growth, the historical institution of Christian marriage might well have developed along very different lines. As it was, the Christian acceptance of monogamy, as the only permissible form of marriage, had its own problematical side effects.[15] The legal monogamy insisted upon by the Greeks and the Romans was often supplemented with institutionalized concubinage and widespread prostitution, and divorce was a recurring problem. In the Roman world at the time of Jesus the marriage rate had declined so seriously that legislation was enacted to penalize the unmarried. Marriage for procreation was a patriotic as well as a religious duty among the Romans. "Single adults," says Gerald Leslie, "were disqualified from receiving inheritances unless they married within a prescribed period."[16] In reaction against the prevailing conditions in Rome, the Christians insisted upon the pure monogamy of the Greco-Roman tradition; and, perhaps to some extent over-reacting, they exalted celibacy over marriage, which they seemed to value mainly as a remedy for concupiscence.[17] Nineteen centuries of Christianity have not entirely removed the ancient concomitants of legal monogamy: concubinage, prostitution, and divorce.

With specific reference to the prohibition against polygamy, Saint Augustine explicitly acknowledged the profound influence of Greco-Roman culture upon the understanding and the structure of marriage among the early Christians. With the other Fathers of the Church, Augustine held that the Christian rule of monogamy was rooted in the teaching of the New Testament.[18] For Augustine it was rooted precisely in the sacramental significance of marriage.[19] At the same time, he argued that polygamy was no longer permitted in New Testament times because of the changed historico-cultural situation: "When polygamy was a common custom, it was no crime; it ranks as a crime now because it is no longer customary."[20] This argument is developed at some length, and in various works, by Augustine: that polygamy was not sinful in former times when it was customary among upright men, when the social conditions of their nation permitted it, and when the needs of that historical period urged it. Moreover, Augustine maintained that polygamy, far from being contrary to the nature of marriage, was "not without becoming beauty,", when it was socially accepted for reasons arising from nature.[21] However, the point to be made here is simply that the historico-cultural situation in which the early Church found itself had something to do with the monogamy rule among Christians. "Now indeed in our time and in keeping with Roman custom," says Augustine, "it is no longer allowed to take another wife, so as to have more than one wife living."[22]

The Roman understanding and structure of marriage was basi-cally accepted and "baptized" by the Church. Must it be as-sumed, therefore, that these things are absolutely and univer-sally constitutive of Christian marriage and that non-Roman ways and laws are somehow less appropriate for Christians? Legions of missionaries, sent out from the Western world, have acted on such an assumption. It is instructive to note, however, that there were some signs of flexibility in the Church's mis-sionary approach to the peoples of northern Europe. One of the great missionary prolems here was the precise conception of marriage and what exactly constituted a valid marriage. "When Christianity spread to the Germanic tribes," according to Edward Schillebeeckx, "it was some time before the Church succeeded in getting her marriage theory of the *consensus,* based on Roman law, accepted." In some of these socio-cultural situations, "mar-riage was seen as a contract between two tribes or extended family groups, rather than a contract between the bride and the bridegroom themselves."[23]

On occasion the official Church went very far indeed. The following directive, astonishing as it may be, is taken from a papal letter written by Gregory II to a missionary in northern Europe:

Gregory, the servant of the servants of God, to Boniface, our most holy brother and colleague in the episcopate . . . . Since you seek our advice on matters dealing with ecclesiastical discipline, we will state with all the authority of the apostolic tradition what you must hold . . . . As to what a man shall do if his wife is unable through illness to allow him his marital rights, it would be better if he remained apart and practiced continence. But since this is practicable only in the case of men of high ideals, the best course if he is unable to remain continent would be for him to marry. Nevertheless, he should continue to support the woman who is sick, unless she has contracted the disease through her own fault . . . . This, my dear brother, is all that need be said with the authority of the Apostolic See.[24]

It would appear from this that a modified form of simultaneous polygamy may have been considered tolerable in the Germanic missionary situation, at least with people lacking "high ideals."[25] Such flexibility would have been consistent with the missionary guidelines articulated by Pope Saint Gregory the Great, at the beginning of the previous century, in his famous letter to Mellitus. Change, when necessary, should be gradual. "It is impossible," said Gregory, "to cut off all abuses at once from rough hearts, just as a man who sets out to climb a high mountain does not advance by leaps and bounds, but goes up step by step and pace by pace."[26]

The very same attitude of tolerant flexibility is reflected also in Gregory's answers to a series of missionary questions, asked by Augustine of Canterbury, respecting the customs of the "rude English people," who were still newcomers to the faith and not yet ready for strong meat. Marriages between near relatives were customary among the English, while such marriages were regarded as evil and sinful by the Church. What then was to be done about the neophytes in the faith, who were already married within the degrees of relationship forbidden by the Church? Gregory answered that all were to be warned against such marriages; but people were not to be punished for marriages they had entered through ignorance and before baptism. As a principle Gregory affirmed that "sometimes a fault must be tolerated in those who have acted through ignorance." In the concrete missionary situation, he pointed out, the Church "corrects certain things through fervor; tolerates certain things through mildness; overlooks and suffers certain things through consideration; often with the result that, by suffering certain things and overlooking them, the Church curbs the evil which it opposes."[27]

While the historical data may permit of various apologetical interpretations, it does appear in general that the pre-Christian marriage customs of the different peoples were, as Schillebeeckx says, "strictly observed" by the Church, "with the aim of preventing any later doubts about the validity of marriage."[28] Although freedom of consent was always insisted upon in theory, there is some considerable evidence to suggest that the lack of consent in practice was widely tolerated by the Church.[29] According to Schillebeeckx, "it was not until the eleventh century that women gained a measure of freedom in the matter of their own consent to marriage."[30]

While most of the theologians of Christendom have consistently maintained the incompatibility of polygamy and the Christian way of life, it should be noted that this form of marriage was almost always discussed by the theologians in apologetical and theoretical terms: it was never a widespread pastoral or missionary problem among Western peoples. The main concern of the theologians was simply to show that the polygamous patriarchs of ancient Israel were not lecherous old men. Following Augustine, Innocent III, and Thomas Aquinas, the usual position was that polygamy was not absolutely forbidden: it could be permitted by divine dispensation. In the Thomistic theory of natural law, polygamy later became a classical example illustrating something that was prohibited by a secondary precept of the natural law.[31]

It was against this academic background that the Fathers of the Council of Trent finally condemned the concrete pastoral proposals set forth by some of the sixteenth-century Reformers. Martin Luther and Philip Melanchthon had attempted to justify the practice of simultaneous polygamy in a few isolated pastoral cases; the most famous cases being those of Henry VIII of England and Philip of Hesse. Since the time of Trent, Roman Catholics have generally assumed that all questions concerning polygamy have been settled once and for all. This assumption is examined elsewhere, and exposed for what it is: a misunderstanding of both the intention and the teaching of the Council of Trent.[32] Later in the present chapter we will see how and to what extent the pope alone, even before the time of Trent, dealt with polygamy as a missionary problem.

What people think about marriage—and therefore what theologians have written about it—is obviously bound up with their particular historico-cultural attitudes toward sex and toward womanhood. Here is an area in which the philosophical anthropology of the pre-Christian Greco-Roman world has had a grim and pervasive influence upon all subsequent Christian thought and conduct. According to Daniel Maguire, the Stoic view that sex is given only for procreation of the species, and not at all for pleasure, was already the traditional opinion among Christians even before the famous Bishop of Hippo started theologizing about marriage.[33] Does Augustine's understanding of sex and marriage perhaps owe more to his own pagan background, and particularly to his Manichean experience, than to his Christian faith?[34] Augustine could not see, by his own admission, "what other help a woman could be to a man if the purpose of generation were eliminated."[35] In his formal teaching on the good of marriage, he affirms also that marital intercourse for the sake of begetting children is without fault; but the husband or wife who has marital intercourse in order to satisfy the desires of the flesh is guilty of venial fault: "to pay the debt of marriage is no crime, but to demand it beyond the necessity of begetting children is a venial fault."[36]

While Pope Gregory the Great was ready to make concessions in other matters, he was intolerant of any compromise concerning the pleasure, and hence the fault, involved in marital intercourse. He was even more austere than Augustine. In the letter to Augustine of Canterbury, already cited, Gregory replied negatively to the missionary's question about the feasibility of allowing married persons to enter the Church and to receive communion after marital copulation. Although other peoples thought differently about this, and had different customs, Gregory observed first that the constant practice of the Romans from

ancient times was to seek purification by washing and for some
time to reverently abstain from entering the Church. Such a
course was to be followed "because this lawful mingling of
spouses cannot be done without pleasures of the flesh." And,
according to Gregory, "this pleasure cannot be without fault."[37]

Several centuries later the same somber view of conjugal
pleasure was still found in the Church's teaching concerning
marriage, and it was strongly reiterated by Pope Innocent III,
himself one of the most important influences in shaping the
Christian understanding of marriage.[38] Indeed, this view may be
regarded as forming a part of the Western Christian traditional
understanding of marriage, although it was later tempered and
eventually abandoned. This view, together with the earlier patristic insistence on seeing marriage almost exclusively as a
"remedy against desire," had an inhibiting effect on the theological development of marriage as a sacrament. The scholastic
theologians, even those who were reaching out for a fuller sacramental understanding of conjugal love, were dominated by the
idea that marriage was a remedy against the evils of sexuality.
According to Schillebeeckx, "the thought which lurked at the
back of everyone's mind at this time was: how could marriage,
which involves 'you know what' (!), be a sacramental source of
grace?"[39]

As Western culture changed in the course of time, so also did
the Western Christian theology of marriage change. According to
Joseph Kerns, "the changes in what Christian writers say from
the second to the twentieth century reflect nothing so much as a
struggle between two cultural views of human sexuality, with the
Christian view gradually prevailing."[40] This is strikingly exemplified in the difference between the official teachings of Pope
Gregory the Great and Pope Pius XII. While Gregory, and so very
many others, taught that conjugal intercourse always involves
sin, Pius XII taught that there is nothing wrong at all when
married persons seek and enjoy this pleasure.[41] Such irreconcila-
ble opinions can be explained only in terms of historical and
cultural conditioning. If Gregory's theology could be so influenced by the ethos of his particular time and place in history, then
we may assume that all theology is apt to be so influenced.

"Thus, too, we can understand," with Josef Fuchs, "how it is possible that different peoples in the history of mankind have had different concepts of marriage as well as different concepts of right and wrong in the relationship between man and woman —and at times very erroneous concepts."[42]

We know now, of course, that there are even today very many different cultural conceptions of the universal human institution of marriage, many different views of human sexuality and conjugal union. If so many centuries were required in the West before "the Christian view" finally prevailed (assuming that it has prevailed), then we should not expect similar developments, indeed profound changes, to be effected more rapidly—even as a precondition for baptism—in the non-Western world. What has the Church actually expected and even demanded of non-Western peoples during the past few hundred years?

IN THE NON-WESTERN WORLD

One of the very first things that the Church has expected of many husbands, as they were just beginning to turn to the Lord in faith, is that they should divorce the mothers of their own children. In practice this has been a necessary condition, on a level of importance with faith itself, for the acceptance of polygamists into the Christian fellowship. It would seem that divorce, with the consequent disruption of the existing family unity and continuity, is somehow supposed to be more compatible with Christianity than is polygamy. With very few exceptions, this has been the regular procedure of Christian missionaries wherever they encountered the social institution of simultaneous polygamy.

Among Roman Catholics this negative requirement for admission into the Church through baptism is expressed in the canonical regulations known generally as the "privilege of the faith." At least since the publication, in 1537, of the constitution *Altitudo* by Pope Paul III, this has been the official solution to the problem of polygamy in the missionary situation. This "privilege" is allegedly based upon, and sometimes confused with, the so-called "Pauline privilege" (cf. 1 Cor. 7:10–15); and it was progressively extended through its application to missionary problems, especially the problem of the polygamist who wished subsequently to become a Christian.[43]

Originally, however, the "privilege of the faith" appears to have been a more general principle based, somewhat tenuously perhaps, on the Petrine power to bind and to loose. From as early as the fourth century in Spain there is evidence of this "privilege" in legislation dealing with the tensions existing then between Christians and Jews.[44] The "privilege of the faith" was used, in principle, by the Third Council of Toledo in 589 to justify restrictions against Jews: against their taking Christian wives, holding authority over Christian groups, and keeping Christian slaves—a thing that only Christians were permitted to do.

The regulations set forth in *Altitudo*, and in the subsequent papal documents that greatly extended the scope of this "privilege," meant, in effect, that the pope authorized the dissolution of marriages previously recognized as valid; and this was done "in favor of the faith" of the would-be Christian spouse, who was then free to marry again. In the common missionary case of simultaneous polygamy, to which the regulations of Paul III were particularly directed, there was a presumption, arising from the Roman conception of marriage, that the greatest claim to validity belonged to the polygamist's first marriage and thus, also, a presumption that the other wives were probably concubines, after the manner of Roman custom. In the event that the husband could not recall exactly which of his wives had been the first one, *Altitudo* allowed him to remarry any one of his previous wives, while the others were to be "sent away." With the one chosen wife, he then made a valid "contract" of matrimony "through consent." What in their particular society might have been required for the social recognition of valid marriages seems to have been ignored. So the stability of the new marriage was based on its external conformity with Roman law; this Roman law having been "baptized," canonized, and more or less universalized.

In these cases it sometimes happened that, after the new marriage, the husband actually did recall that another woman had been his first wife. Then, by the regulations of the constitution *Romani Pontificis*, issued in 1571 by Pope Pius V, and sometimes called *Constitutio Piana,* the new marriage could still be regarded as valid; and the previous marriage to the first wife, in spite of its prior claim to validity, was dissolved. In addition to such cases arising from the practice of simultaneous polygamy, later regulations, given in 1685 by Pope Gregory XIII in his constitution *Populis,* provided also for the dissolution of valid monogamous marriages, with permission to marry again "in favor of the faith." These cases arose originally from the predicament of married slaves who were subsequently separated from one another. In this situation a previously valid monogamous marriage could be dissolved if a separated spouse wished to become a Catholic and to marry a Catholic.

Legalistic minds were able to devise subsequent variations, which tended to extend further the "privilege of the faith," so that it could be used also to solve some nonmissionary problems. The wider possibilities of this principle were not missed when Pope Pius XII shifted the norms from the "favor of the faith" to the "salvation of souls."[45] In an entirely new departure, which goes beyond the limits of the traditional theory and practice of the "privilege of the faith," and against the almost unanimous teaching of theologians and canonists up until a few years ago, the dissolution of valid marriages between non-Christians, neither of whom intends to receive baptism, now comes within the power of the pope.[46] In these cases of recent years the principle —whether it is in "favor of the faith" or for the "salvation of souls"—is invoked in behalf of a third party.

What all of these regulations amount to, in modern language, is a set of rules governing the conditions for divorce and remarriage. In the words of John Giles Milhaven: "The Church, representing God, authorized divorce and remarriage in certain cases."[47] In his more testy treatment of this matter, Noonan regards the present papal practice as evidence "that the scriptural teaching 'What God has joined together, let no man put asunder' is not taken literally or absolutely by the Roman Curia."[48] In any case, what is clearly permitted, under a variety of legal conditions, is *consecutive* polygyny and *consecutive* polyandry—two practices that have always been concomitants of the Western conception of monogamous marriage. What seems never permissible, whether in "favor of the faith" or for the "salvation of souls," is the peculiarly non-Western practice of *simultaneous* polygyny, and perhaps only because this had been forbidden by Roman law, which so profoundly conditioned the historical interpretation of the New Testament teaching about marriage.

Whatever else might be said, it is evident that these canonical norms are more directly traceable to Greco-Roman culture than to the New Testament; and they are clearly not at all in sympathy with the specifically non-Western forms of plural marriage. These forms are still considered to be, at least for Christians, less suitable than the Western forms of plural marriage. So a valid question is raised concerning the extent to which the "privilege of the faith" regulations are truly catholic or transcultural.

This is not to suggest that the "privilege of the faith" regulations were ill-inspired when they were first worked out for the different marriage customs encountered by missionaries among non-Western peoples. Doubtless these regulations, representing a serious and radical effort to come to terms with new customs, were motivated by a keen desire for the "salvation of souls"—especially the souls of men—at a time when it was commonly believed that salvation was practically impossible for persons who were not visibly in communion with the Church. However, the method chosen for solving the problem of polygamy is now seen to have been excessively juridical. An even more serious criticism of this solution is its grossly inconsiderate attitude toward women. A Christian concern for the rights and destinies of the wives, who were "sent away," is not in evidence.

Indeed, the plight of these wives has often been notorious. Their previously contracted conjugal rights, their social status, economic security, and even their relationships with their own children, have been radically compromised; and this, in the name of the Christian ideal of marriage and family life. In African traditional societies it is frequently difficult, and sometimes impossible, for such women to marry again. Many of them must choose to live like nuns or like prostitutes. Their fate is determined by the structures of the particular society in which they live; it is sometimes a cruel fate, especially in societies with strong inhibitions against divorce and remarriage.

Some of the Protestant missionary solutions, while they may be less consistent than the Roman Catholic solution, are a little more humane, although they also reflect the same traditional Western view of women as second-class persons—or, as Thomas Aquinas calls them, "misbegotten males."[49] In general, the various Protestant solutions may be summarized under the following propositions. When the members of a polygamous family have been called to the new life of Christian faith: (1) All the women and children may be baptized, but not the husband. (2) Only those who are not polygamously married may be baptized. (3) The husband may be baptized, if he retains his first wife, while divorcing the others. (4) The husband may be baptized, if he divorces all but the preferred wife. (5) All may be baptized with the understanding that any subsequent plural marriages are forbidden. (6) On the testimony of their faith alone, any of them may be baptized with no other previous conditions.[50]

THE DEBATE IN AFRICA

Each of the six propositions just given has its own history.[51] But the debate within the Anglican communion, from about the middle to the end of the last century, concerning the proper missionary approach to polygamy in Africa, manifests the major tensions behind the practical solutions worked out by the different churches and missionary groups. A study of the arguments for both sides reveals not only a shallow anthropology and a persistent ethnocentrism, but also a consistently naive manner of interpreting the Bible.

Both in Africa and in India some of the early missionaries of the Anglican communion had taken a relatively lenient postion with polygamists who wished to become Christians.[52] But some of the Anglican missionaries in South Africa, under the forthright leadership of Bishop John Colenso of Natal, decided to make an entirely fresh and honest approach to the problem. This precipitated the fullest ecclesiastical debate ever undertaken on the question, which was finally settled negatively by the Lambeth Conference of 1888. After his first ten weeks in Natal, Colenso initiated the historic debate, in 1855, with these words:

I must confess that I feel strongly on this point, that the usual practice of enforcing the separation of wives from their husbands, upon their conversion to Christianity, is quite unwarrantable, and opposed to the plain teaching of our Lord. It is putting new wine in old bottles, and placing a stumbling-block, which He has not set, directly in the way of receiving the Gospel.[53]

There followed a vigorous exchange of letters and pamphlets that served to polarize opinions. Unshaken by any opposition, the Bishop of Natal continuously reaffirmed his stand, and with growing conviction. Thus, in 1860, Colenso wrote this:

With respect to the polygamy question, all my experience has deepened and confirmed the conviction . . . that a most grievous error has been committed all along by our Missionary Societies in the course they have been hitherto adopting with regard to native converts who have had more than one wife at the time of their receiving the word of life in the Gospel.[54]

Already a modest compromise had been proposed by Henry Venn, the influential general secretary of the Church Missionary Society in London. This allowed for the possibility of accepting into the Church the wives of polygamous families, but not the husbands, for the wives were usually regarded as "involuntary victims of the custom."[55] Even the most liberal of the Anglican missionary bishops in Africa refused to go any further than this. So Colenso alone carried the debate to the Lambeth Conference, although he did not live to see the final outcome. From the record of the voting in the Third Lambeth Conference, it appears that "of the hundred and four bishops present, twenty-one were prepared to accept polygamists and thirty-four opposed any concession—even to wives."[56] The resolutions were not binding in the mission areas, where all "difficult questions of detail" were to be worked out on the local level; so no uniformity of practice was dictated by the Conference.

While Lambeth did not entirely close the door against the possibility that "the wives of polygamists may be in some cases baptized . . . since they presumably did not violate the Christian precept which enjoins fidelity to one husband," the official position was that "polygamy is inconsistent with the law of Christ concerning marriage."[57] So the practice of allowing the baptism of the husbands was regarded as completely intolerable. Although the question had not even been adequately researched and prepared by the Lambeth Committee on Polygamy, the general negative attitude of the Conference had very considerable influence over the practical decisions taken subsequently by churches other than those of the Anglican communion. Previous tendencies toward the toleration of polygamy among African Baptists and Methodists, for example, were eventually reversed.[58] But there were exceptions, such as the Bremen Mission, which maintained its positive policy, previously formulated in these words:

> Polygamy existed at the time of Christ and the apostles, but we do not find that monogamy was made a condition for acceptance into the Chruch. Therefore, a man who has several wives must be admitted to baptism and communion; however, all are always to be reminded that monogamy is the true marriage according to God, and that only in this way can the purpose of marriage be reached.[59]

On the whole it is the independent African churches, composed initially of dissident Christians from the Western-based churches, that have taken the more lenient positions. Some of these separatist bodies have repudiated polygamy, while others have merely upheld monogamy more as an ideal than as a normal practice. Still others of them have positively accepted polygamy as a part of their conscious indigenization of Christianity in Africa. The correlation between the occurence of these numerous independent movements and the incidence of polygamy in the same populations, and the fact that independency rarely occurs among peoples with a low incidence of polygamy, suggests that this form of marriage is one of the dynamic factors behind the growth of independent churches.[60] Some of these churches, precisely because of their stand on this question, have been excluded from ecumenical fellowship with neighboring churches; and sometimes, for this reason only, they were not even regarded as authentic Christian communities. Where this happens the law of monogamy becomes a criterion of Christian faith and a mark of the true Church.[61]

The general lack of consistency among the older Protestant

churches shows that they really ought to examine the theological reasons for their various positions. It certainly appears, as the principal of a seminary in Nigeria recently pointed out, that they are concerned more with maintaining positions than with explaining them: "Both the churches that forbid polygamists from being members and the churches that permit such membership would probably be hard put to give a convincing reason for their stand."[62] Even in some of the same churches there are contradictory disciplines, and this fact says something about the arbitrary nature of ecclesiastical decisions that bind upon men "heavy and oppressive burdens" (Matt. 23:4). Anglicans, for example, in West Africa allow the wives of polygamists to be baptized, while in South Africa and elsewhere they are not even admitted to the catechumenate without the authorization of the bishop in each case.[63] In this connection the comments of the Anglican bishop of Malawi are instructive:

> I came to this Diocese from a country where Christianity had been planted largely by the Christian wives of polygamous husbands, and their courage and resourcefulness in living a Christian life . . . and bringing up their children as practicing members of the Church, won my admiration. It was with profound shock that I learned that here none of them would have been admitted to Holy Baptism, not because of any fault of their own, but because they had the misfortune to be brought up in a society where polygamy was the rule. After discussion with the clergy, changes are coming, and baptism will no longer be refused to a woman who was married to a polygamist before her baptism.[64]

"Changes are coming," indeed. The Lutheran Church in Liberia, which is otherwise a very traditional Christian community, has already decided that polygamous husbands as well as their wives may be admitted to baptism and communion, although normally they may not hold official positions of leadership in the ecclesiastical organization. While these Lutherans, and the few other traditional churches now following the same course,[65] firmly uphold the ideal of monogamy, they have also come to recognize that the rejection of polygamy does not always demand the rejection of men who were polygamists before the Christian message was presented to them.

It was only after careful deliberation that the Lutheran Church in Liberia started on this new course in 1951.[66] Fourteen years later these Lutherans undertook a survey to evaluate pragmatically their policy, and they found "no indication that the Church's teaching on monogamy as the standard of Christian marriage is compromised by the practice of baptizing those who had previously entered into polygamy."[67] So, "The Lutheran Church in Liberia stands firm in its conviction that it has been right in its policy of admitting polygamists into full membership in the Christian fellowship."[68] This church was "not inundated with polygamists," and well over ninety percent of its married members are monogamists. Nor is it anticipated that "the proportion of polygamous to monogamous Christians will increase appreciably."[69] Moreover, the survey revealed that "the real problem with respect to the monogamous Christian is not his entering subsequently into a polygamous marriage, but rather the committing of adultery."[70]

A Methodist bishop, reconsidering his church's position in the light of his experiences in Angola and in parts of southeastern Africa, asks these disturbing questions:

> Is it more Christian to have organized prostitution, marital infidelity with impunity, a rapidly growing divorce rate and increasing numbers of illegitimate children, than polygamy? Is it more Christian for young women to become prostitutes, call girls, or mistresses than to become the second or third wife of a respected member of the community? . . . Is permitting youth to choose their own mates necessarily more Christian than an agreement between families? Is a widow any better or happier in the world alone than living intimately with a member of her husband's family?[71]

Certainly there is today among church leaders in Africa a new openness and at least a willingness to discuss the recurring suggestion that the churches may have been mistaken in their previous policies regarding plural marriage.[72] At their 1967 regional conference in Nairobi, some seventy Roman Catholic bishops of eastern Africa were asked to consider the possibility of adopting a new policy regarding polygamy.[73] The discussion was brief, because it came only at the end of a crowded agenda and because most of the bishops had not had time to study the prepared paper on the subject; so there was no serious effort even to debate the issues, much less reach an agreement. It is, however, significant that the question was not simply dismissed with any negative resolutions or anathemas. Instead, the bishops wisely decided that further study was required.

This "further study" has since been urged upon all church leaders in Tanzania, since the government's 1969 proposal that even Christian marriages in Tanzania should be legally recognized as potentially polygamous. In their most ecumenical statement to date, the ecclesiastical leaders of this country offered the government a joint reply—from the Dar es Salaam Committee of Churches: Roman Catholic, Anglican, Lutheran, Presbyterian, Baptist, Mennonite, Salvation Army, and Assembly of God.[74] Their statement points out that monogamy is not a "Western import," that polygamy was previously "justified by historical, social, and economic situations," and that even now there is no need to make this African form of plural marriage illegal for non-Christians.[75] Their defense of monogamy is based simply on the problematical hypothesis, to be examined in Chapter 3, that polygamy is actually disappearing anyway. This hypothesis is supported by the sociological conjecture that the maintaining of this custom would be socially and economically retrogressive. No biblical or theological reasons are offered in support of the traditional Christian position. Basically, therefore, the argument of these church leaders comes to this: The problem will solve itself, as the problem-people, the polygamists, gradually disappear for socio-economic reasons. Is there nothing more to be said?

The problem surely has some other dimensions. As already noted in this chapter, there are questions of justice and charity arising from the practice of "sending away" all but one of the wives of a polygamist who would become a Christian. In areas where polygamy is a preferential and socially integrated form of marriage, missionaries have all too often been seen as persons who come to break-up the natural family unity and to shatter the existing complex of marriage-related human bonds. Jesus clearly taught that marriage should be indissoluble. Yet a polygamist is told that, if he would fully obey the call of Christ, the first thing he must do is to divorce the mothers of his own children. Does this approach reflect the gospel message of unity, liberation, and joy? Is there no suspicion that this traditional approach amounts to little more than a legalistic improvisation? As long as polygamy continues to exist in Africa, even though it may be diminishing generally, there are some questions to be faced by Church leaders.

We cannot simply wait for the whole problem to go away, while in practice the law of monogamy remains on a level of importance with faith. What is the meaning of the Christian *kerygma*, if the law of monogamy must be presented together with it, and, if the external observance of this particular law, no less than faith itself in Jesus Christ, is made a condition *sine qua non* for admission into the Christian fellowship? External conformity to this legal prescription has become so overwhelmingly important and finally decisive in practice that it seems almost to have become a substitute for the real conversion of faith, which alone leads to the newness of the Christian life. The theological problem here is a very old one; and it may perhaps be formulated in the question addressed to the people of Galatia: "Was it through observance of the law that you received the Spirit, or was it through faith in what you heard?" (Gal. 3:2).

So there really is a problem. An increasing number of African church leaders have come to see this problem in its true theological and anthropological dimensions. Bishop Josiah Kibira of the Evangelical Lutheran Church in Tanzania, for example, has this to say about it:

> Our greatest ethical problems are divorce and polygamy and, intertwined with them, the question of church discipline . . . . The Church should not simply stress laws without first making certain that these rules are a help rather than a detriment to those in need . . . . The problem of polygamy is the most difficult. In this area, the Church in Africa is bogged down and badly in need of a way out of the dilemma . . . . Perhaps, by theological study we may find that we should not prevent a pagan polygamist from being baptized if he is called while in that condition.[76]

For Peter Sarpong, the Roman Catholic Bishop of Kumasi in Ghana, the widespread African custom of polygamy is "certainly a pressing pastoral problem." In his opinion, "the African bishops should be conducting studies into the problem . . . . Maybe some theological leeway can be found."[77]

In December of 1973, during a meeting of some sixty-five Roman Catholic bishops of eastern African countries, gathered in Nairobi to plan for the Church in the 1980's, the same point was made once again; this time by Bishop John Njenga of Eldoret in Kenya. In his formal paper on African marriage Bishop Njenga concluded his sympathetic treatment of customary polygamy with a "call for more study, research, education and even re-thinking and revaluation on the part of pastors, theologians and the faithful."[78] In spite of the Apostolic Nuncio's frenzied maneuverings to terminte the subsequent discussion of polygamy, the majority of the bishops agreed that this is indeed an issue which deserves far more study. However, all references to this discussion are curiously missing from the officially published conclusions of the meeting.[79]

NOTES

1. See Edward Schillebeeckx, *Marriage: Secular Reality and Saving Mystery*, 2 vols, trans. N.D. Smith (London: Sheed and Ward, 1965), II; George H. Joyce, *Christian Marriage: An Historical and Doctrinal Study* (London: Sheed and Ward, 1948); Joseph E. Kerns, *The Theology of Marriage* (New York: Sheed and Ward, 1964); and Franz Böckle, ed., *The Future of Marriage as Institution*, Concilium 55 (New York: Herder and Herder, 1970); John T. Noonan, Jr., *Contraception: A History of Its Treatment by the Catholic Theologians and Canonists* (Cambridge: Harvard University Press, 1965).

2. See Jean Daniélou and Henry Marrou, *The First Six Hundred Years*, trans. Vincent Cronin (London: Darton, Longman and Todd, 1964), I, p. 175: "The Christians, adopting the notion of Roman law, regarded consent as constituting marriage. They also kept the practices accompanying the pagan celebration of marriage; . . . they removed only what

was specifically idolatrous: sacrifice and the reading of horoscopes."

3. See Kenneth Scott Latourette, *A History of the Expansion of Christianity*, 7 vols. (New York and London: Harper and Brothers, 1937–1945), I, p. 326.

4. See Jerome Carcopino, *Daily Life in Ancient Rome*, trans. E. O. Lorimer (New Haven: Yale University Press, 1940; Hardmondsworth: Penguin Books, 1964), p. 94.

5. See Joyce, *Christian Marriage*, p. 85.

6. *Ibid.*

7. *Ibid.*, p. 96.

8. See Schillebeeckx, *Marriage: Secular Reality and Saving Mystery*, II, pp. 7, 15; W. Michael Lawson, "Roman Law: A Source of Canonical Marriage Legislation," *Resonance* 3 (Spring 1967) 9.

9. See Schillebeeckx, *Marriage: Secular Reality and Saving Mystery*, II, p, 7: "It was the principle of the household religion which provided the basis of the monogamous and essentially indissoluble character of marriage."

10. See Lawson, "Roman Law," pp. 9–14.

11. Schillebeeckx, *Marriage; Secular Reality and Saving Mystery*, II, pp. 18–19, 20–21, 27–28: "Marriage 'in the Lord' in the first centuries of Christianity meant, as it did for Paul, marrying a fellow Christian."

12. Lawson, "Roman Law," p. 9. For more on the extent to which pre-Christian cultural conceptions and social structures were "baptized" by the early Church, see Henri Irenée Marrou, "The Church and Greek and Roman Civilization," trans. John Griffiths, in *History: Self-Understanding of the Church*, ed. Roger Aubert, Concilium 67 (New York: Herder and Herder, 1971), pp. 47–60.

13. See E. O. James, *Marriage Customs through the Ages* (New York: Macmillan, Collier Books, 1965), pp. 103, 107, 119: Edward Westermarck, *The History of Human Marriage*, 3 vols. (New York: Allerton, 1922), III, pp. 84–86.

14. See Joyce, *Christian Marriage*, pp. 570–571; Joachim Jeremias, *Jerusalem in the Time of Jesus*, trans. F.H. and C.H. Cave (London: SCM Press, 1967), pp. 90–94, 369; L.W. Barnard, *Justin Martyr: His Life and Thought* (London and New York: Cambridge University Press, 1967), p. 46; Salo Wittmayer Baron, *A Social and Religious History of the Jews*, 14 vols., 2nd ed. rev. (New York: Columbia University Press, 1937, 1952, 1962), II, pp. 223–229.

15. See Joyce, *Christian Marriage*, pp. 604–605; Gerald R. Leslie, *The Family in Social Context* (New York and Torento: Oxford University Press, 1967), pp. 168–176; Harry Boer, "Polygamy," *Frontier* 11 (Spring 1968)

24–25; and John T. Noonan, Jr., "Freedom, Experimentation, and Permanence in the Canon Law of Marriage," in *Law for Liberty: The Role of Law in the Church Today*, ed. James E. Biechler (Baltimore: Helicon, 1967), p. 55: "Pope Leo the Great writes to Rusticus, bishop of Narbonne, that girls given by their fathers in marriage to men who already have concubines are without fault, for the concubines are not legal wives."

16. Leslie, *The Family in Social Context*, p. 175.

17. The most famous exponent of this view is Saint Augustine, who emphasized the utility of marriage as a way of bringing lust under lawful control, a means of preventing adultery and fronication. See Augustine's *De bono conjugali*, i cc. 5–6, in *Patrologia Latina* (subsequently designated P.L.) ed. J.P. Migne (Paris, 1844), 40, col. 377. On the generally negative attitudes of the early Christians regarding even monogamous marriage, see John T. Noonan, Jr., "History and the Values of Christian Marriage," in *Marriage in the Light of Vatican II*, ed. James T. McHugh (Washington: Family Life Bureau, U.S.C.C. 1968), pp. 7–9.

18. For a survey of patristic teachings on monogamy, see Joyce, *Christian Marriage*, pp. 562–565; and Charles A. Schleck, *The Sacrament of Matrimony: A Dogmatic Study* (Milwaukee: Bruce, 1964), pp. 60, 143–145.

19. See Augustine, *De bono conjugali*, i, c. 21, P.L. 40, cols. 387–388. For Augustine's understanding of the *sacramentum* as a symbol of stability, see Noonan, *Contraception*, pp. 161–163; and Schillebeeckx, *Marriage: Secular Reality and Saving Mystery*, II, pp. 67–73.

20. Augustine, *Contra Faustum Manichaeum*, xxii, c. 47, P.L. 42, col. 428. For the development of this argument, see also *De bono conjugali*, i, cc. 15–20, P.L. 40, cols. 384–386; *De doctrina Christina*, iii, cc. 12–14, P.L. 34, cols. 73–74. Polygamy was not wrong, according to Augustine, when it was considered to be a necessary means of multiplying offspring and populating the world. In Augustine's time polygamy had ceased to be necessary and customary, since the world had already been sufficiently populated. Hence, the practice of polygamy had become morally wrong: it would arise only from an "excess of lust," not from any natural or social need.

21. *De bono conjugali*, i, c. 20, P.L. 40, col. 387.

22. *Ibid.*, c. 7, col. 378.

23. Schillebeeckx, *Marriage; Secular Reality and Saving Mystery*, II, pp. 33, 36, 38: "For the Western Goths betrothal and marriage were above all tribal affairs, as they were for the Germanic tribes."

24. Pope Gregory II, "Replies to Questions Put by Boniface" (November 22, 726), in *The Anglo-Saxon Missionaries in Germany*, trans. and ed. C.H. Talbot (London and New York: Sheed and Ward, 1954), pp. 80–81; Letter 14, P.L. 89, col. 525. Although this letter would seem to

be concerned with a case of simultaneous polygamy, since the time of Gratian it has been discussed only in reference to consecutive polygamy. See Noonan, "Freedom, Experimentation, and Permanence in the Canon Law of Marriage," p. 61.

25. Plural marriage seems not to have been a general missionary or pastoral problem among the Germanic peoples. Polygamy, according to Tacitus, was "exceedingly rare" and found only among some men of high rank. See Tacitus, "Germania," 18, in *Tacitus on Britain and Germany*, trans. H. Mattingly (Harmondsworth: Penguin Books, 1948), p. 115.

26. See Pope Gregory the Great "Epistola LXXVI ad Mellitum Abbatem," P.L. 77, cols. 1215–1215, English translation from Stephen Neill, *A History of Christian Missions* (Hardmondsworth: Penguin Books, 1964), p. 68.

27. Pope Gregory the Great, "Epistola LXIV ad Augustinum Anglorum Episcopum," P.L. 66, cols. 1190–1191. On the authenticity of this letter, see Noonan, *Contraception*, p. 188, Note 9.

28. Schillebeeckx, *Marriage: Secular Reality and Saving Mystery*, II, p. 36.

29. See Noonan, "Freedom, Experimentation, and Permanence in the Canon Law of Marriage," pp. 53–56, 65–67; "History and the Values of Christian Marriage," pp. 3–5, where Noonan points out how very slowly the Church moved not only in the matter of authentic freedom of consent but also in the matter of slave marriages: "It is not, however, until the twelfth century that you find strong efforts by the universal church to legitimate slave marriages."

30. Schillebeeckx, *Marriage: Secular Reality and Saving Mystery*, II, p. 39. See also Noonan, "History and the Values of Christian Marriage," p. 5; "It was only in the thirteenth century that there were serious papal efforts to provide some remedy if a person had been coerced into marriage and even these remedies were hedged about with various restrictions. Protection . . . from simple fear of parents exercising their authority unjustly becomes operative in any substantial degree only in the seventeenth century."

31. For a discussion of the Thomistic understanding of polygamy and natural law, with the appropriate references, see Liam Ryan, "The Indissolubility of Marriage in Natural Law," *Irish Theological Quarterly* 31 (1964) 62–77; and Joyce, *Christian Marriage*, pp. 566–568: "The representative Scholastics . . . are agreed that natural law prescribes that marriage should be monogamous; but that the law is not of that absolute character which renders all exceptions impossible. . . . It follows (according to Aquinas) that nature sets monogamy before us as the true form of marriage, but that in certain altogether special circumstances

polygamy may become permissible. . . . he [Aquinas] does not suppose
that the law of monogamy was enforced by a positive divine command
(IV Sent., d. xxxiii, q. 1, art. 2): and elsewhere he gives it as his opinion
that, where secondary laws of nature are concerned, human authority
can judge where a dispensation is required (IV Sent., d. xxxiii, q. 2, art. 3,
q. 1, art. 1). "Aquinas also accepts uncritically Augustine's ill-founded
demographic theory that polygamy is an efficient means of increasing
the world's population.

32. See Appendix: "Polygamy and the Council of Trent."

33. See Daniel Maguire, *Moral Absolutes and the Magisterium*
(Washington and Cleveland: Corpus Papers, 1970), p. 8; Noonan,
Contraception, pp. 6, 165–166, 171; Philip Sherrard, "The Sexual Relationship in Christian Thought," *Studies in Comparative Religion* 5 (Summer
1971) 153–161; Joseph Blenkinsopp, *Sexuality and the Christian Tradition*
(Dayton: Pflaum, 1969), p. 9; and Josef Fuchs, "The Absoluteness of
Moral Terms," *Gregorianum* 52 (1971) 420: 'It could scarcely be supposed
that the Stoic, Judaic and Diaspora-Judaic ethos which Paul represents
was in all respects a timeless ethos. If it is self-evident to us today that
the Pauline directives concerning woman's position in marriage, in
society, and in the Church . . . are to be regarded as conditioned by his
times . . . we must indeed ask ourselves with what criterion we decide
that those directives which Paul seeks to validate, even theologically, are
historically conditioned and thus not absolute (i.e., universal).''

34. See Oscar E. Feucht, ed., *Sex and the Church: A Sociological, Historical, and Theological Investigation of Sex Attitudes* (St. Louis: Concordia,
1961), pp. 51–53; Noonan, *Contraception*, p. 151; Maguire, *Moral Absolutes*, p. 8: "On matters of sex and marriage . . . Augustine the Christian
was never fully free from Mani."

35. Augustine, "On Genesis according to the Letter," 9, 7, in *Corpus
scriptorum ecclesiasticorum latinorum* (Vienna, 1866), 28:275; as cited by
Maguire, *Moral Absolutes*, p. 9.

36. Augustine, *De bono conjugali*, i, c. 6, P.L. 40, cols. 377–378.

37. Pope Gregory the Great, "Epistola LXIV, Ad Augustinum Anglorum Episcopum," P.L. 77, col. 1196. See also cols. 1197–1198. The same
negative view of conjugal pleasure is found also in Gregory's "Regulae
pastoralis liber," pars 3, Admonitio 38, P.L. 77, cols. 101–103.

38. Pope Innocent III, "Comment. in VII Psalmos Poenitent., Psal.
IV." P.L. 217, cols. 1058–1059. See also Noonan, *Contraception*, pp.
242–243.

39. Schillebeeckx, *Marriage: Secular Reality and Saving Mystery*, II, p.
134. For more evidence of the generally negative attitude toward mar-

riage in the Western Christian tradition, and for signs of a gradual shift toward a more positive attitude, see Kerns, *Theology of Marriage*, pp. 41–83.

40. Kerns, *Theology of Marriage*, p. 90. For the Christian understanding of marriage in the twelfth century, see M. D. Chenu, *Nature, Man, and Society in the Twelfth Century*, trans. and ed. J. Taylor and L.K. Little (Chicago and London: University of Chicago Press, 1968), pp. 153–154; "Matrimony was considered as serving procreation more than conjugal love, and woman was an instrument of procreation more than a personal object of such love."

41. For the views of Gregory the Great, see Note 37 above. For Pius XII, see his encyclical letter "Sacra virginitas," in *Acta Apostolicae Sedis*, 43 (1951) 851.

42. Josef Fuchs, "The Theology of the Meaning of Marriage Today," in *Marriage in the Light of Vatican II*, ed. James T. McHugh (Washington: Family Life Bureau, U.S.C.C., 1968), p. 15.

43. For this and the following two paragraphs, see John de Reeper, *The Sacraments on the Missions* (Dublin: Browne and Nolan, 1957), pp. 282–320; and especially Paul E. Demuth, "The Nature and Origin of the Privilege of the Faith," *Resonance* 3 (Spring 1967) 60–73.

44. See Demuth, "Privilege of the Faith," pp. 63–65. See also Noonan, "Freedom, Experimentation, and Permanence in the Canon Law of Marriage," p. 63: According to the Fourth Council of Toledo (canon 63; Mansi 10: 634), "the right to divorce an unbelieving spouse may be turned by the Church into a duty, and the Church can legislatively destroy the marriage of two Jews, one of whom becomes a Christian."

45. See Demuth, "Privilege of the Faith," p. 70.

46. *Ibid.*, p. 71; René Leguerrier, "Recent Practice of the Holy See in Regard to the Dissolution of Marriages between Non-Baptized Persons without Conversion," *The Jurist* 25 (1965) 453–465; and John T. Noonan, Jr., "Indissolubility of Marriage and Natural Law," *The American Journal of Jurisprudence* 14 (1969) 92–94.

47. John Giles Milhaven, *Towards a New Catholic Morality* (Garden City, N.Y.; Doubleday, 1970), p. 29.

48. Noonan, "Indissolubility of Marriage and Natural Law," p. 94.

49. Thomas Aquinas, *Summa Theologiae* (Ottawa: Impensis Studii Generalis, O. Pr. 1941–1945), Suppl., q. 52, art. 1, ad 2: "Et quando natura non potest perducere ad maiorem perfectionem, inducit ad minorem, sicut quando non potest facere masculum, facit feminam, quae est 'mas occasionatus', ut dicitur in xvi *De Anim.* (Aristoteles, *De gen. Anim.*, II, iii)."

50. See Alan Tippett, "Polygamy as a Missionary Problem: The Anthropological Issues," *Church Growth Bulletin* 5 (March 1969) 60–63.

51. For a more detailed account, with the appropriate references, see Lyndon Harries, "Christian Marriage in African Society," in *Survey of African Marriage and Family Life,* ed. Arthur Phillips (London: Oxford University Press, 1953), pp. 329–359.

52. *Ibid.,* pp. 341–342. See also J.B. Webster, "Attitudes and Policies of the Yoruba Africa Church Towards Polygamy," in *Christianity in Tropical Africa,* ed. C.G. Bäeta (London: Oxford University Press, 1968), pp. 224–226.

53. John William Colenso, *Ten Weeks in Natal: a Journal of a First Visitation among the Colonists and the Zulu Kafirs of Natal* (Cambridge: Macmillan, 1855), p. 140. See also Colenso, *Remarks on the Proper Treatment of Cases of Polygamy as Found Existing in Converts from Heathenism* (Pietermaritzburg: May & Davis, 1855), p. 16.

54. Colenso, "Letter of 8th February 1860 to F.D. Dyster," as cited by George W. Cox, *The Life of Bishop John William Colenso* (London: W. Ridgway, 1888), I, p. 122.

55. See Harries, "Christian Marriage in African Society," pp. 344–345.

56. Webster, "Attitudes and Policies of the Yoruba African Church," p. 225.

57. See Harries, "Christian Marriage in African Society," pp. 351–352.

58. See Webster, "Attitudes and Policies of the Yoruba African Church," pp. 225–226.

59. Bremen Mission, Church Rules, 1976, par. 62, as cited by E. Grau, "Missionary Policies as Seen in the Work of Missions with the Evangelical Presbyterian Church, Ghana," in *Christianity in Tropical Africa,* p. 68.

60. See David B. Barrett, *Schism and Renewal in Africa* (Nairobi, Addis Ababa, Lusaka: Oxford University Press, 1968), pp. 117–118; Barrett, "Church Growth and Independency as Organic Phenomena: An Analysis of Two Hundred African Tribes," in *Christianity in Tropical Africa,* pp. 269–288. See also Webster, "Attitudes and Policies of the Yoruba African Church," pp. 227–228.

61. See Harold W. Turner, "Monogamy: A Mark of the Church?" *International Review of Mission* 55 (July 1966) 313; and Lesslie Newbigin, *Honest Religion for Secular Man* (London: SCM Press, 1966), pp. 73–74: "In the history of missions in Africa it has been more or less taken for granted that the abandonment of polygamy is always and at all times an essential mark of conversion."

62. Harry Boer, "Polygamy," *Frontier* 1 (Spring 1969) 24.

63. See R.M.C. Jeffrey, "Marriage and Baptism Regulations," Report

ME/SR/4, Church of England, London, no date (c. 1966) mimeographed, pp. 4–5.

64. The Bishop of Nyassaland, *Ecclesia*, July 1964, as cited by Jeffrey, "Marriage and Baptism Regulations," p. 5.

65. Two traditional Christian Churches in East Africa are following the same course as a matter of policy, but they do not wish the fact to be publicized, lest this information should occasion some misunderstanding among their church members in other parts of the world. According to Adrian Hastings, in his personal letter to the author (November 4, 1971), the Lutheran Church of Transvaal in South Africa has recently decided to follow the same course, and the Anglican Church in the Diocese of Victoria Nyanza in Tanzania has also taken some steps aimed at eventually adopting the same policy.

66. The theological and practical reflections behind this departure are contained in an unpublished paper by Harvey J. Currens, "Polygamy in the Church in Native Africa." Chicago: Lutheran Theological Seminary, January 1950 (typewritten).

67. G.E. Currens and R.J. Payne, "An Evaluation of the Policy of the Lutheran Church in Liberia on the Baptism of Polygamists," Monrovia, June 1965 (mimeographed), p. 3. See also G.E. Currens, "A Policy of Baptizing Polygynists Evaluated," *Africa Theological Journal* 2 (February 1969) 71–83.

68. Currens and Payne, "An Evaluation of the Policy of the Lutheran Church," p. 3.

69. *Ibid.*, p. 2.

70. *Ibid.*

71. Ralph E. Dodge, *The Unpopular Missionary* (Westwood, N.J.; Revell, 1964), p. 145. See also Noel Q. King, *Religions of Africa* (New York, London, and Evanston: Harper and Row, 1970), p. 75; There is a good deal of justification for the generalization that until outsiders came, prostitution (and there is some justification for adding promiscuity and homosexuality) was scarcely known in the interior of Africa. Polygamy in the form of polygyny was widely practiced, but its rules were strict and it was not a form of licentiousness. . . . No one should take it for granted that the present subsequent polygyny of some extreme forms of Western marriage is 'better' than the contemporaneous polygyny of traditional Africa."

72. For evidence of this new openness among Anglicans, see the survey of current opinions and practices, by Edward G. Newing, "The Baptism of Polygamous Families; Theory and Practice in an East African Church," *Journal of Religion in Africa* 2 (1970) 130–141. See also *The*

Lambeth Conference, 1968: Resolutions and Reports (London and New York: S.P.C.K. and Seabury Press, 1968), p. 37, Resolution 23, which asks each province of the Church to "re-examine its discipline" concerning polygamy and other such marriage problems.

73. See *Pastoral Perspectives in Eastern Africa after Vatican II*; AMECEA Study Conference Record (Nairobi, 1967), pp. 97–98 and Appendix.

74. See "The Committee of Churches of Dar es Salaam on the Government's Proposals for a Uniform Law of Marriage," *Tanzania Standard*, November 28, 1969, pp. 4, 5, 9. This refers to the Tanzania Government's proposals, *Mapendekezo ya Serikali juu ya Sheria ya Ndoa* (Dar es Salaam: Government Printer, September 1, 1969), pp. 1–12. See also Chapter Three, Note 50.

75. *Ibid.*

76. Josiah Kibira, "The Church in Buhaya: Crossing Frontiers," in *The Church Crossing Frontiers: Essays on the Nature of Mission, in Honor of Bengt Sundkler* (Uppsala, Sweden: Boktryckeri Aktiebolag, 1969), p. 196. See also G.C. Oosthuizen, *Post-Christianity in Africa: A Theological and Anthropological Study* (London: C. Hurst and Co., 1968), p. 199, where the author quotes from a 1962 report prepared for the Christian Council of Nigeria: "Of all the problems that confront the Church in West Africa, polygamy is the most difficult with perhaps the least light. Like an ominous dark cloud it seems to haunt the Church in all areas."

77. Peter Sarpong, as quoted by Desmond O'Grady, "The Church in Africa: Coming into Its Own," *U.S. Catholic* 38 (February 1973), p. 32.

78. John Njenga, "Customary African Marriage," *African Ecclesiastical Review* 16 (1974) 120.

79. See Appendix II, under the heading "Marriage and the Christian Family," *African Ecclesiastical Review* 16 (1974) 260.

CHAPTER II

CULTURE AND CHRISTIANITY

> To us this confusing of the European
> way of life with Christianity was a
> contradiction of terms.
>
> TOM MBOYA

Because of man's necessary involvement in, and his essential dependence upon, the contingencies of time and place, every concrete moral judgement and ethical system is historically conditioned and culturally formed; and so it is also with each of man's religiously inspired moral acts.[1] It is now widely recognized, as Lesslie Newbigin expresses it, "that every human life and every articulated body of human thought has been shaped by the particular epoch in which it occurred and shares the relativity of that epoch."[2] This humble acknowledgement of human finitude, if we really accept it, leads to some difficult questions about the alleged universal and objective (transcultural and suprahistorical) teachings of traditional Christian ethics and moral theology.[3]

It may be taken as a universally objective moral imperative, or a primary precept of the natural law, that every man should do good and avoid evil. But how readily discernible is the good and the evil beneath the variegated camouflage of history in the changing circumstances of diverse cultures? While it may be quite clear on a general and theoretical level that all men should do good and avoid evil, it is by no means always and everywhere evident just what is good and what is evil in particular instances.

47

"In matters of action," as Thomas Aquinas puts it, "truth or practical rectitude is not the same for all."[4] On this aspect of the Thomistic natural law theory, Liam Ryan offers the following pertinent comment:

> The *philosophical* factor in human nature necessarily gives rise to immutable moral rules. Beyond a certain point, however, human nature is variable, being shaped by physical and social environment, and so the moralist who follows the principles of St. Thomas will take careful account of this *cultural* factor in human nature and will not be likely to transfer a judgement which is really proper to one society or historical period to another society which is characterized by significantly different social life and customs.[5]

Slavery provides a dramatic example of this sort of moral relativity. The present attitude of Christians toward this socio-economic institution is, as Peter Berger reminds us, "anything but timeless."[6] Good Christians, great theologians, and diligent ecclesiastical officials have not always and everywhere seen slavery as universally and objectively incompatible with the natural law and the teaching of Jesus.[7] Surely, we cannot just dismiss all these Christians of former times as morally unrefined. Dare we suggest that Christians today have a greater moral sensitivity than our forefathers had? No indeed. The reason for the difference between now and then will be found rather in the different socio-cultural situations that gave rise to profoundly different moral viewpoints on the institution of slavery: the moral vision of each generation, ours no less than theirs, is limited by the circumstances of time and place. Later generations will see, better than we do now, just how limited our own horizons are today. The point here is that there is a kind of moral relativity which is unavoidably determined by one's socio-cultural and historical vantage point. In other words, the Christian "way" can be followed by men here and now only in the terms of their particular history.

With a view to situating the missionary and pastoral problem of African plural marriage in its wider human context, as one of many similar problems arising from mankind's cultural diversity and the Church's unifying significance, the following reflections are offered on the perennial tension between culture and Christianity. Both the explicit presuppositions and the tacit assumptions of our theological moralizing deserve to the reexamined in the light of this general tension. What is called for, in other words, is a radical historico-cultural hermeneutic.[8] Culture, as well as history, must be taken more seriously than has been the wont of theologians, moralists, canonists, and missionaries in the past. In the very first place, this means that a number of obstacles, inherited from the past, must at least be indicated and recognized for what they are, even if perhaps they cannot be entirely cleared away: certain uncritical habits of thinking, especially the use of ethnocentric standards of valuation.

Ethnocentrism is a term used by sociologists and anthropologists to designate the tendency that each of us has to judge the ways of other peoples according to the norms that prevail in our own culture, instead of trying to understand the others according to the norms that are considered appropriate in their respective cultures. In some parts of the world this way of judging others is called "racism"; in Africa it is usually called "tribalism." A professor of sociology describes ethnocentrism in the following terms:

> Once people of a particular culture have identified their own way of life with nature, they tend to judge other cultures according to the standards which prevail in their own. They tend to define as wrong or evil or un-natural the cultural practices which constitute the way of life of people of a culture different from their own. . . . Once people of one culture have defined their way of life as "natural", and it is inevitable that they will do so, once they have begun to define the way of life of others as wrong or un-natural, the possibility of communication is limited. People of Culture A see in Culture B only the meaning that things have for them in their own culture. They do not perceive the meaning which things in Culture B have for the people in Culture B.[9]

In an effort to be "objective," men pretend to see reality from a divine vantage point outside of history and above culture. But this cannot be done with the eyes of men. The result is ethnocentrism, against which we must be always on guard; for this kind of blindness leads all to readily, as we know from recent and ancient history, to things more wicked than the cultural obtuseness of well-intentioned missionaries.

The focus of attention in this chapter will be particularly upon culture: the universal problem of cultural obtuseness, the meaning of culture itself, the fact of cultural diversity, and the inevitable tension with Christianity. While reference is made here especially to the African scene, the principles involved obviously have a much wider relevance. Perhaps these reflections may also be taken, therefore, as a modest contribution to the effort of those who are today trying to redeem Christian ethics and moral theology by providing them with a method that is more conscious of the historico-cultural dimensions of human nature.[10]

Since this newer methodology has not yet been fully elaborated, some of the ideas expressed here should be regarded as tentative probings and suggestions, rather than definitive statements. Again, the primary concern of the present study is to raise the right questions, and to set them in their proper perspectives, rather than to answer them. For it is impossible to find authentically Christian answers to questions which have not been considered, first, in all of their human complexity.

CULTURAL OBTUSENESS

Missionaries, ill-acquainted with the findings of the social sciences and burdened with the cultural pride of their own Western world, have been notoriously obtuse in their approaches to the peoples of the larger world. Many of them, so like the "Judaizers" in the very first period of the Church's missionary history, have become Christianity's self-assured "Westernizers." For them, Euro-American social institutions and cultural values were inseparable from Christianity; so their evangelical mission was very much a matter of what Jomo Kenyatta refers to, with appropriate scorn, as "civilizing and uplifting poor savages."[11] Where indigenous social structures and cultural patterns were not condemned, they were gradually supplanted or merely ignored. This, at any rate, was the usual procedure. For the usual type of missionary imagined that what was good for the peoples of the

West would also be good for the peoples elsewhere; so these foreigners, as Stephen Neill says, "tended to reproduce as nearly as possible a replica of the society in which they grew up"; and the missionaries' insistence on the monogamy rule is "the classic example of the perils involved in the transference of the principles of one society, without due consideration, to another society which has been developed on very different principles."[12]

Far from understanding the universal significance of the circumcision debates recorded in the Acts of the Apostles, some of these missionaries insisted even upon "uncircumcision" as a condition for participation in the sacramental life of the Church.[13] In his spirited criticism of the Roman Catholic approach to the evangelization of the non-Western world, Bernard Häring reminds us that the theologians, who should have known better, "did not dare to speak up when ecclesiastical authorities and organizations declared the Latin language and the Latin culture to be *sopracultura* and ascribed to the church the task of civilizing the barbarians with the aid of Latin theology and the Latin liturgy."[14] What very few missionaries seem to have understood is the significance of culture, as expressed so clearly by Jomo Kenyatta some thirty years ago: "It is the culture which he inherits that gives a man his human dignity as well as his material prosperity."[15]

The results are well known. Countless Western spiritual colonies have been established throughout the world in imitation gothic, romanesque, baroque, etc. The myriad cultures of men, the only proper foundations of human dignity, have become for millions of Christians sources of embarrassment and anxiety. In parts of Africa there has emerged a new anthropological category which President Julius Nyerere calls "Black Europeans": those who have come to believe, as a result of a Westernizing system of education, that "we had no indigenous culture of our own, or that what we had was so uncouth as to be a cause of shame to us, and not a cause of pride."[16] As the late Tom Mboya expressed it:

> In the early days the church objected to the African dances as primitive and uncivilized, and for years there was complete conflict between the church and those Africans who wanted to continue

African traditions and customs and stood for African culture. . . . To us this confusing of the European way of life with Christianity was entirely a contradiction of terms.[17]

This persistent and widespread display of ethnocentrism, which is certainly not a weakness of missionaries only, nor of Western peoples exclusively, prompted the erudite President of Senegal to say that Europeans and North Americans "have no idea of the preeminent dignity of the human person."[18] Another articulate African observer of the missionary achievement remarked that "it is an irresponsible Christian, a half-Christian, that is being created; and the fruit of this work reflects more the glory of European Christendom that it does the glory of Christ and of God."[19] It is, he went on to say, "a facile type of success"; for it has been achieved by ignoring, if not condemning outright, many indigenous cultural values, deeply rooted customs, and meaningful social structures.

The same criticism was expressed more recently by Professor Bolaji Idowu of the University of Ibadan. In his words, the missionary effort in Africa "succeeded not only in enlightening, but also in enslaving the mind, in as much as it inculcated that the only way to human dignity and full-grown personality was to be in everything like Europeans and to despise their own culture."[20] Even today, in the opinion of two other Ibadan professors, "many scholars are so emotionally and unyieldingly attached to Western civilization that they cannot help adopting a rather negative attitude towards indigenous African religious ideas and idioms, festivals, rituals and institutions, much of which remain part of the spiritual life of African Christians, and are not repugnant to Bible Christianity, but have found no place in institutionalized Christiantiy in Africa."[21]

There is behind all of this an excessive measure of Western cultural arrogance: a naive belief that Western culture is not only superior totally and cumultatively to all other cultures, but that it is also more human and, thus, the only appropriate instrument for the communication and incarnation of Christianity. As Belloc expressed it, "Europe is the faith; the faith is Europe."[22] This is not the opinion of merely one man—it is a reflection of the Western mentality up until very recently.

The thought of Ernst Troeltsch on this matter is significant. He considered Christianity to be so "indissolubly bound up with elements of the ancient and modern civilization of Europe" that it "stands or falls" with this particular civilization.[23] He even found a sign of Christianity's validity and divine origin (but not its exclusive truth) in the fact that it is the religion of Europeans. "Christianity," in the opinion of Troeltsch, "could not be the religion of such a highly developed racial group if it did not possess a mighty power and truth."[24] So it would seem to follow that the encounter in faith with Christ among the "less developed races" can take place only in terms of Western culture and, thus, only among Western peoples or among others who have become Westernized. Troeltsch, more than most of his contemporaries, had a generous appreciation of non-Western cultures. But he saw no way of making the Christian message intelligible in non-Western terms; so he inclined to the view that the West should not even send missionaries to the rest of the world.

Troeltsch's fellow Christians solved this problem by sending out missionaries who would present Christianity as a package inextricably intertwined with their own Western ethnic conventions and social institutions, as "a substitute from the higher religion and culture" of the West, as something to be simply accepted or rejected in its totality.[25] What Bernard Häring said of Roman Catholic missionaries is generally true also, *mutatis mutandis*, of all other Christian missionaries sent to Africa during the nineteenth century and most of the twentieth century:

> The education in ethics which we gave to our missionaries was largely a mixture (seemingly unproblematical) of elements taken from the Gospel and from the Roman practice of law. It mirrored the culture of peoples living near the Mediterranean. Our ethics were far too European. The ease with which we declared that our own particular customs and conceptions were the eternal law of nature was not only a sign of our ignorance of other cultures and traditions but also a mirror of our European pride. We held ourselves to be "the cultured people" while we left to others only the right to learn from us and be instructed by us.[26]

Given this sort of widespread cultural obtuseness, it is not surprising that so many missionaries, with the best of intentions, should have acted as they did. Their historically conditioned outlook may account also for the curious "fusion of economic and

spiritual aspirations" which characterized so much of this early
missionary enterprise in Africa.[27] Somehow, in spite of everything, Christianity has taken root in Africa while Western civilization manifests itself there mostly in the accoutrements of com-
mercial trading.

In fairness, however, it must be added immediately that there
has always been a minority of missionaries who, in the authentic
spirit of Saint Paul, strove to transcend the limitations of their
own cultures of origin and to accomplish their task with full
respect for the diverse cultures of the peoples they served. The
most famous names in this tradition are Robert de Nobili and
Matteo Ricci, but many others have tried to follow the same
general principles.[28] And the highest officials of the Roman
Catholic Church have consistently issued missionary directives
and guidelines which, although seldom followed in fact, belong
to this same tradition. Here is one of the more striking examples,
taken from an official instruction to missionaries in 1695:

> Do not regard it as your task, and do not bring any pressure to bear
> on the peoples, to change their manners, customs and uses, unless
> they are evidently contrary to religion and sound morals.[29]

The supposition here is that all the manners and customs of the
peoples are good, and to be regarded as compatible with the
Christian faith, unless the opposite is patent. The burden of
proof, therefore, rests upon those who feel that a particular
custom, practice, or institution cannot be harmonized with Christian belief. This general missionary principle—that an indigenous custom or institution has a prior claim to validity—is supported in the same instruction by this pragmatic consideration:

> It is the nature of men to love and treasure above everything else
> their own country and that which belongs to it; in consequence there
> is no stronger cause for alienation and hate than an attack on local
> customs, especially when these go back to venerable antiquity. This
> is more especially the case when an attempt is made to introduce the
> customs of another people in place of those which have been
> abolished.[30]

While it is fashionable these days to dramatize the very many real
shortcomings of the missionary enterprise, honesty demands a

more contextual type of criticism than is usually given to missionaries. As men, working in this or that particular time and place, their horizons were necessarily limited. Some day it will be seen that the horizons even of their present critics are limited. This is what it means to live within the dimensions of history. However, a careful analysis of the abundant phenomenological evidence might show that, in spite of all the blindness, the missionary achievement considerably outweighs the mischief.[31] African nationalists are among the most perceptive of critics; and one of them, until recently a leading political figure in Nigeria, offered this interesting observation:

> When African historians come to write their own account of the adventure of Africa with imperialism, they will write of the missionaries as the greatest friends the African had.[32]

Thanks to the enlightening influence of the social sciences, the present renewal of theological reflection, and the new attitudes of the postcolonial period, many missionaries today, and a growing number of the local pastoral clergy of the young churches in Africa, accept the validity of the criticisms previously cited. They would agree that the time has come, in this last hour of the Christian missions as we have known them, for some positive action toward a cultural indigenization of Christianity in Africa. If indeed it is possible to learn from history, the missionaries of the future, whether they will be sent out from the young churches of Africa or from the older churches of the West, should find it somewhat easier to appreciate the central importance of understanding and respecting the cultures of the peoples to whom they may be sent.

Nevertheless, this sensitivity to the cultures of other peoples cannot be regarded, even today, as something that is acquired casually, without conscious effort and persistent care. One example, which is quite relevant to the contemporary African scene, may serve to illustrate the point. The *Pastoral Constitution on the Church in the Modern World,* issued by Vatican Council II, is obviously a contemporary document; and it is addressed not only to Roman Catholics and "to all who invoke the name of Christ, but to the whole of humanity" (GS 2). Yet none of the Council fathers seems to have noticed that the writers of this document rather obtusely consigned polygamy (without even bothering to distinguish its very different forms) to the same category as "the plague of divorce, so-called free love, and other disfigurements" that obscure the excellence of marriage (GS 47). There is here a curious lack of care, if not a complete failure of understanding.

Cultural arrogance is congenital, however unconsciously it may be expressed by well-intentioned people; so the African writer, Joseph Okpaku, was expressing a righteous indignation when he remarked that "the West has always had a pejorative attitude toward Africa," and this is "self-evident."[33] On the grounds of invincible ignorance, one may perhaps excuse the early missionaries who tended to condemn or ignore customs which they did not even try to understand in terms of African culture. But this sort of blindness is inexcusable today. Jomo Kenyatta's cogent plea, made more than thirty years ago, for a more enlightened and respectful approach to customary plural marriage in Africa was not heeded by missionaries and moralists who could see polygamy only in terms of sexual excess and moral inferiority.[34] Now, in a tone which suggests that African forbearance is unlimited, John Mbiti asks again:

> I plead with people from other cultures and backgrounds, to try to understand the meaning behind African marriage and family life, and to be patient in passing harsh judgments on our traditional marriage customs and ideas.[35]

For those who cannot hear such a modestly formulated request, there are the more specific and vigorous words—more like an admonition than a plea—of A. J. Ade. Ajayi and E. A. Ayandele, for whom the "most obvious example" of Western negativism regarding African culture is "the great amount of fuss made about the issue of monogamy, as if it were the most fundamental dogma of the Christian Church, and possessing indubitable scriptural validity."[36] These are the words of two reputable African historians whose allegations cannot be lightly dismissed:

> Even scholars who have presented in their writings sociological data that demonstrate in bold relief the merits of polygamy in African society have failed to expose the fallacy of the doctrine that

monogamy was divinely ordained and not an accretion of European cultural development. Till this day, nearly all European scholars and Westernized Churches in Africa continue to indulge in moral condemnation of the institution of polygamy in a manner prejudicial to scientific objectivity.[37]

What, then, is the meaning of "scientific objectivity" in the moral theology of a Church which aspires to be at home among all peoples?

THE MEANING OF CULTURE

In modern anthropology the word culture refers to the whole complex of learned patterns of thought and behavior which belong commonly and characteristically to the members of a permanent human group who share a sense of common history and destiny who regard themselves, and are recognized by other such groups, as a people apart in the family of mankind. Since men experience human existence only in the limited dimensions of particular historical times and places, and since permanent culture groups normally grow from the seeds of biologically related family and clan units, there is necessarily in the world a plurality of cultures and an ethnic background (real and/or fictive) to each culture.

Instead of speaking of African culture as such, it is therefore necessary to speak of the cultures of African peoples or tribes or nations. It is within these ethnological groups—as total, concrete and cohesive entities—that cultures are created, developed, and handed on. This process really does not occur within groups that are merely conventional or legal, such as may be constituted by an army or by an aggregate of factory workers. Thus, real as they are throughout Africa, political nation-states are not by themselves the creative bearers of culture, unless they happen to be at the same time ethnological and linguistic units bound by a common sense of historical destiny, as well as common socioeconomic interests. There is, of course, much more than this to be said about the relationships between peoples, environments, cultures, languages, economies, and nation-states in modern Africa. But, for our purpose, the word culture has the meaning just indicated and as understood in contemporary scholarly literature.[38]

The patterns of a particular culture are delicately interwoven multicolored threads. They form a web of thought categories, values scales, emotional responses, communication media, religious aspirations, moral ideals, artistic expressions, aesthetical norms, and educational methods. The complex includes, also, techniques of survival, food production, household management, economic insurance, child-rearing, social control, mutual assistance, as well as all those activities and functions that might come under such headings as manners, myths, laws, rites, taboos, customs, traditions, institutions, games, practices, habits, styles, folkways, social systems, and organizational structures. All of these represent the genius of many human generations who discovered, invented, borrowed, and integrated the elements available and useful to them for their human existence in their bioclimatic region of the earth.

All of these functional elements are dynamically interrelated, vitally depending one upon the other, in the manner of a living organism. This is why no socio-cultural element can be correctly understood in isolation, without reference to its particular place and function within the total system to which it belongs.[39] All of these elements are, as it were, alive in each strand of the web. The interaction is for the most part unconsciousness; yet everything is experientially learned by each member of the culture group, in the same way that each one learns his own native language. This is the work of a lifetime, the primary educationtional experience of every man, the labor of becoming human. This can be done only within one's own culture group, by accepting one's social heritage: receiving it, learning it, integrating new elements into it, transmitting it within the group, and offering to share it with those outside.

Each culture is thus a human achievement laid over, and largely dependent upon, the bioclimatic environment in which a people finds itself. The achievement amounts to what Bronislaw Malinowski calls "an organized system of purposeful activity,"[40] guided by a carefully worked-out scale of values, an order of means and ends, with a measure of adaptablity, directed to the living of a harmonious and dignified human life. All the values of a particular system—economic, biologic, as well as those values which are less tangible and not even articulated—are concerned with what is regarded as the good human life of all who belong to the group. The ideal of the good life may seldom, if ever, be realized; but most people are convinced that their way of life is the best way of becoming truly human. In this sense, all peoples are basically ethnocentric and culture bound. As Ruth Benedict says, "no man ever looks at the world with pristine eyes."[41]

So fully and profoundly are we influenced, permeated, and circumscribed by our own culture that we tend to become its prisoners. Every human act is culturally conditioned. Not only our external behavior, but our every judgment, even our inner-most thoughts and emotional responses, are formed and shaped and colored by our own particular cultural experience and histor-ical vantage point.[42] Yet each culture represents, conserves, and communicates something of the total human experience and the creative genius of the species. Each does this in its own limited but unique fashion. No single culture group encompasses the whole wealth of the human experience; but each one expresses some irreplaceable aspects of it—nuances that other peoples, engaged in different historico-cultural situations, have missed. The nature and the multiplicity of languages may be taken as an example of this uniqueness.

Each language, with its unmentioned presuppositions and silent gestures as well as its spoken sounds, is able to say some things that no other language is capable of expressing quite so well. And how much of our self-expression, even our ability to think, is confined within the limits of our own particular lan-guage? Together with all the other phenomena of culture, lan-guage molds discourse, as Levi-Strauss says, "beyond the con-sciousness of the individual, imposing on his thought conceptual schemes which are taken as objective."[43] Among another people, even when we have studiously acquired a knowledge of their language, we can be rendered deaf, mute, and blind by their supple manipulation of thier own means of communication. Im-portant as linguistic ability may be, this alone is not enough for real intercultural communication which takes place only to the extent that we are able to participate in the culture of those with whom we seek to communicate. Participation is the primary mode of learning; and we all have much to learn from one another.

The starting point for any meaningful encounter between the members of different cultures is, therefore, a humble realization that every man, ourselves included, is intelligible to himself and to others only in the context of his own culture and experience. It is only in these terms, conditioned as they are by the circumstances of particular times and places, that human life is lived, reflected upon, and expressed. So, to reach some understanding of the behavior patterns and social systems of an alien culture, there is required, first of all, an unequivocal disposition and willingness to learn. On the part of the learner this presupposes at least a conscious suppression of the tendency to pass comparative judgments on the ways of others, especially those critical judgments based upon the arrogant assumption—which is *a priori* and self-evident only to ourselves—that "our ways are of course superior and more human."

To learn from others: this is a call to transcend our own cultural limitations and congenital blindness. To do this, even partially, is to achieve a measure of liberation, a new vantage point, a broader horizon, a fresh vision of the world, a better look at humanity and what it means to be human. The new vantage point also enables us to criticize our own culture and ourselves. We all need this, and more. We also need, and we desire, to glimpse at least the possibility of human unity in multiformity. This is a primordial and universal aspiration arising from the very nature of the human predicament. Man's repeated attempts to impose uniformity in the name of unity have always been futile, and often ghastly, ever since the erection of the first Tower of Babel.

CULTURAL DIFFERENCES

It is clear enough that cultures differ. But it is quite another thing to regard them as better or worse, higher or lower, more or less human. Nor should they be seen as simple or complex, primitive or advanced, savage or civilized. Such terminology has too many pejorative connotations. Besides, how are such comparisons to be verified when the only criteria are those which have been invented within, and for the purposes of, particular cultures? With such norms the members of each culture are apt to demonstrate merely the superiority of their own respective cultures. Lacking the divine perspective, and without universal norms that are readily accepted among all peoples, the most that we can say honestly is that each culture is different. Cultures, as totalities, are not subject to the comparative terminology that earlier social scientists used so uncritically.[44]

Instead of accepting the Western experience as an *a priori* norm for comparing all societies, and categorizing them as "savage" or "barbarous" or "civilized," it is now generally recognized, with Robert Lowie, that "in the sphere of social life there is no objective criterion for grading cultural phenomena."[45]

It should be obvious today that Western peoples cannot afford to speak any longer of "savage" or "barbarous" societies in comparison with their own "civilized" societies, although it might be correct to say that savagery and barbarism, which are found among all peoples just below the cultural surface, are generally better organized and more efficiently exercised in the West.[46] Nor is it particularly helpful to speak of "primitive" peoples in the world today. The popular connotations of this misleading term are rooted in a naive cultural evolutionism which was formerly taken to be scientific. Anyone might use this same obsolete hypothesis to show that his own people are more "advanced" than others. It depends merely upon the criteria of value that are taken as the norms of comparison.

If, for example, we evaluate societies by their contribution to mankind's long-range survival potential, then the so-called "primitive" societies must be rated superior to the so-called "civilized" societies which have recently "progressed" to the point of threatening to annihilate mankind in a variety of scientific ways: through nuclear or chemical or biological warfare, or by rendering the environment incapable of sustaining human life, or by tampering with the genetic processes of the human species. Another example: If the chosen norm of valuation is the authenticity, multiplicity, and complexity of personal relationships within the human group, then again the "noncivilized"

societies are apt to be rated "higher" than the industrialized
societies of the Western world.[47]

Moreover, according to the theory of biological evolution,
upon which cultural evolutionism has been resting precariously
since the end of the last century, there are in the world today no
primitive peoples.[48] All of our contemporaries are equally distant
from the remote beginnings of the human sojourn; so none of the
living cultures, through which men are actually achieving and
expressing their human existence, can rightly be described as
"backward" or "retarded" or "archaic."[49] Another way of putting it: archeologists and paleontologists are properly concerned
with primitive man, while social anthropologists are interested in
contemporary man as he exists in a multitude of different cultural
contexts, each with its own long history and many changes, each
with its own world view and balance of functional structures
which have been worked out in the course of countless generations. In the words of Claude Levi-Strauss:

> So-called primitive societies, of course, exist in history; their past is
> as old as ours, since it goes back to the origin of the species. Over
> thousands of years they have undergone all sorts of
> transformations. . . . But they have specialized in ways different
> from those which we have chosen. Perhaps they have in certain
> respects remained closer to very ancient conditions of life, but this
> does not preclude the possibility that in other respects they are
> further from these conditions than we are.[50]

Following the insights of the German historian Ranke, who saw
that each generation is as immediate to God as any other generation, and that each generation is therefore capable of experienc-
ing a fullness of the human spirit, Peter Berger urges the total
rejection of "the vulgar progressivism that sees one's own moment in history as history's pinnacle,"[51] and he warns us not "to
think of history as a straight line of 'progress,' ascending of
necessity to ever greater knowledge of the truth about man."[52]
For, a variety of truths about the human experience—and many
different ways of achieving a refinement of the human spirit
—can be discovered, lost, rediscovered, emphasized, or overlooked in the course of history which is not "a giant escalator

ascending to the point at which we happen to be standing."[53]

Considering each generation's immediacy to God, and with due respect to each generation's socio-cultural situation in history, "it is in no way certain, but altogether possible, that we know some things about the scope of *humanitas* that have never been known before."[54] At the same time, still following Berger's line of thought, "it is also possible that there was a secret conclave of Aztec priests who knew something we have not even dreamed of—and that this truth perished with them, never to be rediscovered." Not only each past generation, but also every different cultural context today should be carefully studied for whatever signs of transcendence, wisdom, and human refinement might belong to it uniquely.[55]

A very long view of history is necessary if we are going to think seriously about the progressive and/or retrogressive aspects of all human cultures. If elaborate technology and mass literacy are not required for the refinement of the human spirit and for the attainment of a full and noble human existence, then, in terms of what it means basically to be human, can we affirm with any degree of certitude that *homo occidentalis mechanicus* represents any real progress beyond the level of human refinement already achieved by Cro-Magnon man?[56] It is even possible to raise the question, as some scholars have done recently, as to whether the human species, at least in some of its Western segments, is not now caught in a process of degenerative evolution.

"Contemporary geneticists," writes Paul Ramsey, "are increasingly being driven to varying degrees of gloom regarding the future of mankind because of the inexorable degeneration of the human genetic pool under the conditions of modern life."[57] While the life styles of modern Western man certainly offer many short-term advantages to a small segment of the contemporary world population, it could well be that what is good for this particular segment is at the same time ominous in its long-term implication for humanity as a whole. Where the biological process of natural selection becomes progressively less significant in determining which members of the species will reproduce themselves, there are certain inevitable and perhaps irreversible consequences which Ramsey describes as "an insidious genetic deterioration that will leave us less fit than when we began."[58]

In addition to the gloomy consensus among geneticists, account must also be taken of the forebodings of many other students of human life. While "all thoughful persons worry about the future of the children who will have to spend their lives under the absurd social and environmental conditions we are thoughtlessly creating," René Dubos poignantly reminds us that "even more disturbing is the fact that the physical and mental characteristics of mankind are being shaped *now* by dirty skies and cluttered streets, anonymous high rises and amorphous urban sprawl, social attitudes which are more concerned with things than with men."[59] The progressive "dehumanization of life" appears to be an unavoidable result of Western man's "aggressive behavior for money or for prestige" and his calculated waste of the world's natural resources.[60]

The substantive questions just touched upon provide a background which should help us to understand the larger dimensions of the immediately practical issue before us: the tendency to make ill-founded comparisons between different cultures and, thus, to reach pejorative conclusions about the ways of alien peoples. It must be said repeatedly that to excel in one area or another of human experience—whether in technology or social organization or economic development, whether in the marketing of soap or in polar-bear hunting or in some department of knowledge or in the accumulation of knowledge itself—is not at all the same thing as excelling in the total realm of being human.

To pursue excellence in one particular area is, at the same time, to forfeit similar initiatives in many other areas. Eskimos are excellent technicians, but poor sociologists, while the reverse is true of the Australian aborigines.[61] An illiterate Masai herdboy knows more about the uses of the steppe andvegatation of East Africa than does a Western graduate student in botany. Humanistic developments in each culture are uneven, as are also the achievements of applied sciences. But these are differences of degree, not of kind.[62] Without a total understanding of all the knowledge, wisdom, problems, and functional factors of each culture, we cannot begin to compare cultures against one another and against some allegedly absolute norm of human excellence.

The problematical character of cultural progress is demonstrated throughout history. The classical culture of ancient Greece, with its emphasis on wisdom and beauty and freedom for the sake of an elite group, was developed together with, and in dependence upon, the corrupt socio-economic institution of slavery. [63] Indeed, this large-scale degradation of human beings was a major factor in the cultural development and productivity of the great city-states of the Far East as well as those of the Mediterranean basin; and a somewhat similar form of institutionalized inhumanity accompanied the Western cultural transformations associated with the technological and industrial progress in Europe and North America. [64] And what is the price of the economic advancements that have produced the modern American culture of obscene affluence and luxurious waste? Given about twenty more years of the present rate and uncontrolled style of this technological and economic "progress," the bioclimatic substratum of the American way of life will have been reduced to an inhospitable wastland. Techinical efficiency can destroy social efficiency. Any number of additional questions might be raised concerning the moral vulgarity that is so blatantly displayed in the American cultural patterns of economic development and progress. [65]

So, progress in one area should always be evaluated against retrogression in other areas of the same culture. Probably the only truly universal norm of human progress is the concern, respect, and love that men should have for one another. A very high level of such sensitivity may be accompanied by the use of inadequate techniques. A case in point is the New Testament's good Samaritan who, while manifesting the highest type of human behavior, used a medical technique that might have done more harm than good: pouring oil and wine into wounds. We know, also, and it is hardly necessary to cite examples, that the most up-to-date knowledge and the most efficient techniques are compatible with a low level of moral sensitivity, and even with a general regression in all other aspects of being human.

While whole cultures as such are not comparable, it is possible, as we have just illustrated, to use comparative terminology (better, worse, etc.) with reference to some of the isolated elements of particular cultures. The technique of curing malaria with chloroquin, for example, may be regarded as better than trying to do it by means of magical charms or blood-letting. When this is actually seen to be the case, then chloroquin is very likely to be incorporated into the culture of those who preciously used much less efficient means. For it is not only through discoveries and inventions, but also by borrowing things that serve their human aims and purposes, that cultures are enriched, developed, and changed.

One thing leads to another; and even a modest adaptation may result eventually in far-reaching changes. As already noted, innovations in one area of a culture can also bring about deterioration in other areas. Newly accepted elements, which are not harmoniously integrated into the whole culture, can even initiate a process of disintegration and dehumanization. Briefly, the dynamics of social change may be summed up in the words of Raymond Firth:

> A change in established patterns tends to bring unforeseen results in its train. The functional interrelation of activities is very delicate. So people who have adopted an innovation may find themselves facing a situation to which they must conform, though very much against what they would have chosen in the beginning could they have known. These new situations, in which unwanted changes are enforced on some members of the society and unforeseen effects encountered by others, pose fresh organizational problems. So the stage is set for further efforts at change. The essence of the dynamic process lies in the continuous operation of the individual psyche, with its potential of unsatisfied desires . . . within the universe of its social system.[66]

CULTURE AND CHRISTIANITY IN TENSION

The fact that Christianity has become an integral part of all Western cultures does not mean that these have become Christian cultures. Although Christianity and particular cultures have had far-reaching influences upon one another, no single culture stands over and above all the others as *the* Christian culture. No particular set of cultural patterns and social structures is in itself specifically Christian. Aside from a short-lived experiment in radical communalism, the earliest Christians generally continued to follow the basic patterns and structures of the societies in which they lived prior to their acceptance of the Christian "way." Even "the ethical teaching of the early Church," says C.H. Dood, "falls into a scheme of practical precepts for everyday living, a scheme based upon a realistic recognition of the structure as it then was, and following in general outline the patterns of ethical teaching which were being set forth by the teachers of other schools."[67]

Even if they had wished to do so, the first Christians could not have created a whole new socio-cultural complex, with its own new ethical system, to guide them in their new lives as Christians. They could not have done this any more than they could have invented a new language. It was expected, of course, that the Christian gospel, acting after the manner of a leaven, would profoundly influence all cultures.[68] Thus, the unity of mankind would be, hopefully, signified through the multiform manifestations of the same faith in the diverse cultures of the tribes and peoples and nations who constitute the whole of humanity in the extension of different historical times and places.[69]

It was in keeping with the logic of the Incarnation that the first Christians should have expressed their new faith in their own indigenous cultural forms. These happened to be Judaic and Greco-Roman. Perhaps because he participated in both of these cultures, Saint Paul was better able than most men to achieve a measure of cultural transcendence. He provided the theological rationale for the cultural multiformity of Christianity. Indeed, the whole of his theology is best understood as a response to those who imagined that the Judaic culture alone provided worthy patterns and structures for the expression and development of their new faith.[70] This very question of culture and faith provoked the first great theological crisis in the Church: the first of many similar crises that have since arisen from the ethnocentrism of dedicated ecclesiastical functionaries.[71] With the acceptance of Paul's views, however, the principle was at least established that Christianity not only could, but should, take on the cultural flesh of one new people after another in the course of history.

It is not suprising, therefore, that elements which are recognizably Christian in their inspiration, if not always in their actual functioning, should have developed in many societies as a result of the Church's missionary outreach. But no single culture has become *the* Christian culture, just as no man has become a perfect follower of Christ: none of us. We are all "pagans" trying, sometimes, to become Christians. At the same time, elements that are recognizably "pagan" in their inspiration were drawn into the service of the Church: Platonism, Stoicism, Roman law, Aristotelianism, pontifical trappings, Christmas trees, etc., And such things as racism (tribalism), found today in many Christian communities, owe nothing to the spirit of the gospel, but everything to the cultural attitudes of men who would become Christians. So it is, also, with the pernicious economic system through which nature is despoiled and human relationships are reduced to naked self-interest. The ambiguity of Christianity in its various historical manifestations, as well as the ambivalence of Christians in their daily lives, may be seen as inevitable consequences of the historical relationship between culture and Christianity. This relationship is sometimes incarnational and sometimes merely symbiotic; and, where culture and Christianity are both alive, there is always tension.

These two notions, incarnation and symbiosis, may be used to describe the normal historical situation of Christianity in the world. The Lord himself fully accepted the Judaic culture into which he was born and which formed him as a human being. It was within the limited historical framework of this culture that Jesus accomplished his mission. His approach was incarnational. But, with many elements of his native culture, his relationship was merely symbiotic. Although his life contradicted some of the contemporary religio-ethical patterns of Judaic culture, he nevertheless expressed himself through these very patterns, even manifesting an astonishing respect for religious and moral structures that were already obsolete and extensively tainted by the selfishness of men.[72] It was not every day that Jesus drove the money-changers from the temple. And he firmly ordered the cured leper to make the legally prescribed offering to the priest. For the revolutionary vision of Jesus is more radical than that of utopian dreamers who imagine that institutions, rather than men, are the principal bearers of evil.

The methodology of Christianity, to put it briefly, is to be present in the world as it is, and among all peoples, after the manner of a leaven. This is not at all the same thing as an extrinsic and legalistic "Christianization" of social structures, according to some latter-day conception of the ancient *Corpus Christianum*—as though new laws and foreign institutions were capable of renewing the hearts of men. Nor can we expect the leaven to function where Christians are not positively and creatively engaged in the dynamic processes of their own cultures. The reform of social structures and moral systems is a consequence, rather than a cause, of authentic changes within men and their cultures. This inner *metanoia* cannot be imposed from the outside. How many centuries passed before Western Christians came fully to realize that their faith is essentially incompatible with the socio-economic institution of slavery?

Moreover, Christianity's essential universalism, so manifest at least in the pristine Pentecostal spirit of the earliest Christians, precludes the total identification of Christianity with any particular culture. The second-century writer of the *Epistle to Diognetus* took note of this in the following words:

> Christians are not to be distinguished from other men by country, language, or customs. They have no cities of their own, they use no peculiar dialect, and they practice no extraordinary way of life. Residing in cities of the Greek world and beyond it, as is the lot of each, they follow the local customs as in clothing, diet, and general manner of life.[73]

With this same sense of universalism and awareness of mankind's cultural multiformity, the fathers of Vatican II repeatedly urged the Church to move more generously toward the concrete realization of cultural catholicity in all forms of Christian life:

> Sent to all peoples in every time and place, the Church is not bound exclusively and indissolubly to any race or nation, nor to any particular way of life or any customary pattern of living, ancient or recent. Faithful to her own tradition and at the same time conscious

of her universal mission, she can enter into communion with various cultural modes, to her own enrichment and theirs too (GS 58).[74]

This ecumenical outlook, in the New Testament sense of the world *oikumene* (cf. Mt. 24:14; Rom. 10:18), is based on the belief that all men are equal before God. "There is no distinction: all have sinned," and "all have the same Lord" (Rom. 3:22f; 10:12). The salvation announced and accomplished in Christ is not the salvation of a favored elite, but of humanity. Hence, the same saving grace is universally available to all men, whenever and wherever they may experience their brief participation in the history of redeemed mankind.[75] All the works of men are, therefore, under the influence not only of sin but also of grace. So the general unevennes of cultural development is reflected also, and perhaps especially, in the area of morality. The diverse ethical systems devised by men, but not by them alone, in the course of history reflect at once the shame and the glory of man. No particular system, just as no individual human being, is entirely bad or entirely good. It is precisely on this assumption that the whole Christian ministry of reconciliation is based—not on the opposite assumption that some peoples and their cultures are bad, while others are good.[76]

Anthropologists have never encountered a people without an ethical system: an interlocking set of judgments, norms, and rules for the guidance and evaluation of human conduct in relation to the common good of the society which formed, and continuously reforms, its own morality.[77] This cultural creation is a "social cement" which holds together in relative harmony the structures and institutions of each society. Without some such system, dignified human existence is not possible. Moral decisions have to be made and structured for the purpose of guiding and controlling human behavior, which otherwise tends to become inhuman.

If family life, the elementary social unit upon which all larger societies are based, is to be maintained, then obviously it is necessary to have some socially accepted structures for restraining and regulating sexual activity. Every human society has its own ways of controlling sex, by surrounding it with checks and balances, taboos and permissions.[78] Even in the hordes of primates "random promiscuity is rare and usually the result of some kind of social breakdown."[79] Unregulated sexual activity is, of course, not the only threat to social harmony. The common good demands that such things as greed and violence should also be systematically curbed. Thus a whole network of interrelated and interacting norms, prohibitions, and licenses is developed together with, and as a dynamic element within, each culture.

A culturally integrated ethical system represents a long sequence of historically conditioned moral choices made by men who are at the same time fallen and redeemed. No ethical system represents the best of all possible choices. There must always be some painful exceptions to the established rules of behavior, some human compromises, adaptations, and even radical changes of position. We have only to recall, for example, the ambivalence of Christians in their moral attitude toward war and peace during the course of Western history. After Constantine the theory of the just war, borrowed from "pagan" antiquity, was baptized; and this represented a new morality in contrast to the earlier position articulated by such persons as Justin, Athenagoras, Tertullian, Cyprian, Origen, Minucius, and Arnobius.[80]

Men must live with the ethical system that happens to be available and intelligible to them where they are, at least until new possibilities for change arise from within their own historico-cultural situation. The presence of the Church in each culture is supposed to be a leaven; and Christian revelation provides its believers with a norm for questioning, criticizing, evaluating, and reforming the content of thier own indigenous ethical system.[81] The community itself, enlightened by God's grace, is alone competent to discern the values that protect and promote its own well being; so it belongs properly to the community to question, criticize, evaluate, and reform its own patterns of behavior—and to do this in relation to their understanding of Christian revelation. It is only as persons experience life together in the same historico-cultural world, as they reach out together for what is good and true in their situation, that they find the most appropriate ways of articulating verbally and in their social structures the values that promote the life and destiny of their community.[82]

What is suggested here is that the Church cannot improve the moral life of a people by issuing decrees from the outside, by importing readymade ethical rules, or by imposing extrinsic modifications that have been borrowed from some foreign culture, some profoundly different historico-cultural experience of life together. Moral changes, if they are to be coherently integrated and deeply influential in the normal functioning of existing cultures, must come from inside these cultures. For example, it is notorious that moral and social disintegration have been directly consequent upon the imposition by missionaries, and by colonial governments, of Western individualistic moral and legal codes. This situation is, of course, exacerbated by the Church's typically Western experience of, and insistence upon, individuality in all aspects of religion as well as morals, almost as though these were private affairs, and not societal realities.[83]

If all morality is culturally formed and historically conditioned, always and only in the terms of some concrete society, then no particular ethical system stands, in some kind of abstract Platonic objectivity, over and above all human behavior. For this behavior, and therefore all morality, is real only where men actually live, in the diversity of their particular historico-cultural experiences. The content of every ethical system, whether it is labeled "Christian" or not, exists as a functional element in some ephemeral cultural complex. In this sense, whatever is called Christian ethics is really pre-Christian or secular. In the words of John G. Milhaven:

> In short, any Christian ethics must rest on a secular base, man's experience in the world, his experience, for example, in marriage. The secular experience is irreducible; it cannot be altered by religious faith or theological understanding. All the values, responsibilities and obligations the Christian recognizes—except those pertaining directly to God, such as prayer—are forged first of all in this human experience.[84]

Fundamentally, therefore, it would seem that there is in reality no specifically Christian ethics.[85] Nor is any ethical system essentially inimical to the leaven of the gospel. (Periodic outbursts of savagery, as occurred for example in Germany under Nazism, do not signify the presence of an evil ethical system, but rather the breakdown of a good one.) For all positive moral striving has the same source. All morality rests on common ground; and this common ground is nothing other than the historical nature of man, fallen and redeemed. Whether they know about it consciously or not, there is only one final destiny to which all men are summoned by the same saving grace of God in Jesus Christ (cf. Jn. 1:3, 9; 4:42; 12:32; Acts 4:2; 10:36; Rom. 8:19-24; I Cor. 8:6; Eph. 1:9-11; Col. 1:15-20; Heb. 1:3).[86] Unless we regard this as a kind of pious fiction, we must accept the implication that the victorious and superabounding grace of God is universally operative among all men in terms of their respective historico-cultural experiences. "If men do not reject this grace," says Josef Fuchs, "they accept it."[87]

All upright moral behavior—and Christians certainly have no monopoly on this—is therefore a manifestation of God's grace at work among men of all times and places. This understanding of grace prevents us from imagining, even without any convincing evidence, that Christians are somehow morally better than the rest of men—as though Christians experience a kind of love which is not found among non-Christians.[88] "The work of Christ," according to Fuchs, "is not meant to proclaim a higher moral standard, but rather salvation, which the love of the Father grants us through Christ."[89] Is this just some novelty invented by contemporary theologians? No. This very idea, that "Christian morality is *in essence* a true human morality," and that "no new moral directives are given by Jesus Christ beyond those dictated by human virtue,"[90] is found also in the teaching of Thomas Aquinas on the contents of the New Law.[91] What is new is that this idea, with its practical implications, is being taken more seriously these days than heretofore.

If the content of all morality is pre-Christian, and if the same grace of God inspires moral uprightness or holiness among non-Christians no less than among Christians, what then is the significance of the morality we call "Christian"? Fuchs gives this reply:

We must call the morality of Christians the explicit and Church-
societal form of this morality, which non-Christians, too, realize in
an implicit manner. . . . The Christians are those who, in an explicit
manner and in a Church-community, direct the moral formation
and organization of their life and world towards the person of
Christ. . . . The visibility of the morality founded on Christ's person has just this task: to help the non-Christian to a more explicit
comprehension of not only the single elements, but also the deepest
sense of the morality founded in Christ, which fundamentally con-
stitutes their own morality.[92]

What Christian revelation adds, then, to this world of human
values and to pre-Christian morality is not a new set of rules or
norms, but a new perspective, a new understanding, a new
consciousness, a new motivation, and, consequently, a new challenge to the blind selfishness that permeates the entire human
condition. Christian faith, in other words, offers a new vantage
point for a fresh approach to the meaning of all human values and
moral systems, a new incentive and criterion for self-criticism
and for continuous conversion, and a new hope in the possiblility
of realizing the potential for love that is in every man.

This is not a matter of saying that Christians should tolerate
any ethical system. Rather, they must live with the operative
system of the particular culture within which they find themselves. For it is only through this sort of incarnation or symbiosis
that it will become possible for the gospel to lay its transcendent
claims on all the works of men, and to act as a transforming
leaven within each culture and among all peoples. Man's struggle
with his own selfishness, blindness, prejudice, stupidity, and
wickedness—as also his altruistic aspirations and transcendent
desires—must be expressed, and can be realized, only within his
own concrete historico-cultural context. So the best culture for
the manifestation and development of each man's Christian faith
is his own culture, because normally this is the only one available
to him; and he can hardly find himself in some foreign culture. To
say all this is simply to affirm the principle of incarnation.

At the same time it is recognized that some cultural elements
can stand only in a tentatively symbiotic relationship to Christianity. We may recall, for example, the self-righteous pharisaism
that so marked God's revealed religion in the time of Christ and
the vested interests then associated with worship. Self-

righteousness is still the major temptation, and sometimes even the outward sign, of those who see themselves as God's "chosen people." For centuries the Christian conscience was undisturbed by the socio-economic institution of slavery that was so well integrated into cultures which were regarded as Christian. And how many Christians in our own time are actively participating, for their own material advantage, in a system of economic imperialism that works for "the increasing enrichment of the rich, and the increasing impoverishment of the poor"?[93]

While working against all forms of individual and collective egoism, we must realistically accept the well-attested fact that we will never fully succeed; for this same selfishness is quite alive in all of us. While each culture preserves much that is good, beautiful, unique, and irreplaceable, each one at the same time has its own ways of institutionalizing human selfishness. So the transformation of the world, insofar as this is to be signified through the visible witness of Christianity among all peoples, is a task to be accomplished within, and in the terms of, each culture. It cannot be done by transferring from one culture to another various rules and institutions that seem to be pure, and thus solely Christian. What looks pure to the members of one culture might be taboo in a different historico-cultural context.

NOTES

1. See Paul Tillich, *Theology of Culture* (New York: Oxford University Press, 1964), pp. 42, 47–49, 137; Gregory Baum, "Does Morality Need the Church?" in *The Catholic Theological Society of America: Proceedings of the 25th Annual Convention* 25 (June 1970), 163: "Studies in the sociology of knowledge have shown how deeply embedded moral convictions are in the life of the community and how much a social component affects even those views and values that seem most spiritual and private." See also M.B. Crowe, "Human Nature: Immutable or Mutable," *Irish Theological Quarterly* 30 (1963), 213 and 218: "The point of present interest in this whole discussion is the suggestion that the nature of man, even the metaphysical nature, must be taken in its historical setting. . . . In general, human morality has its universal and invariable aspect and its aspect relative to this or that particular culture."

2. Lesslie Newbigin, *The Finality of Christ* (Richmond, Virginia; John Knox Press; London: SCM Press, 1969), p. 10.

3. See, in addition to works cited in Note 1 above, Hans Rotter, "Tendenzen in der heutigen Moral Theologie," *Stimmen der Zeit* 185 (1970) 259–268; Josef Fuchs, "The Absoluteness of Moral Terms," *Gregorianum* 52 (1971), 415–458; Richard McCormick, "Notes on Moral Theology: Specificity of Christian Morality," *Theological Studies* 42 (1970) 71–78; Charles Fay, "Human Evolution: A Challenge to Thomistic Ethics," *International Philosophical Quarterly* 2 (1962) 50–80; Carl Wellman, "The Ethical Implications of Cultural Relativity," *The Journal of Philosophy* 60 (March 28, 1963) 169–184; Charles E. Curran, "Methodological and Ecclesiological Questions in Moral Theology," *Chicago Studies* 9 (Spring 1970) 169–184; Charles E. Curran, and others, *Absolutes in Moral Theology?* ed. C.E. Curran (Washington and Cleveland: Corpus Books, 1968); Philip Ekka, "Anthropology and the Idea of a Universal Moral Law for Socity," in *Light on the Natural Law*, ed. Illtud Evans (London: Burns and Oates, 1965), pp. 100–125. The recognition of diverse ethical systems does not imply an acceptance of total moral relativity; but it does urge theologians to locate the true objectivity of morality in a more historically and culturally conscious understanding of the traditional natural law theme: an understanding based not on mere philosophical abstractions, but on the way things are in the real world of different times and places. On the need for thologians to abandon the classicist notion that only one culturally conditioned ethical system (their own) is truly human and universally normative, see Bernard Lonergan, *Method in Theology* (New York; Herder and Herder, 1972), especially pp. 49–51, 78–81, 123–124, 300–302, 326–329.

4. Thomas Aquinas, *Summa Theologiae*, I-II, q. 94, art. 4. On the mutablity of human nature, and thus the possiblity of changes in the natural law itself, see Liam Ryan, "The Indissolubility of Marriage in Natural Law," *Irish Theological Quarterly* 31 (1964) 62–70.

5. Ryan, *op. cit.*, p. 76. According to Ryan (p. 74), "St. Thomas's insight into the variability of natural law . . . goes much deeper than the mere question of the application of precepts to contingent circumstances. He envisages the case where the change occurs not in the external conditions in which human nature exists but in the internal constitution of human nature itself."

6. Peter Berger, *A Rumor of Angels: Modern Society and the Rediscovery of the Supernatural* (Garden City, N. Y.: Doubleday Anchor Books, 1970), p. 73.

7. See John T. Noonan, Jr., "Making One's Own Act Another's,' in

The Catholic Theological Society of America: Proceedings of the 27th Annual Convention 27 (1972) 33: "The institution of slavery was not challenged by those most qualified to attack its assumptions and its concepts. . . . Christian law did not create this dehumanizing institution, but it failed spectacularly to criticize it." For more on slavery, see Chapter Six.

8. See Yves Congar, "Church History as a Branch of Theology," trans. Jonathan Cavanaugh, in *Church History in Future Perspective*, ed. Roger Aubert, Concilium 57 (New York: Herder and Herder, 1970), p. 87; Avery Dulles, "Dogma as an Ecumenical Problem," *Theological Studies* 29 (1968), 406: "A competent interpreter of any doctrinal statement will have to examine the entire historical and cultural context out of which it arose in order to discern its true significance. The modern believer cannot and should not be asked to accept the world view of ancient or medieval Christians." See also Edward Schillebeeckx, *God the Future of Man*, trans. N.D. Smith (New York: Sheed and Ward, 1968), pp. 18–19, 42–43; and Hendrik Kraemer, *The Bible and Social Ethics* (Philadelphia: Fortress Press, Facet Books, 1965), pp. 4–5, 13.

9. Joseph P. Fitzpatrick, "Faith, Freedom, and Cultural Difference: Cuernavaca and Christian mission," *International Review of Mission* 59 (July 1970) 336: "All men have a deep and consistent tendency to identify their own culture with nature. . . . Americans consider it 'natural' to work in order to 'get ahead.' They do not realize that most people in the world consider the competiveness of American society not only unnatural but even inhuman. . . . When the ordinary American man and woman observe the subordinate role of woman in Latin America, they tend to define this as 'demeaning' to the woman, as a lack of respect for her dignity and position. On the other hand, when Latin American men and women observe the role of women in the United States, they tend to define it as disrespectful, bold, and destructive of the dignity of woman as they define it." There is, of course, much more to be said about the notion of ethnocentrism, especially as it is reflected in the absolutizing of ephemeral institutions and structures and as it is expressed through the exclusion of "foreign" forms, structures, institutions, norms, values and tastes.

10. See Note 3, above.

11. Jomo Kenyatta, *Facing Mount Kenya: The Tribal Life of the Gikuyu* (London: Secker and Warburg, 1938), p. 120: "There has been too much of 'civilizing and uplifting poor savages.' This policy has been based on preconceived ideas that the African cultures are 'primitive,' and as such, belong to the past and can only be looked upon as antiquarian

relics. . . . Europeans should realize that there is something to learn from the African and a great deal about him to understand."

12. Stephen Neill, *Call to Mission* (Philadelphia: Fortress Press, 1970), pp. 28, 31.

13. See John V. Taylor, *The Primal Vision* (London: SCM Press, 1963), p. 114.

14. Bernard Häring, *A Theology of Protest* (New York: Farrar, Straus and Giroux; Toronto: Doubleday Canada Ltd., 1970), p. 141.

15. Kenyatta, *Facing Mount Kenya*, p. 304.

16. Julius Nyerere, *Hotuba ya Rais wa Jamhuri katika Baraza Kuu la Taifa, Tarehe 10 Desemba, 1962,* (Dar es Salaam: Tanzania Government Printer, 1962), p. 9.

17. Tom Mboya, *Freedom and After* (London: Andre Deutsch, 1963), p. 20.

18. L.S. Senghor, "What is Negritude?" (an address given at Oxford University, October 1961), as quoted by Joseph Gremillion, *The Other Dialogue* (Garden City, N. Y.: Doubleday, 1965), p. 253.

19. Alioune Diop, "Colonization and the Christian Conscience," *Cross Currents* 3 (Summer 1953) 353–355.

20. Bolaji Idowu, *Towards an Indigenous Church* (Oxford University Press, 1965), p. 5.

21. J.F. Ade. Ajayi and E.A. Ayandele, "Writing African Church History," in *The Church Crossing Frontiers; Essays on the Nature of Mission, in Honor of Bengt Sundkler* (Uppsala, Sweden: Boktryckeri Aktiebolag, 1969), pp. 93–94.

22. Hilaire Belloc, *Europe and the Faith* (London, 1920), p. 331.

23. Ernst Troeltsch, *Christian Thought* (London: University of London Press, 1923), p. 24.

24. *Ibid.*, p. 26.

25. *Ibid.*, p. 29. Under the influence of a naive evolutionism, or progressivism, even the best Western thinkers of the nineteenth century tended to see all non-Western cultures, and all previous Western experience, as the lower rungs of an evolutionary ladder on the top of which they themselves were perched; the highest rung of the ladder being, of course, the cultural experience of nineteenth-century Western man. This viewpoint, still reflected to some extent in modern Western thought —as, for example, in the notion that contemporary Western man (in certain universities, anyway) is "the vanguard of humanity come of age"—is questioned in the following paragraphs, which owe much to the insights expressed by G. Collingwood, *The Idea of History* (London, Oxford, New York: Clarendon Press, 1946; Oxford University Press,

1956), pp. 321–334; and Herbert Butterfield, *Christianity and History* (London and Glasgow: G. Bell and Sons, 1949: Collins, Fontana Books, 1957), *passim*.

26. Häring, *A Theology of Protest*, pp. 140–141. For documentation on the erroneous and arrogant assumptions of the nineteenth- and early twentieth-century missionaries, see Poikail John George, "Racist Assumptions of the 19th Century Missionary Movement," *International Review of Mission* 59 (July 1970) 271–284; and also Israel K. Katoke, "Encounter of the Gospel and Cultures," *Lutheran World* 19 (1972) 24–41.

27. See C.G. Bäeta, "Introductory Review: Facts and Problems," in *Christianity in Tropical Africa*, ed. C.G. Bäeta (London: Oxford University Press, 1968), pp. 7–10.

28. See Stephen Neill, *A History of Christian Missions* (Harmondsworth: Penguin Books, 1964), pp. 162–164, 183–164, 183–185; William A. Visser 't Hooft, "Dynamic Factors in the Ecumenical Situation," *The Ecumenical Review* 21 (October 1969) 324–326.

29. *Collectanea S. Congregationis De Propaganda Fide* (Rome, 1907), I, p. 42. English translation in Stephen Neill, *A History of Christian Missions*, p. 179.

30. *Ibid.*

31. See J.B. Schuyler, "Conceptions of Christianity in the Context of Tropical Africa: Nigerian Reactions to its Advent," in *Christianity in Tropical Africa*, ed. C.G. Bäeta (London: Oxford University Press, 1968), pp. 101–223; Stephen Neill, *Call to Mission*, pp. 24–70.

32. Dennis Osadebay, as quoted by Schuyler, "Conceptions of Christianity," p. 208.

33. Joseph O. Okpaku, "Let's Dare to Be African," *Africa Report* 13 (October 1968) 13.

34. See Kenyatta, *Facing Mount Kenya*, pp. 260–262, 304–305.

35. John Mbiti, *African Religions and Philosophy* (New York and Washington: Praeger, 1969), p. 134.

35. Ajayi and Ayandele, "Writing Church History," p. 94.

37. *Ibid.*

38. See Claude Levi-Strauss, *The Scope of Anthropology*, trans. S.O. Paul and R.A. Paul (London: Jonathan Cape, 1967), pp. 23–24; George P. Murdock, *Africa: Its Peoples and Their Cultures* (New York, Toronto, London: McGraw-Hill, 1959), *passim*; Paul Bohannan, *Africa and Africans* (Garden City, N.Y. The Natural History Press, 1964), pp. 124–128; C.H. Dodd, *Christ and the New Humanity* (Philadelphia: Fortress Press, 1965), pp. 7–11; Vatican II, "Pastoral Constitution on the Church in the Modern World," no. 53, Milton M. Gordon, *Assimilation in American Life: The Role*

of Race, Religion, and National Origins (New York: Oxford University Press, 1964), pp. 23–34; E.K. Francis, "The Nature of the Ethnic Group," *American Journal of Sociology* 52 (March 1947) 393–400.

39. See Raymond Firth, *Elements of Social Organization* (Boston: Beacon Press, 1963), pp. 33–35; Levi-Strauss. *The Scope of Anthropology*, pp. 14, 18–19, 31.

40. Bronislaw Malinowski, *A Scientific Theory of Culture and Other Essays* (New York Oxford University Press, 1960), p. 52.

41. Ruth Benedict, *Patterns of Culture* (New York: Mentor Books, 1958), p. 2.

42. See Tillich, *Theology of Culture*, p. 42.

43. Claude Levi-Strauss, *Structural Anthropology*, trans. Claire Jacobson and B.G. Schoepf (Garden City, N. Y.; Doubleday Anchor Books, 1967), p. 20. The fact that I cite here, and elswhere, some of the anthropological insights articulated by Levi-Strauss does not mean that what I am trying to say is dependent upon an acceptance of his theory of structuralism; for these particular insights may also be reached independently of structuralism.

44. See, for example, Edward B. Taylor, *Anthropology: An Introduction to the Study of Man and Civilization* (New York: D. Appleton and Co., 1891), pp. 24–25, 401: "So far as the evidence goes, it seems that civilization has actually grown up in the world through these three stages, so that to look at the savage of the Brazilian forest, a barbarous New Zealander or Dahoman, and a civilized European, may be the student's best guide to understanding the progress of civilization, only he must be cautioned that the comparison is but a guide, not a full explanation. . . . Now, no doubt, the life of these less civilized people of the world, the *savages* and *barbarians*, is more wild, rough, and cruel than ours is on the whole, but the difference between us and them does not lie altogether in this. . . . Savage and barbarous tribes often more or less fairly represent stages of culture through which our own ancestors passed long ago." For more of this kind of ethnocentrism, see the treatment of "high gods and low races," by Andrew Lang, *The Making of Religion* (London, 1898).

45. Robert H. Lowie, *Primitive Man* (New York; Boni and Liveright, 1920), p. 438, and pp. 439, 440: "The appraisal of sociological features is wholly different from that of technological features of culture. The latter may be rated according to the closeness with which they accomplish known ends; the former have unknown ends or ends whose value is a matter of philosophic doubt, hence they can be graded only on subjec-

tive grounds and must scientifically be treated as incommensurable.
. . . Neither morphologically nor dynamically can social life be said to
have progressed from a stage of savagery to a stage of enlightenment."
See also Christopher Dawson, *Progress and Religion* (Garden City, N. Y.:
Doubleday, Image Books, 1960), pp. 45–77; E.O. James, *The Beginnings of
Religion* (London: Hutchinson's University Library, n.d.), pp. 9–27; and
G. Charbonnier, *Conversations with Claude Levi-Strauss*, trans. John and
Doreen Weightman (London: Jonathan Cape, 1969), pp. 18, 22–23.

46. See Lesslie Newbigin, *The Finality of Christ*, p. 12: "The western
white man has been guilty in recent centuries of genocide, wholesale
exploitation of subject peoples, the opium wars, the slave trade, the
colour bar, apartheid and the use of weapons of mass destruction on
civilian populations. . . .Plenty of material here for a bad conscience."

47. See Levi-Strauss, *Structural Anthropology*, pp. 363–364; Gerald R.
Leslie, *The Family in Social Context* (New York and Toronto: Oxford
University Press, 1967), p. 33; Ashley Montagu, *Man's Most Dangerous
Myth: The Fallacy of Race* (New York and Cleveland: World Publishing
Co., 1964), p. 382: "We speak of 'primitive' peoples—the nonliterate
peoples of the earth. What do we mean when we use the term? We mean
that such peoples are, in comparison with ourselves, underdeveloped;
in many respects that is true. . . . But it is very necessary to point out
that, in certain respects, such cultures are more highly developed than
are most civilized cultures. For example, Eskimos and Australian
aborigines, to take two of the so-called most 'primitive' cultures known
to anthropologists, are very much more generous, loving, and coopera-
tive than are most of the members of civilized societies. . . .Members of
these 'primitive' cultures are honest, dependable, cheerful, and
courageous, in all these respects to a degree which comparatively few
civilized men manage to be. Who is more developed in these respects?"

48. See Montagu, *Man's Most Dangerous Myth*, p. 383: "No culture, as
we know it today, is as it was in prehistoric times. It may even be that
some of the so-called 'primitive' cultures are much less like those of
prehistoric times than some that appear to be more
advanced. . . . Cultures differ from one another in the history of the
experiences they have undergone and, therefore, in the kind of development they have realized. . . . Too often we identify 'primitive
man' with contemporary non-literate peoples when the only legitimate
use of the phrase 'primitive man' is when it is applied to prehistoric
man."

49. See Levi-Strauss, *Structural Anthropology*, p. 98: "A primitive peo-

82   POLYGAMY RECONSIDERED

ple is not a backward or retarded people; indeed it may possess, in one realm or another, a genius for invention or action that leaves the achievements of civilized peoples well behind."

50. Levi-Strauss, *The Scope of Anthropology*, p. 46. See also his *Structural Anthrolology*, pp. 3, 59–101, 108–110, 114.

51. Berger, *A Rumor of Angels*, p. 45.

52. *Ibid.*, p. 73.

53. *Ibid.*

54. *Ibid.*, p. 74.

55. *Ibid.*, p. 79.

56. See Montagu, *Man's Most Dangerous Myth*, pp. 100–107, 112–113, and especially p. 384: "In the works of art of prehistoric men who lived between 15,000 and 30,000 years ago, we have the clearest evidence that these men, as artists, were as accomplished as any who have lived since. When it is remembered that these works were not really executed as works of art but as magico-religious rituals . . . that the conditions under which these works were created were usually of the most difficult kind . . . the achievement becomes all the more remarkable. There can be little doubt that individuals capable of such skills were endowed with an intelligence potentially no less great than that possessed by contemporary civilized man." See also René Dubos, *So Human an Animal* (New York: Charles Scribner's Sons, 1968), pp. 37–38: "Cro-Magnon man was established over much of Europe some 30,000 years ago. . . . Although he lived chiefly as a hunter, he seems to have been very similar to us both anatomically and mentally; his tools and weapons fit our hands; his cave art moves our souls; the care with which he buried his dead reveals that he shared with us some form of ultimate concern. Every trace of prehistoric man in the world provides further evidence for the view that the fundamental characteristics of *Homo Sapiens* have not changed since the Stone Age."

59. Paul Ramsey, *Fabricated Man; The Ethics of Genetic Control* (New Haven and London: Yale University Press, 1970), p. 1.

58. *Ibid.*, p. 8; see also pp. 2–9; and Ernst Mayr, *Animal Species and Evolution* (Cambridge: Harvard University Press, 1963), pp. 650–651.

59. Dubos, *So Human an Animal*, p. xi.

60. *Ibid.*, p. 4.

61. See Levi-Strauss, *Structural Anthropology*, p. 3.

62. See Raymond Firth, *Human Types: An Introduction to Social Anthropology* (New York: New American Library, 1958), p. 41.

63. During the "golden age" of Greek culture, even while monogamy was the normative form of marriage, "women were little better off than

slaves," although they had been "virutally the equals of their husbands" during the earlier agricultural period. See Gerald Leslie, *The Family in Social Context,* p. 166.

64. See Levi-Strauss, *The Scope of Anthropology,* p. 48. See also Noonan, "Making One's Own Act Another's" p. 35: "Slavery in the Western world which lasted until little more than a century ago owed its beginnings to the men of Spain, Portugal, France, the Netherlands, and England, all nations molded by Christian thought. . . . The omissions of church law left open gulfs of dehumanization into which European civilization plunged, in which American civilization foundered."

65. For a perceptive commentary on Western man's narrow vision of progress, and on the ambivalent character of technology, see Richard Dickinson, "So Who Needs Liberation?" *The Christian Century* 88 (Januray 13, 1971) 43–46; and also David French, "Does the U. S. Exploit the Developing Nations?" *Commonweal* 86 (May 19, 1967),257–259.

66. Firth, *Elements of Social Organization,* p. 86.

67. C.H. Dodd, *Gospel and Law* (New York: Columbia University Press, 1951), p. 25. For more on the extent to which the early Christians, as also those of the Middle Ages, borrowed their ethics from the pre-Christian Greco-Roman world, see Heinrich A. Rommen, *The Natural Law,* trans. Thomas R. Hanley (St. Louis and London: B. Herder, 1948), pp. 3–5, 21–22, 34–39; John Giles Milhaven, *Toward a New Catholic Morality* (Garden City, N. Y. : Doubleday, 1970), pp. 37–39, 145; Gerard Watson, "Pagan Philosophy and Christian Ethics," in *Morals, Law and Authority,* ed. J.P. Mackey (Dublin: Gill and Macmillan, 1969), pp. 39–59; and Hendrik Kraemer, *The Bible and Social Ethics,* pp. 11-12.

68. See Yves Congar, *This Church That I Love,* trans. Lucien Delafuente (Denville, N. J.: Dimension Books, 1969), p. 60: "Where the tension between the Church and the world is keenly felt, the Church is considered a leaven in the mass, carrier of a message and a life meant for the benefit of the whole world."

69. See H.C. Dodd, *Christ and the New Humanity,* pp. 1–7; Vatican II, "Decree on the Missionary Activity of the Church," no. 22.

70. See John L. McKenzie, *The Power and the Wisdom* (Milwaukee: Bruce, 1965), p. 202.

71. See Eugene Hillman, *The Wider Ecumenism* (New York and London: Herder and Herder, Burns and Oates, 1968), pp. 151–152.

72. See Rudolf Schnackenburg, *The Moral Teaching of the New Testament,* trans. J. Holland-Smith and W.J. O'Hara (New York and London: Herder and Herder, Burns and Oates, 1965, 1965), pp. 56–65.

73. *Epistle to Diognetus* 5–6, abridged, as cited by Dodd, *Christ and the*

New Humanity, pp. 3–4. See also Edward Schillebeeckx, *Marriage: Secular Reality and Saving Mystery*, trans, N.D. Smith (London and Melbourne: Sheed and Ward, 1965), II, p. 18.

74. See also Vatican II, "Dogmatic Constitution on the Church," no. 13, "Decree on the Missionary Activity of the Church, nos. 21–22, "Constitution on the Sacred Liturgy," no. 37; "Declaration on the Relationship of the Church to Non-Christian Religions," no. 2.

75. See Hillman, *The Wider Ecumenism*, pp. 34–59; and Gregory Baum, *Man Becoming: God in Secular Experience* (New York: Herder and Herder, 1970), pp. 28–36.

76. See Dodd, *Christ and the New Humanity*, p. 14.

77. See Firth, *Elements of Social Structure*, p. 213: Anthropology reveals "the existence of standards of right and wrong, and sensitive judgements in their terms, in all human socieities studied. . . . Morality is a social cement between individual means and social ends."

78. See George P. Murdock, *Social Structure* (London: Collier-Macmillan, 1949; New York: The Free Press, 1965), p. 4.

79. Robin Fox, *Kinship and Marriage* (Harmondsworth, Baltimore, Victoria: Penguin Books, 1967), p. 29.

80. See Daniel Maguire, *Moral Absolutes and the Magisterium* (Washington and Cleveland: Corpus Papers, 1970), pp. 4–7.

81. See Franz Böckle, "The Problem of Social Ethics," *American Ecclesiastical Review* 163 (November 1970) 347; and Johannes B. Metz, "Religion and Society in the Light of Political Theology," *Harvard Theological Review* 61 (October 1968) 514.

82. For this and the previous sentence, see Gregory Baum, "Does Morality Need the Church?" *The Catholic Theological Society of America: Proceedings of the 25th Annual Convention* 25 (June 1970) 163.

83. See Metz., "Religion and Society," pp. 507, 509–510, 512–513; Stephen Neill, *Christian Faith and Other Faiths; The Christian Dialogue with Other Religions*, 2nd ed. (London: Oxford University Press, 1970), pp. 148–149; Jomo Kenyatta, *Facing Mount Kenya*, pp. 115, 117–118, 188; and Bernard Häring, *A Theology of Protest*, p. 144: "The moral theology of the last century sanctioned the individualistic concept of private property as entertained by the ruling class and by an individualistic European culture. Christian ethics . . . was for a long time uncritical with regard to this individualistic concept of property with its many effects. The moralists were uncritical not only because they have grown up in this climate and for the most part came from the bourgeoisie, but also because they themselves knew little about the missionary apostolate of the church to all classes and all cultures. . . . Moreover, this individu-

alistic concept of private property was utterly alien to most African and Asian cultures."

84. Milhaven, *Toward a New Catholic Morality*, p. 37.

85. See Böckle, "The Problem of Social Ethics," p. 347: "The Bible does not wish to offer a complete material ethic which would claim validity for all times as the specifically Christian one. . . . In this sense, there is no specific Christian material ethics." See also John Macquarrie, *Three Issues in Ethics* (New York, London, Evanston: Harper and Row, 1970), pp. 82–110; Charles E. Curran, *Contemporary Problems in Moral Theology* (Notre Dame, Indiana: Fides, 1970), pp. 223–234; 236; *Christian Presence and Responsibility*, ed. Philip D. Morris (Notre Dame, Indiana: Fides, 1970), pp. 114–115: "This is the precise sense in which I deny existence of a distinctively Christian ethic; namely, non-Christians can and do arrive at the same ethical conclusions and prize the same proximate dispositions, goals and attitudes as Christians." Josef Fuchs, "Is There a Specifically Christian Morality?" *Theology Digest* 19 (Spring 1971), 39–45; and *Human Values and Christian Morality*, trans. M.H. Heelan, Maeve McRedmond, Erika Young, and Gerard Watson (Dublin and London: Gill and Macmillan, 1970), pp. 112–147; R. Simon, "Spécificité de l'éthique chrétienne," *Le Supplément de la Vie Spirituelle* 23 (Feburary, 1970), 74–104; Bas van Iersel, "The Normative Anthropology of the Gospel," trans. David Smith, in *Man in a New Society*, ed. Franz Böckle, Concilium 75 (New York: Herder and Herder, 1972), pp. 48–57.

86. See Note 75, above.

87. Fuchs, *Human Values and Christian Morality*, p. 69.

88. See George Crespy, "The Grace of Marriage," in George Crespy, Paul Evdokimov, and Christian Duquoc, *Marriage and Christian Tradition*, trans. Agnes Cunningham (Techny, Illinois: Divine Word Publications, 1968), p. 50: "Christians in no way enjoy a monopoly by which they are secretly admitted to a kind of love which unbelievers can never experience. They love as all men love, with the ambiguity attendant upon love."

89. Fuchs, *Human Values and Christian Morality*, p. 76; see also p 77: "Joy in Christ and in his law sometimes encourages the Christian to compare this law with the law of non-Christians, as if there existed a twofold moral law, one for Chritians and one for non-Christians, for the latter maybe even a purely natural law. Yet the conception which makes such a comparison is guilty of an under-valuation of the law of Christ."

90. *Ibid.*, pp. 120–121. See also pp. 122–125, where Fuchs goes on to explain how, and in what sense, it is possible to speak of a specifically Christian morality.

91. See Thomas Aquinas, *Summa Theologiae,* I-II, q. 108, art. 2.

92. Fuchs, *Human Values and Christian Morality,* p. 70; and see also p. 131: "When one speaks of *human* morality as such, one is really speaking of Christian morality, even if under a particular aspect, its human aspect." According to John Macquarrie, *Three Issues in Ethics,* p. 110, "There is no conflict between the ideals of a Christian ethic and the moral ideals to be found in humanity at large. . . . Christianity does not establish a new or different morality, but makes concrete, clarifies, and, above all, focuses on a particular person, Jesus Christ, the deepest moral convictions of men. Christ declared he was fulfilling the law, not abolishing it."

93. Yves Congar, "Poverty in Christian Life in an Affluent Society," in *War, Poverty, Freedom: The Christian Response,* Concilium 15 (New York: Paulist Press, 1966) 65.

CHAPTER III

THE OCCURRENCE OF POLYGAMY

*It is clear that polygynous society will
not disappear for some time to come.*
DAVID B. BARRETT

Missionaries and foreign administrators in Africa have long believed that the disappearance of customary plural marriage
would be "just a matter of time." According to this widely accepted hypothesis, polygamy would be rendered obsolete almost
in proportion to the growth of Christian communities, the rising
levels of literacy, the introduction of a cash economy in place of
the traditional subsistence economy, and the general process of
"Westernization."[1] Thus, in an encyclical letter addressed to the
peoples of Africa in October 1967, Pope Paul VI could affirm
confidently that "the system of polygamy, widespread in pre-
Christian and non-Christian societies, is no longer linked, as it
was in the past, with social structures today; and, fortunately, it is
no longer in harmony with the prevailing attitude of African
peoples."[2]

Whether, and to what extent, African social structures are still
linked with polygamy will be seen in the chapter following this
one. The present chapter deals with the actual occurrence of
preferential polygamy in sub-Saharan Africa: the feasibility, the
incidence, and intensity of this form of plural marriage. On the
basis of the available demographic data, together with some
sociological reflection, it should be possible to determine with

greater empirical accuracy what "the prevailing attitude of African peoples" really is with respect to this traditional institution.

PREFERENTIAL POLYGAMY

As previously noted, plural marriage in Africa almost always means that a husband has more than one wife at the same time: simultaneous polygyny. This form of marriage is preferential in areas where there is a relationship of mutual support and reinforcement between polygamy and culture, polygamy and tradition, polygamy and public opinion, and where polygamy enjoys superior prestige, as compared with monogamy; so that respected males in the society will normally seek to acquire more than one wife.[3] In other words, polygamy is preferential when it is a social ideal.

Even where this is a social ideal, it will always be found that at any one time monogamous unions actually outnumber polygamous ones, although, at the same time, monogamous unions will usually tend to be potentially polygamous.[4] The reasons for this will be seen, shortly, when we consider the factors which make it possible for many men to have more than one wife. But a society may be regarded as polygamous "wherever the culture permits, and public opinion encourages, a man to have more than one wife at the same time, whether such unions are common or comparatively rare, confined to men of outstanding prestige or allowed to anyone who can afford them."[5] Regardless of the number of men who actually attain this social ideal, polygamy is assumed to be culturally normative, so long as it "enjoys superior prestige and is not the exclusive prerogative of a very small status group."[6]

THE FEASIBILITY OF POLYGAMY

Official population figures for sub-Saharan African countries indicate that, in general, the number of females tends to be somewhat greater than the number of males.[7] According to a demographic inquiry in Guinea, for example, there are in that country about 122 females for every 100 males.[8] The recent population census in Tanzania provides another example of the numerical preponderance of females.[9] The total population of Tanzania, exclusive of the islands, was almost twelve million persons in 1967. The sex ratio of this mainland population was about 95.1 males per 100 females. This amounts to a surplus of almost 300,000 females. The ratio varies, of course, from one region to another and from one district to another. But look at the situation in Kilimanjoro Region of Tanzania. Here there were, according to the census, only 316,488 males, while the number of females was recorded at 334,045. There is a surplus here of more than 17,000 females.

Even allowing for the fact that many of the men of Kilimanjaro Region are working in other parts of the country, the numerical differential favoring females over males appears to be significant in this one region. Because this regional population has been particularly responsive to many years of intensive Christian missionary activity, it might be suggested, at least as a hypothesis, that the Christian law of monogamy has something to do with the difficulty some women, reportedly, have in finding husbands.[10] In this connection, the question might also be raised about the notable percentage of prostitutes which this region allegedly supplies to the towns of Tanzania and the unusually large number of applicants to the religious sisterhood.

Similar to Europe and North America, however, it appears that more males than females are actually born alive in Africa.[11] But the African sex ratio tends to fluctuate, especially during childhood. Although the differential mortality factors are only imperfectly known, the male mortality rate appears higher at all ages, with the exception of some of the child-bearing years. This sex-differential mortality leads almost inevitably to a varying female predominance in the adult populations of the different African peoples. Male infanticide is so rare that it does not count in this analysis; and only in relatively few areas does male mortality, in warfare or raiding, contribute significantly to the surplus of females. The differential mortality rate is probably due, more than anything else, to the preferential treatment of females in the family environment, and the greater hazards to which males are exposed by reason of their proper occupations of farming and herding.

In any case, it is clear that one of the factors that would make polygamy possible is the higher mortality rate in the male populations. However, this alone accounts for such a modest surplus of women that it is not in itself a sufficient explanation for the number of polygamous marriages found among these peoples. At the same time, it should be noted that any lowering of the general mortality rates, through improved diets, sanitation, and medical facilities, will normally have the effect of increasing the female predominance.

Another factor, which might contribute somewhat to the possibility of polygamy, is male celibacy. In some few African societies there are some men who never get around to marrying, while spinsterhood is practically unknown. In the Gikuyu language, for example, there is not even a term to designate the status of unmarried women.[12] However, the percentage of celibate males in Africa is very much lower than in Europe and North America; so male celibacy may be regarded only as a very minor, and almost insignificant, factor in relation to the widespread practice of polygamy.

By far the most important single factor that makes polygamy possible is the chronological age gap between males and females at the time of marriage.[13] Men marry relatively late in life, while women marry relatively early. This age discrepancy, more than anything else, provides an adequate "pool" of marriageable females, although other important contributing factors are at work: the natural annual increase in the whole population, the relatively high mortality rate in the male segment of this population. The interrelationship of these factors is described succinctly by R.E. Hanin:

> Women, as a rule, marry at an earlier age than males, so men in the younger age-groups are excluded from the pool of "marriageable" ages. Further, if it is assumed that the number of births is increasing from year to year, then if women aged 15 marry men aged 20, they marry men born five years earlier than their own date of birth. But five years earlier fewer births were occurring. A large difference between the ages at marriage of men and women in a population of

high mortality with increasing numbers of births tends greatly to reduce women's chances of marriage in a monogamous society.[14]

What Jomo Kenyatta says of the Gikuyu society may be said of all societies in which polygamy is customary: "In every generation there are more women of marriageable age than men."[15] The actual discrepancies in the marriage age of males and females differ according to the cultural patterns of the various peoples; according to the cultural patterns of the various peoples; but the average discrepancies are so great that this fact alone could account for the surplus of marriageable-age women, which makes African polygamy feasible; and this would be true, as Dorjahn says, "even where the sex ratio of the adult population shows a male predominance."[16] Among the Nyakyusa, for example, polygamy "is made possible by the ten years of difference in the average marriage age of men and women."[17] Among some other peoples the age differences may be even greater.[18]

Various social mechanisms and traditional practices are at work in determining the marriageability of men and women in each society. Where great deference in all things is shown to older persons and all important social decisions are in the hands of elder males, there is a tendency for them to have priority with respect to the women who are available for marriage.[19] This may even become a monoply, so that younger men wishing to marry can do so only with the help of elder relatives and friends. There is here a function of social control. Younger men are thus obliged to behave themselves, to work hard, and to manifest a sense of responsibility before they can hope to obtain a wife and full acceptance into the mature community. Social control implies, also, various systems of sexual regulation.

The early age of the girls' betrothal and marriage if often due to the traditional system of sexual control, as well as to the conventional sense of propriety, especially where an unwed mother is a disgrace to her family, and an illegitimate child is a threat to family harmony when questions of inheritance arise. In many societies girls are expected to be virgins at the time of marriage;[20] and among some peoples an unwed mother is punished harshly. The Batem people of Tanzania, for example, send these unfortunate girls into exile to bear their illegitimate children among alien peoples; and only then, after much difficulty and delay, may they be permitted to come back into the tribal community.[21] The Batem have very few illegitimate children. But in such circumstances, especially where there are many unmarried young men roaming about, it is a matter of some importance for girls to marry as soon as they reach the age of puberty, if not sooner.

Another consideration might be the wishes of parents, and even of the girls themselves, to form marriage alliances with "good families." A man who has already proved himself to be a responsible husband is often preferred. So there are in some societies preferential mating patterns. For example, girls may be normally expected to marry into families from which the wives of their brothers have come or will come. Some peoples prefer the practice of sororal polygyny in which sisters become the wives of the same husband; because, as Gerald Leslie points out, "co-wives who are sisters are more likely to get along with one another than are co-wives who are not sisters."[22] Such matching patterns may sometimes require long delays before a man's first marriage, as he may have to wait a long time before the preferred partner becomes old enough for marriage. Betrothal arrangements frequently begin even before a girl is born. This is common practice among the Masai of East Africa. A man who is looking for a wife, or for an additional wife, will give gifts to a pregnant woman and her husband with the understanding that, if they accept his gifts, they will remember him if a girl is born to them.

In combination with such factors and many other interacting considerations, there would also be the very important matter of wealth. By his wealth, usually symbolized in livestock, a man shows how reliable, hard working, and sober he has been, and how responsible a husband he is apt to be. In this respect, a married man is already in a more favorable position than one who has not yet obtained his first wife; and the polygamist is well ahead of both. As will be made clear in the following chapter, marriage in Africa is not merely a personal matter between two individuals: it is always, also, and in the first place, a mutually rewarding socio-economic affair with important implications for the whole community. The well known African custom of "bride-wealth," paid by a man to the parents or guardians of his wife, is not only intended to be a support to the permanence of marriage and a compensation to the family which gives away a member, but it is also a pledge of a man's ability to provide adequately for his wife and children. This payment signifies, among other things, a man's willingness and ability to help his in-laws; and it shows that he loves his prospective wife more than his hard-earned possessions.

In a relatively poor, developing country, and especially in communities based on a marginal subsistence economy, it takes young men some time to achieve the measure of economic security (wealth) that is considered a necessary prerequisite to marriage. This factor, probably more than anything else, although not in isolation from everything else that makes up the whole cultural fabric of his society, is responsible for the late age at which a man enters his first marriage. It is this delay, related to the early marriage age of women, that really makes it possible for polygamy to become widespread. Male lust does not figure at all among the factors that make this a preferential form of marriage.[23]

A final word of caution may be added here, lest it be imagined that polygamy causes the late marriage of men and the early marriage of women. The matter is not at all that simple.[24] We will do well, therefore, to heed these words of Etienne van de Walle:

> One would not be warranted in concluding from the evidence presented here that polygyny causes a difference between the sexes in the age at marriage, or that polygyny condemns adult men to celibacy. Moreover, sex differences in the age at marriage, though a necessary condition for a high frequency of polygyny in a closed population, does not necessarily cause polygyny. Polygyny is merely one of a set of interrelated factors, including age at marriage of both men and women and remarriage rates of the widowed and divorced persons in the population, as well as social structure and cultural values. It is impossible to foresee how a change in one of these factors may affect the others.[25]

THE INCIDENCE OF POLYGAMY

According to the largest and most reliable sociological data matrix, compiled and analyzed in 1967, there are some 742 different tribes in Africa to the south of the 15th parallel north.[26] (For the sake of analysis, a tribal unit was taken to be the "tribe-within-a-nation"; so, for example, the Masai people were counted as two tribal units, since they are partly in Kenya and partly in Tanzania.) From this total of 742 clearly identified socio-cultural units, it was found that in 580 of them polygamy is accepted as a preferential form of marriage. In other words, polygamy is traditionally and socially normative in 78 percent of these anthropological groups, although the incidence is not the same in all of them.[27]

Further analysis shows that in 34 percent of all these sub-Saharan tribes the incidence of polygamy is more than 20 percent, while it is common, although restricted to certain types (either sororal or nonsororal) in another 44 percent of these societies. In the remaining 22 percent of these societies this form of plural marriage is either "very limited, restricted, infrequent or nonexistent."[28] In general, therefore, it may be said that, according to the widest and most reliable data analysis, polygamy is regarded as a socially valid form of preferential marriage among the majority of peoples in Africa south of the Sahara.

The same conclusion may be reached by approaching the matter from another sociological viewpoint and by using a different method for making estimates on the basis of the available data.[29] After taking account of the variable and doubtful factors (and omitting the East Horn and Eastern Sudanic areas, owing to the lack of sufficient data), it is estimated that the mean incidence of polygamy in sub-Saharan Africa, as measured by the percentage of all married people who are polygamous, averages about 35 percent. Within this 35 percent there is an intensity of about 245 wives per 100 polygamously married men. But, taking monogamously and polygamously married men together, there is an average of about 150 wives per 100 husbands. According to this estimate, "the mean number of wives per married man is 1.5, and the ratio of married women to married men is 3 to 2."[30]

Most of the data available for this estimate were synchronic; but, in the few areas where there were subsequent re-studies of the same populations, it was found that polygamy is decreasing among some peoples and increasing among others. Trends in both directions are found also in the ethnographic literature dealing with different peoples and areas. The overall picture indicates little change, one way or the other, during a period of some forty years. Lacking the necessary quantitative data, however, especially of a diachronic character, it is not possible to say precisely that the general incidence of polygamy is either increasing or decreasing.

Most of the churches have fairly consistently, and sometimes very persistently, opposed polygamy; and in certain areas the custom has declined notably. Yet, even in some of the regions where Christianity has become firmly rooted, the incidence appears not to have fallen in the slightest. This is the situation among the Akan people of Ghana, and their case may be taken as fairly typical.[31] Missionaries in the Central African Republic also report that plural marriage is definitely increasing, even in Christian communities, and that this increase is directly related to the change-over from a subsistence to a cash economy.[32] Indeed, there is a positive correlation between the incidence of polygamy and the increase of personal income. This trend was noted some twenty years ago in what was then the Belgian Congo:

> While the number of wives held by polygamist husbands has been reduced, one may say, by half in the majority of tribes, the number of polygamist husbands has increased. Nowadays anyone who, by trading or working for Europeans, earns the necessary cash can afford the luxury of polygamy. Optimistic hopes for the speedy disappearance of the custom are not likely to be realized.[33]

On the face of it, the assumption seems reasonable enough: that the introduction of a sound cash economy, (especially in association with urbanization, Western systems of education, incomes from salaries, and the desire for exotic goods and luxuries) will create a new situation in which men are less dependent upon their kin relationships and cultural traditions, with the result that they will be able to marry at an earlier age. Not only marriage, but also divorce, becomes easier to accomplish. Under such conditions it would seem that polygamy should be regarded as an economic liability; so it should gradually cease to be a common practice and a social ideal.

But there is an abundance of evidence to show that these new conditions do not always and everywhere yield the expected results regarding marriage and family life. Of all human institutions those involving marriage and family are probably the least susceptible to erosion. Among the Koko people of Cameroon, for example, there was a period in which polygamy declined for forty years; but in 1962 the old custom was on its way back again at a steadily increasing pace *in the urban areas.*[34] The same tendency is recorded in a United Nations report on plural marriage in African towns, where the proportion of males is usually greater than females: "Despite the relative freedom of choice for women in urban areas, and the law of supply and demand operating in their favor, polygamy is still maintained and is even on the increase in many towns."[35] The studies that have been made on this question indicate that customary plural marriage is still a tradition to be reckoned with, not only among the majority of the peoples in the rural areas, but also among increasing numbers in the urban areas.[36] There the incidence of polygamy is apt to increase with the upward curve of income.[37]

Even though there are, at the same time, indications of declining polygamy in urban areas, it is by no means certain that the practice is actually dying out considering these new socioeconomic influences. A demographic survey in Lagos, in 1964, revealed that the majority of marriages were "performed according to customary laws, thus showing the influence of the cultural and traditional system on marriage patterns in this premier city."[38] Moreover, "polygynous marriages accounted for nearly 14 percent of the marital conditions within households, and the number of such wives resident in Lagos at the time of the survey ranged from two to five, while the wives of some of these polygynous households were living away from Lagos."[39]

Another survey, undertaken in the same year but in a different section of Lagos, was equally instructive in its findings.[40] The rate of monogamous marriages in this city is probably higher than elsewhere in West Africa. Still, "the noticeable incidence of polygyny, in such a nonagricultural urban setting as Lagos, illustrates the fact that for many people it is an expression of a way of life with deeply embedded religious and cultural obligations." While non-Christians exhibited a higher rate of polygamy, it was found that 17.3 percent of the Catholics and 23.3 percent of the Protestants were also polygamously married. It was also found that "many women, even among those married to monogamists . . . did not disapprove of polygyny." Approval was expressed by 17.3 percent of the Catholic women interviewed and by 24.1 percent of the Protestant women interviewed. The majority of these women gave as their reason the social, economic, and domestic advantages of belonging to a polygamous household, while another 20.7 percent of them mentioned the importance of polygamy as a means of making a large family, ensuring it of a number of children, with particular reference to the possibility that one wife alone might not be a guarantee of this. In Lagos, anyway, it appears that a sizable minority will probably continue to favor plural marriage; and the reasons for this "have their roots in tradition, which dies hard."

The facts alone, on the incidence of polygyny, urge us to accept today the judgment made almost thirty years ago by an African writer:

> The practice of polygamy is at present the rule in Africa. Women have not only reconciled themselves to their position; some even consider it a disgrace to be the only wife of a man. They give all sorts of reasons for desiring a partner or co-wife and sometimes help their husbands to prepare for the necessary expenses of having another wife. As long as this idea remains, polygamy will no doubt remain.[41]

THE PREVAILING ATTITUDE

The sociological data and analysis, just presented in a summary manner, tell us something about "the prevailing attitude of African peoples" with regard to the practice of polygamy. There are, however, a few more indications worth noting.

We might recall that most of Africa's famous public figures of the past, and some of them today, are social models associated with the traditional forms of plural marriage. Nationalistic movements, moreover, are now turning more and more for inspiration to the original cultural sources of African peoples. This search for re-identification with an authentically indigenous way of life involves much more than styles of dress.[42] And polygamy is not one of those traditions that faded away under Western colonial influence. Although African Christian communities may

tend to abandon this custom, the fact remains that the vast
majority of the African populations are not Christian, and the
traditional religio-ethical values are still very much in force
among most of the peoples. Because it is already more numerous
to start with, the non-Christian population as a whole will naturally continue to increase more rapidly than the Christian population. Even allowing for the growth of the Christian communities
through conversions as well as births, the most optimistic estimates indicate that at best Christians might become about 50
percent of the total population by the year 2000.[43] In any case,
whether one takes an optimistic or a pessimistic view of church
growth in Africa, it must be assumed that the stronger traditional
social institutions will still be very much in force by the year 2000.

Up to now, the opponents of plural marriage have not done
very well in their various efforts to introduce legislation against
the custom. Indeed, very few independent African countries
have enacted any legislation against polygamy; and in some of
these countries, Mali, for example, the new marriage codes represent an "ingenious compromise" with customary laws.[44] In
Kenya the government-appointed commission on marriage legislation has recommended that "the law should recognize two
distinct types of marriage: the monogamous and the polygamous
or potentially polygamous."[45] During the hearings of the commission the Kenya Minister of Health strongly supported the
customary laws which permit polygamy; and at least one local
branch of *Maendeleo ya Wanawake* (a society for the advancement
of women) suggested that the number of wives should be limited
to four.[46] "Women" they pointed out to the commission, "were
normally willing to share a husband."[47] The report of the commission chairman was a surprise to few:

> There is undoubtedly a considerable body of opinion in favour of
> retaining polygamy. Of those who oppose it, many thought it
> would be unwise to abolish it by law, believing it should be left to die
> out under the pressure of social and economic circumstances, par-
> ticularly the cost of education and land shortage.[48]

A recent government "white paper" in Tanzania proposed that,
with a view to eliminating any conflict between civil and religious

law, even Christian marriages should be recognized as potentially polygamous.[49] An articulate and well-organized minority
of Christians, who would question such a proposal, is assured of
an adequate hearing. But the fact remains that the less articulate
majority is made up of non-Christians who traditionally subscribe to plural marriage; and, in a religiously pluralistic society
like Tanzania, Christians are not totally or even generally en-
dogamous. In their initial reaction to this government proposal,
the Roman Catholic Bishops of Tanzania issued a mild statement
which, while affirming that monogamy "pertains to the essence
of Christian marriage," explicitly recognized that "it is not the
Government's responsibility . . . to enforce religious laws as
though they were the laws of the country."[50] Instead of trying to
prove that Christian marriage is always and everywhere essentially monogamous, the statement was concerned simply with
pointing out that monogamy is not a "foreign Western custom"
standing over against "the traditional African way" of polygamy.

In any case, the problem of enforcing a new law of monogamy
would be formidable in any country where traditional plural
marriage is intimately bound up with the kinship systems, the
norms of land tenure, inheritance regulations, social control,
economic security, family continuity, notions of prestige, etc. It
must be remembered that the populations of sub-Saharan Africa
are still predominantly rural and that, for economic reasons, they
must continue to remain so in the foreseeable future. For
economic development in this part of the world "must be based
pre-eminently upon agriculture and industry associated
therewith."[51] This means that the traditional social institutions
and cultural values will continue to influence profoundly the
lives of most people. The thinking of the relatively few educated
and Christian elites in the cities, however well articulated and
widely publicized, does not always reflect the thinking of the less
"schooled" and non-Christian masses in the rural areas.

It is important to realize that African cities really are not, as
some outside observers might imagine, melting-pots that produce a homogeneous cultural pattern based on Western values
and life-styles. Exotic influences are tangible enough, to be sure.
But the urban populations of Africa, especially as they tend to be

grouped in ethnic (or tribal) ghettoes, are profoundly and extensively influenced by the much larger rural populations. Urbanization, first of all, is not everywhere in Africa a consequence of
contact with the Western world. Particularly in parts of West
Africa, city living is quite traditional. Some of the urban centers of
the Yoruba, Hausa, and Mali peoples date back to the thirteenth
century. The traditional towns and cities have, of course, grown
rapidly during the past seventy-five years, while also many new
cities have come into existence. Still, it is estimated that only
about 9 percent of the population of sub-Saharan Africa is found
in the urban areas.[52]

Moreover, there is a continuous flow of people, back and forth,
between the urban and the rural areas. There is a considerable
turn-over of the city populations, as many people return to the
rural villages after spending some time in the cities. "African
urbanism," as William Schwab points out, "must be understood
with regard to its overwhelming rural background."[53] Schwab
continues:

> The average African lives in a small village and leads a life structured
> around personal relationships. Usually, he owes his economic, re-
> ligious and social security and identity to a kin group, which con-
> trols and dominates his life. Without this kin group or lineage, the
> average African would be unable to satisfy his needs or be able to
> achieve the goals or opportunities that his cultural world provides
> for him. To an African his village and his kin group are the major
> factors controlling his behavior, and the great city is viewed as a
> distant and remote place of splendor and evil . . . . African cities
> are not only populated by village migrants, since so few are born in
> cities, but are islands in a sea of rurality and are surrounded by the
> conservative rural tradtiions which emanate from the villages.[54]

Whether we regard it as "fortunate" or not, all the evidence at
hand suggests that the practice of polygamy is still very much "in
harmony with the prevailing attitude of African peoples."[55] As
Barrett says, "it is clear that polygynous society will not disappear for some time to come.[56] Indeed, we may expect this custom
to be defended, and even reaffirmed, among the 580 different
peoples who accept it as a traditional social institution. "Hence,"
Barrett continues, "we can see that in those societies where the

institution is or has been common, this factor will continue to be present as a powerful component of the *Zeitgeist*.[57] Another noted sociologist who shares this view is Aidan Southall:

> Africa remains a continent of polygamy. Polygamy is the undoubted goal of men in rural society, though comparatively few reach it until their later years. This is a built-in value for societies based on patrilineal descent groups . . . . Economic change has undermined the economic basis of the compound polygynous family in towns and other employment centers, but the early results of this have been that the same norms and values have found expression in new forms. The usual male reaction has been either to practice successive monogamy instead, which is certainly polygynous from the dia-chronic point of view, or to combine official monogamy with concubinage . . . . We are therefore justified in assuming that most Africans still consider that sexual access to a plurality of women is a male right. Islam supports this and Christian teaching has made little headway against it.[58]

Social change is inevitable always and everywhere, and the pace of change is manifestly rapid in many parts of Africa. But the vitality of traditional African cultures should not be underestimated. The old ways are not being simply obliterated in favor of a totally new culture imported from the West. What is going on may be better described as a fusion. The efforts to work out what is called "African socialism" exemplify this. What may seem to be merely an uncritical imitation should be seen, rather, as a process of borrowing and testing. . There remains "a strong pulse of African life below the European clothes and forms," as Guy Hunter says:

> Beneath the outward forms of change in marriage or Parliament or trade, there remains a world of contacts and understanding be-tween Africans which is almost wholly hidden from European eyes . . . . Private messages that pass from man to man, the long branching channels through which social life and action flow, the unspoken assumptions, the ultimate reserves of energy and emo-tional force upon which an African will rely in a time of testing —these are deep currents on the stream of African life which the outside watcher sees only here and there when they break against a rock.[59]

NOTES

1. For this hypothesis, see M.F. Nimkoff, *Comparative Family Systems* (Boston: Houghton Mifflin, 1965), pp. 348–349; Kenneth Little, "Some Urban Patterns of Marriage and Domesticity in West Africa," *Sociological Review* 21 (July 1959) 65–82; and Remi Clignet, *Many Wives, Many Powers: Authority and Power in Polygynous Families* (Evanston: Northwestern University Press, 1970), p. 102: "There is no doubt that in the long run social change is accompanied by the emergence of a nuclear type of family and hence by a decline in the incidence of plural marriage."

2. Pope Paul VI, "Africae terrarum," in *Acta Apostolicae Sedis* 59 (December 1967) 1092–1093; English translation from *African Ecclesiastical Review* 10 (January 1968) 81.

3. See George P. Murdock, *Social Structure* (London: Collier-Macmillan, 1949; New York: The Free Press, 1965), p. 27.

4. See Gerald R. Leslie, *The Family in Social Context* (New York and Toronto: Oxford University Press, 1967), pp. 30–31: "Where it exists, polygyny is usually accorded higher status than is monogamy. . . . Polygyny is more widely valued but monogamy is more widely practiced."

5. Murdock, *Social Structure*, p. 28.

6. *Ibid.*

7. See Vernon R. Dorjahn, "The Demographic Aspects of African Polygyny" (Ph. D. diss., Northwestern University, 1954), pp. 375–377; Dorjahn, "The Factor of Polygyny in African Demography," in *Continuity and Change in African Cultures*, ed. William R. Bascom and Melville J. Herskovits (Chicago: University of Chicago Press, 1959), pp. 95–96, 105–109. See also John C. Caldwell, "Introduction: The Demographic Situtation," in *The Population of Tropical Africa*, ed. John C. Caldwell and Chukuka Okonjo (New York: Columbia University Press, 1968), pp. 11, 21; and Etienne van de Walle, "Characteristics of African Demographic Data," in *The Demography of Tropical Africa*, ed. William Brass (Princeton, N.J.: Princeton University Press, 1968), pp. 38, 43.

8. See Van de Walle, "Marriage in African Censuses and Inquiries," in *The Demography of Tropical Africa*, p. 218.

9. See Tanzania Government, *Preliminary Results of the Population Census Taken in August 1967* (Dar es Salaam: Government Printer, 1967), pp. iv, 1, 9.

10. This question was suggested in an interview, in 1967, with two pastors who had been working for many years in Kilimanjaro Region.

11. For this and the following two paragraphs, see Dorjahn and Cald-

well, as cited in Note 7; also J. Hajnal, "European Marriage Patterns in Perspective," in *Population in History: Essays in Historical Demography*, ed. D.V. Glass and D.E.C. Eversley (Chicago: Aldine and Edward Arnold Ltd., 1965), p 127; and R.A. Henin, "Marriage Patterns and Trends in the Nomadic and Settled Populations of the Sudan," *Africa* 39 (July 1969) 239.

    12. See Jomo Kenyatta, *Facing Mount Kenya: The Tribal Life of the Gikuyu* (London: Secker and Warburg, 1938), p. 168.

    13. Cf. Dorjahn, as cited in Note 7; also Hajnal, "European Marriage Patterns," p. 129, n. 43: "A remarkable feature of European marriage data is that there is often a relatively small excess (only 2 or 3 years) of the mean ages of men at first marriage over those of women. This is surprising because, other things being equal, a great excess reduces the chances of women at marriage. Yet it is in Europe that the percentage of women remaining single has been the highest. The solution of the paradox is that among non-Europeans the great excess of the male over the female age at marriage is counterbalanced by other factors, notably a greater degree of polygamy (successive or simultaneous). In fact a high frequency of (simultaneous) polygamy is possible usually only in a society where young men remain unmarried for a comparatively long period and then marry wives much younger than themselves. . . . Indeed, by varying the relationship between the ages at marriage of the sexes, the rates of first marriage and remarriage etc., one could construct imaginary marriage patterns which are very strange to Western ideas, but in which most or all women are married and hence adequate reproduction would be possible."

    14. Cf. Henin, "Marriage Patterns and Trends," p. 248.

    15. Kenyatta, *Facing Mount Kenya*, p. 170.

    16. Dorjahn, "The Factor of Polygamy in African Demography," p. 109; see also Van de Walle, "Marriage in African Censuses and Inquiries," pp. 214–221.

    17. See Monica Wilson, *Good Company: A Study of Nyakyusa Age-Villages* (London, New York, Toronto: Oxford University Press, 1951), p. 14.

    18. See Paul Spencer, *The Samburu* (London: Routledge and Kegan Paul, 1965), p. 96; Kenyatta, *Facing Mount Kenya*, p. 170; United Nations Economic Commission for Africa, "Polygamy, the Family and Urban Phenomenon," in *Workshop on Urban Problems; The Role of Women in Urban Development* (United Nations Document, mimeographed, E/CN, 14/URB/6, July 25, 1963), p. 21.

    19. For one example of this, see Elliott P. Skinner, "Labor Migration

among the Mossi of Upper Volta," in *Urbanization and Migration in West
Africa*, ed. Hilda Kuper (Berkeley and Los Angeles: University of
California Press, 1965; London: University of Cambridge Press, 1965), p.
62.

20. See Ethel M. Albert, "Women of Burundi: A Study of Social
Values," in *Women of Tropical Africa*, ed. Denis Paulme, trans. H.M.
Wright (London: Routledge and Kegan Paul, 1963), p. 195.

21. This information is from interviews, in 1966, with members of the
Batem tribe in Tanzania.

22. Leslie, *The Family in Social Context*, p. 29; and Murdock, *Social
Structure*, p. 31: "Our data show preferential sororal polygyny to be
exceedingly widespread."

23. See Leslie, *The Family in Social Context*, pp. 26–27: "Americans are
prone, when they hear the word polygamy, to think immediately of the
sexual aspects of marriage. Because of our almost complete restriction of
sexual activity outside of marriage and our frequent preoccupation with
the erotic, we are likely to imagine polygamy as one long sexual orgy.
Nothing could be further from the truth."

24. A contrary viewpoint is presented by Jacques Binet, *Le marriage en
Afrique noire* (Paris: Du Cerf, 1959), pp. 73 and 92.

25. Van de Walle, "Marriage in African Censuses and Inquiries," p.
221.

26. For the data and analysis summarized in this and in the following
paragraph, see David B. Barrett, *Schism and Renewal in Africa* (Nairobi,
Addis Ababa, Lusaka: Oxford University Press, 1968), pp. 116, 150 n. 2,
240–241, 324–326, 329 n. 1. For a more recent sociological analysis of this
data, together with the data provided by Dorjahn, see Clignet, *Many
Wives, Many Powers*, pp. 16–19.

27. For some samples of the incidence in different African societies,
see James L. Giibs, ed., *Peoples of Africa* (New York, Toronto, London:
Holt, Rinehart and Winston, 1965), *passim*; and also Murdock, *Social
Struture*, pp. 28–32.

28. Barrett, *Schism and Renewal in Africa*, p. 116. See also John Mbiti,
Africa Religion and Philosophy (New York and Washington: Praeger,
1969), p. 144: "The proportion of polygamous families would not exceed
more than twenty-five per cent of the population even in societies where
polygamy is most practiced. The proportion is slowly diminishing, but it
is also giving way to new marital situations and problems."

29. For the data and analysis summarized in this and in the following
paragraph, see Dorjahn, "The Factor of Polygamy in African Demography," pp. 98–105.

30. *Ibid.*, p. 105.

31. See S.G. Williamson, *Akan Religion and the Christian Faith* (Accra: Ghana University Press, 1965), p. 145; and, for another example of this, among the Luo people of Kenya, see Barrett, *Schism and Renewal in Africa*, p. 10. See also Clignet, *Many Wives, Many Powers*, p. 32.

32. This information is from interviews, in 1969, with two missionaries working in the Central African Republic. They expressed the opinion that, while fewer men these days can afford a large number of wives, more men can afford a second wife; so the practice has become less intensive than in former times, but at the same time more extensive.

33. J. van Wing, "Polygamy in the Belgian Congo," *Africa* 17 (April 1947) 101–102.

34. See R. Bureau, "Ethno-sociologie religieuse des Duala et apparentés," *Recherches et études camerounaises*, IRCAM, 7–8 (1962), p. 190, as cited by Barrett, *Schism and Renewal in Africa*, p. 117.

35. United Nations Economic Commission for Africa, *Polygamy, the Family and Urban Phenomenon*, p. 7. See also Clignet, *Many Wives, Many Powers*, p. 31: "Indeed, with one notable exception, many observers of the contemporary African scene agree that the incidence of polygyny in cities tends to increase with the length of time spent there and with the higher levels of occupation achieved."

36. See *ibid.* Also Guy Hunter, *The New Societies of Tropical Africa* (London: Oxford University Press, 1962), pp. 34–35; and International African Institute (London), *Social Implications of Industrialization and Urbanization in Africa South of the Sahara* (Paris: UNESCO, 1965).

37. See United Nations Economic Commission for Africa, *Polygamy, The Family and Urban Phenomenon*, p. 20; and Clignet, *Many Wives, Many Powers*, p. 359: "In the short term, we have suggested that participation in urban and modern structures is not necessarily associated with an immediate decline in the incidence of polygynous arrangements."

38. C.N. Ejiogu, "African Rural-Urban Migrants in the Migrant Areas of the Lagos Federal Territory," in Caldwell, *The Population of Tropical Africa*, p. 325.

39. *Ibid.*

40. For the data and analysis summarized in this paragraph, see P.O. Ohadike, "A Demographic Note on Marriage, Family, and Family Growth in Lagos, Nigeria," in Caldwell, *The Population of Tropical Africa*, pp. 380–382.

41. S.I. Kale, "Polygamy and the Church in Arica," *International Review of Mission* 31 (April 1942), 222–223.

42. Cf. Anthony Allott, "Legal Systems in Africa," in *Africa: a Hand-*

book to the Continent, ed. Colin Legum (New York and Washington: Praeger, 1966), p. 435.

43. See David B. Barrett, "AD 2000: 350 Million Christians in Africa," *International Review of Mission* 59 (January 1970), 41–47. This estimate, it must be noted, includes the expected membership of the numerous and rapidly growing African "independent" churches, many of which accept the custom of polygyny.

44. See J.F. Salacuse, "Developments in African Law," *Africa Report* 13 (March 1968) 39–40; and Allott, "Legal Systems in Africa," p. 434. According to Clignet, *Many Wives, Many Powers,* p. 5, Tunisia has also enacted legislation against polygamy, while only two sub-Saharan African countries have taken such action: Ivory Coast and Guinea.

45. Kenya Government, *Report of the Commission on the Law of Marriage and Divorce* (Nairobi: Government Printer, 1968), p. 23.

46. Kenya News Agency, report in *Daily Nation* (Nairobi), September 14, 1967, p. 4. Still, it seems reasonable to assume that an increasing number of African women, perhaps even a majority of those who pass through Western-style schools, will no longer regard polygyny as a preferential form of marriage. However, the fact that many educated men tend to support the custom of polygyny is highly significant: cf. Aidan Southall, "The Position of Women and the Stability of Marriage," in *Social Change in Modern Africa,* ed. Aidan Southall (London, New York, Toronto: Oxford University Press, 1961), p. 53: "In general, the traditional male values persist in only slightly modified form, strengthened by Islam and to an increasing extent condoned by western secular opinion, while Christian orthodoxy has made little headway against them. The impact of female criticism of male behaviours is slight because of the political dominance of men. But male criticism of laxity in female behaviour carries considerable weight, backed by traditional values, Islamic and Christian teaching." According to Clignet, *Many Wives, Many Powers,* p. 33, the schooling of girls is the only social change that has had a negative effect on polygyny.

47. Kenya News Agency, *Report on The Law of Marriage,* p. 4.

48. Mr. Justice Spry, as quoted by Moya Neeld, "Many Favor Polygamy," *Daily Nation* (Nairobi), December 1, 1967, p. 1.

49. See R.W. Apple, Jr., "No. 1 Topic in Tanzania," *New York Times,* October 9, 1969, p. 18; and also "Tanzania Debates Polygamy," *Christian Science Monitor,* October 27, 1969, p. 2.

50. Catholic Bishops of Tanzania, "Draft Statement" (in response to Tanzania Government proposals for a uniform marriage law), *Pastoral Orientation Service,* No. 8 (Mwanza: Bukumbi Pastoral Institute, 1969), p. 4. See also Chapter One, Note 74.

51. John Phillips, *Agriculture and Ecology in Africa: A Study of Actual and Potential Development in Africa South of the Sahara* (London: Faber and Faber, 1959), p. 376. See also Melville J. Herskovits, *The Human Factor in Changing Africa* (New York: Knopf, 1962), p. 148; Guy Hunter, *New Societies*, pp. 50–51, 59–60; and René Dumont, *False Start in Africa*, trans. Phyllis N. Ott (New York: Praeger, 1966).

52. Cf. William B. Schwab, "Urbanism, Corporate Groups and Culture Change in Africa Below the Sahara," *Anthropological Quarterly* 43 (July 1970) 187.

53. *Ibid.*, p. 190.

54. *Ibid.*

55. But see p. 87.

56. Barrett, *Schism and Renewal in Africa*, p. 241.

57. *Ibid.* See also Schwab, "Urbanism," p. 200: " . . . and polygyny, although curtailed, has not been greatly reduced as it is still preferred by men. Most children continue to be reared in the traditional compound with the socialization process of the child remaining as one of the primary functions of the lineage."

58. Southall, "Position of Women," p. 52. See also the general conclusions of Clignet's extensive study of African polygamy, *Many Wives, Many Powers*, p. 259: "that participation associated with an immediate decline in the incidence of polygynous arrangements."

59. Hunter, *New Societies of Tropical Africa*, p. 92. See also Bernard Magubane, "A Critical Look at the Indices Used in the Study of Social Change in Colonial Africa," *Current Anthropology* 12 (October-December 1971) 431: "Where two cultures, differing in their technological development, meet, adjustments are inevitable. Yet the culture that is 'inferior' in terms of technology does not simply yield to the other. The two cultures yield to one another, undergoing profound modifications."

CHAPTER IV

POLYGAMY IN SOCIETY

The custom fits well into the think-
ing of the people, serving many
useful purposes.

JOHN MBITI

The social significance of African polygamy, more precisely called simultaneous polygyny, may be seen by considering the place and functions of this institution within its own socio-econonic and cultural context. While this functionalist viewpoint is not the only possible way of considering the matter at hand, it is, nevertheless, a widely accepted viewpoint among contemporary anthropologists; so it may be taken as a valid frame of reference for a proper understanding of traditional plural marriage in its tropical African setting. The following considerations should suffice, therefore, to indicate whether, and to what extent, polygamy and African social structures are still linked together and whether, and to what extent, this immemorial custom is still in harmony with the prevailing attitudes of African peoples.

MARRIAGE AND KINSHIP

"Birth, and copulation, and death." These are the basic facts of human existence, as summarized rather succinctly in *The Four Quartets* of T.S. Eliot. There is, to be sure, much more than this to be said about the human experience; but nothing less can be said. It is on these three common facts that all socio-cultural systems rest.[1] On these elementary biological foundations and the social bonds proceeding from them, men have erected in the course of history the structures required for their survival and their existence in community. Through the study of kinship systems, social scientists have attempted to understand just what the diverse peoples of the world have accomplished in the way of social organization and why a people has organized itself in its own particular way rather than in the way of some other people. In the words of Robin Fox:

> The study of kinship is the study of what man *does* with these basic facts of life—mating, gestation, parenthood, socialization, sibling-ship, etc. Part of his enormous success in the evolutionary struggle lies in his ability to manipulate these relationships to advantage. And this is important. He does not simply play games with them for sheer intellectual excitement. . . . He utilized them in order to survive, and beyond survival, to prosper. At some level he is bound to adopt one mode of adaptation rather than another; but he is free to vary this within limits and to his advantage.[2]

Each social system represents a different historical response, with its own peculiar solutions to the common human problems. "It is clear," as C.J. Snoek says, "that a multiplicity of cultures will lead to a multiplicity of customs and institutions designed to socialize and institutionalize sexuality."[3] Animals of the same species must follow the same patterns of behavior. But men, because they survive by intelligence rather than instinct, solve their problems through imagination, reflection, humor, invention, and free selection from a variety of possible solutions. Human solutions are never perfect, and no two systems of social organization are quite the same. But the various patterns of social behavior, followed by different peoples, do not generally represent better or worse systems: not higher and lower ways of life.[4] They are simply alternative ways of structuring community life, with a view to making human existence both possible and bearable. The varied institutionalizations of sexuality may, therefore, be regarded as valid "to the extent that, within their cultural context, they serve to promote and actualize the ideal of humanity in general."[5]

To cope with the far-reaching implications of birth and mating and death, each people has its own laboriously devised and constructed complex of social institutions with a concomitant network of interacting human relationships and attitudes. Mating has obvious consequences: gestation, protection, sexual control, parenthood. Offspring must be supported, educated, and integrated into society. So mating requires the structuring of rights and duties: mutual human responsibilities.[6] Children, at least in African societies, are expected to care for their parents in old age. Provision must be made for filling social gaps left by death, which calls, also, for the careful redistribution of responsibility as well as property. For the life of the community must continue with a measure of security and stability.

Social structures are needed for human existence, and the conjugal family is a central structure in all known social units of men.[7] The forms and implications of the conjugal family are many, but the institution itself is quite universal. "For human society always demands formal marriage . . . and then uses it as building blocks by which to make a structure of bigger units."[8] Thus, all the social relationships and attitudes of a particular people are largely determined by their historico-cultural conception and experience of family life. It is "incontrovertible" that "the family image is at the foundation of the images of all social relationships."[9] Marriage establishes firm human relationships of affinity. Mating produces relationships of consanguinity. Families, clans, tribes, and peoples are built up and bound together through the multiplication of relationships based on affinity and consanguinity. These relationships constitute kinship systems: groups related "by real, putative or fictive consanguinity."[10]

Kinship systems may not be of great practical importance for a minority of mankind living in the Western world during the past hundred years more or less; but for the majority of humanity, considered both contemporaneously and totally, kinship systems provide highly significant social services in response to various "recognizable pressures within a framework of biological, psychological, ecological, and social limitations."[11] Kinship systems are important because of the needs they answer. In the traditional societies of sub-Saharan Africa, kin relationships tend to be the most important of social realities.[12]

In these societies an individual's self-understanding, social status, and the patterns of behavior proper to him—as well as his

sense of security, his particular responsibilities, and his expectations in life—are largely determined by his place within the
kinship system of his people. There are, of course, other factors
that shape the individual's destiny, vision, and values. There is,
for example, among some peoples the age-grade system which,
as a structure of social stratification, also determines human
relationships, functions, loyalties, and responsibilities. Here we
are concerned only with the kinship system; it is within this
system that marriage functions as a dynamic, integrating force.

How is this system described? "Man's practical intelligence
devises arrangements for human living," writes Bernard Lonergan in his philosophical analysis of community dynamics, "and,
in the measure that such arrangements are understood and accepted, there necessarily results the intelligible pattern of relationships which we have named the good of order."[13] This concept, "the good of order," may be taken as an apt description of
the kinship system:

> It consists of an intelligible pattern of relationships that condition
> the fulfilment of each man's desires by his contribution to the
> fulfilment of the desires of others and, similarly, protects each from
> the object of his fears in the measure he contributes to warding off
> the object feared by others.[14]

In societies that are held together by strong kin relationships,
individuality is rarely, if ever, asserted as an explicit value in
itself. The person is not generally seen in isolation from the
community. Rather, his personal individuality is affirmed and
fulfilled only in relation to the good of others; and this is explicitly
recognized as normative, to the extent that the individual is
expected to follow the socially established patterns. What is good
for the larger community is, for that reason, presumed to be good
for each of its members. In this sense, each man lives for others;
and his personal development is always community-oriented.
Such an ideal, with its self-effacing discipline, is not easily
achieved in practice by many people. But the ideal is consciously
presented both in positive and in negative terms. Among the
Masai-speaking peoples, for example, the word *nganyet*
designates the highest norm of human behavior.[15] One who

manifests in his life this rarely achieved quality of *nganyet* would probably deserve to be called, in traditional Christian terminology, a saint: one who lives for others. Among the Gikuyu an individualist is given the pejorative name of *mwebongia*: one who works only for himself. [16]

Altruistic ideals are hard to realize in any society. So there is no need to pretend that the social structures of this or that particular African society represent anything like a perfect situation. Nor should we, for the same reasons associated with the nature of man, imagine that the Western exaltation of individuality signifies some special high point in the evolution of the human spirit. (The opposite might just as easily be argued.) For our purpose, anyway, it should suffice to note Jomo Kenyatta's summary of the matter. As he sees it, "individuality is the ideal of life" among Western peoples, while the ideal in traditional African societies is "the right relations with, and behavior to, other people." [17]

It could well be that the current Western understanding of marriage, based on interests that are almost exclusively individualistic, represents a progressive diminishment of family and community feelings. [18] The increasing frequency of divorce and the decreasing number of offspring might also suggest the possible emergence in the West of an entirely new cultural system of marriage in which consecutive polygamy (or serial monogamy) might eventually become preferential. [19] However, the point to be made here is that any system of marriage is a central part of a whole socio-cultural ethos, with its own ephemeral forms, practical arrangements, and imperfectly realized values. Since most Christians live within the cultural sphere of the Western world, the Christian theology of marriage rests almost entirely upon the Western experience, conception, and institutionalization of marriage and family. In order to put this whole matter into its proper perspective, it is, therefore, important to note that the typically Western patterns of marriage are unique in the world. [20] They are not found elsewhere, nor do most married people live in the West.

Kinship and marriage may be seen, therefore, as a set of social arrangements which make it possible for persons to live together, cooperating with one another, in an orderly social life. Their social system "links persons together by convergence of interest and sentiment," while at the same time controlling and limiting "those conflicts that are always possible as a result of the divergence of sentiment or interest."[21] To understand any particular feature of such a system, it is necessary to see how this feature or custom functions as a part of the total system. Hence the need to consider polygamy as a functional part of a functioning whole. Since all social systems change in the course of history, the consideration of polygamy should be on two levels of analysis: static and dynamic. As A.R. Radcliffe-Brown says, the analysis should be both synchronic and diachronic:

> This kind of understanding of a kinship system as a working system linking human beings together in an orderly arrangement of interactions, by which particular customs are seen as functioning parts of the social machinery, is what is aimed at in a synchronic analytic study. In such an analysis we are dealing with a system as it exists at a certain time, abstracting as far as possible from any changes it may be undergoing. To understand a process of change we must first learn all that we possibly can about how the system functioned before the changes that we are investigating occurred. Only then can we learn something of their actual probable effects. It is only when changes are seen as changes in or of a functioning system that they can be understood.[22]

POLYGAMY AS A SOCIAL FUNCTION

Where simultaneous polygamy is a culturally accepted form of marriage it is normally preferred because of its socio-economic functions. Not only does this custom serve as a dynamic principle of family survival, growth, security, continuity, and prestige; but it has, also, an integrating function within the kinship system. There are a number of fairly obvious ways through which polygamy can contribute to the solidarity and prosperity of groups on different levels of society.

A large number of offspring is regarded as a matter of socio-economic urgency in an area where subsistence food production depends on the labor force that each family provides for itself, where the average rate of child mortality is very high, where the continuation of the family through male heirs is a grave responsibility, where each marriage contract multiplies the number of mutually helpful relatives, where leadership qualities are developed only through the good management of large families, where personal relationships are always regarded as more valuable than the possession of things, and where a large number of well-brought-up children is looked upon as the greatest of human achievements. Where the desire for as many children as possible is paramount, as it is in the family units of almost every African society, the practice of polygamy may be seen as an efficient means of realizing socially approved goals and social ideals.[23] A man with more than one wife is normally going to have in his family more children than a man with only one wife.

In tropical Africa, let it be noted, mortality rates are among the highest in the world.[24] Infant mortality at the one-year level is estimated to range from a low in some areas of 100 deaths per 1,000 live births to a high in other areas of 300 deaths per 1,000 live births. This may be compared with the *highest* infant mortality rate of Europe and North America: 50 deaths per 1,000 live births in Chicago's black ghetto.[25] Such a rate, considered catastrophic in Europe and North America, would signify a great improvement if it could be achieved in many African countries. In the cities of Ghana, for example, the figure is said to be 123 deaths per 1,000 live births during the first year and 167 per 1,000 in the rural areas. In the rural areas of Nigeria infant mortality "has been documented at 300 (per 1,000) and may reach much higher."[26] Another comparison may help to dramatize the significance of these figures: "The infant mortality rate in rural Senegal is five times that of France."[27]

Subsequent child mortality, at the level of one year to four, must also be considered. This is generally quite high in Africa, in many areas equalling or even surpassing the rate of infant mortality. Among children of this age in Senegal "the mortality rates are fifteen to forty times higher" than in France.[28] Then another high toll is taken in later childhood. Hence, the security and stability of monogamous households in Africa would seem to be more precarious than that of polygamous households in-so-far as socioeconomic security and family stability depend upon the number of children in the household. In such a situation a plurality of wives clearly makes for greater security and stability in-so-far as two wives are likely to produce more children than one wife.

"It is obvious," writes Jomo Kenyatta, "that, owing to the polygamous system of marriage, a family or *mbari* unit increases rapidly, and in one generation it is possible for a *mbari* to have a hundred members or more."[29] This extension of the family, through the multiplication of relationships of both affinity and consanguinity, is also regarded as a very desirable contribution to the general vitality, security, harmony, and prosperity of the whole ethnic and neighborhood community. Each new relationship gives a greater cohesion, not only to the clan and sub-clan, but also to the aggregates of social units that make up the tribe or people or nation.[30] Hence the father of many is esteemed by all in a society which sees the destiny of each individual in terms of his family, his clan, his tribe, or his people. In such a society each member is to many others in some degree a brother, or sister, or mother, or father, son or daughter; for each one belongs to the same ethnico-cultural family, often with the same legendary common ancestors. In corporate groups of this kind, as Lonergan points out, the primordial intersubjective dynamics of social unity reach out into different times and places:

> The bond of mother and child, man and wife, father and son, reaches into a past of ancestors to give meaning and cohesion to the clan or tribe or nation. A sense of belonging together provides the dynamic premise for the common enterprise, for mutual aid and succor, for the sympathy that augments joys and divides sorrows.[31]

The deep sense of solidarity, which may even be traced back mythologically to common parents "in the beginning," imposes the duty to continue each family through offspring. This vital continuity of past and future generations is concretely symbolized in the special relationships, and the titles used, between grandparents and grandchildren. Among the Gikuyu, for example, a boy is called by his grandmother "my husband," and a girl is called "my co-wife." The grandfather calls the boy "my equal," and he calls the girl "my bride."[32] Similar family titles of address are used throughout sub-Saharan Africa. A Masai may address his son with the title "my father." In some societies the first sons and daughters must be given the names of their respective grandparents. Consanguinity may be fictively attributed even to some non-kin relationships. Among the Masai people, for example, the deepest of interpersonal relationships may be signified by the term *osotwa*, which literally means "the umbilical cord."

Where strong feelings of family solidarity are deeply rooted in the psychology as well as the practical experience of a whole people, the failure to leave behind a sufficient number of offspring to ensure the continuation of the family is a major disaster. Among the Bantu-speaking peoples there is a strong bond between the living and the dead: a person lives on, after death, somehow through, or in relation to, his progeny. This belief has profound significance in relation to the practice of polygyny. As R.M. Janssen expresses it:

> Procreation is the link with after-life and overcomes absolute death. Because of this, polygamy is fairly widespread, for if a marriage remains childless a man marries again. To forbid polygamy to the Bantu can mean a question of survival or extinction.[33]

Hence, the fear that a man might die without a surviving male child is one of the factors behind the practice of polygamy.[34]

Not only among the Bantu-speaking peoples, but in many other societies as well, the sense of family solidarity and continuity, especially with practical reference to such things as rights of inheritance and land usage, is explicitly associated with the motives for the practice of polygamy.[35] Family continuity is, moreover, as important for maintaining cultural traditions as it is for the propagation and stability of society. A man deprived of culture could no more survive than culture itself could survive without human beings to carry it on. Culture, as well as ethnic continuity, is largely a family affair.[36]

Polygyny is motivated by more than the need for children. There is also the practical need to form alliances between family and clan groups. Where marriage is conceptualized as an arrangement between such groups, and only concomitantly between husband and wife, the bonds of marriage and the "payments" that support the stability of marriage, may be seen in terms of social alliances.[37] In other words, polygamy is a function of social solidarity on the level of the extended family, the clan, and the tribal or ethnic community. Each new marriage sets up new relationships of affinity between two different kin groups, that of the husband and that of the wife; and their children are kin to both groups. A variety of new mutual assistance patterns are thus established. As the Gikuyu say, "the corpses of relatives-in-law fall together."[38] However these various relationships may be defined in each society, the emerging alliances are considerably increased when a man's wives have come from different kin groups. The network of alliances, with their concomitant chains of association, are extended according to the intensity with which polygamy is practiced.

As each new relationship implies mutual duties and benefits, the social prestige of the polygamous family is bound to be greater than that of the monogamous family. As the alliances multiply relationships, the sense of security expands and deepens in the polygamous household. This is well illustrated when a region of the tribal land in afflicted by periodic drought or pestilence. Those who have many relatives in other regions know that they have not been permanently impoverished; nor do orphans, widows, and grandparents ever suffer the trauma of being without a family to sustain them. This sort of social insurance is based on the number of marriage relationships and associations that have been established by the heads of families. Hence the importance of polygamous families in societies that structure their social security and cohesion on the basis of multiple marriage relationships.

In a society that stresses the importance of large families, a woman naturally sees her own personal self-fulfilment through childbearing; and the mother of several children is greatly respected by her relatives and neighbors. "Children are the glory of marriage," says Mbiti, "and the more there are of them the greater the glory."[39] At the same time, every woman is aware of the possibility that she may perhaps find herself among that unfortunate minority who fail to bear children. The importance of this is duly emphasized by Mbiti:

> To lack someone close who keeps the departed in their personal immortality is the worst misfortune and punishment that any person could suffer. To die without getting married and without chil-

dren is to be completely cut off from the human society, to become disconnected, to become an outcast and to lose all links with mankind.[40]

In the traditional African social context, barrenness is surely the most severe psychological trauma that a woman can suffer. But the sharp edge of this suffering may be dulled through her active participation in the larger family life of the polygynous household. Here she may occupy herself with, and bestow her affection upon, the children of co-wives. Among the Masai it is normal procedure to give a barren wife one of the infants of a co-wife who has had several children, and this is done with the full consent of all concerned.[41] Sociological parenthood can, and does, override physiological parenthood in such situations.[42] A similar practice is that of keeping a grandmother happy by entrusting to her, as her own, one of her grandchildren. Thus, the joys and sorrows of family life are shared.

If loneliness is never a problem for the members of polygamous households, neither is hospitality. While both polygamists and monogamists subscribe to the hospitality patterns dictated by their common culture (and African hospitality tends to be very expansive), it is clear that the larger family more easily acquires the prestige associated with generous hospitality. As Monica Wilson points out:

> Plural marriages breed wealth, for the polygynist is likely to command the labour of many sons and several wives, and in due course he expects to receive the marriage cattle of many daughters. . . . Wealth carries authority and prestige only in so far as it is used generously, in hospitality: one man is great and distinguished . . . because he feeds people, another of little account because he is poor or mean.[43]

This can be a source of acute embarrassment for a monogamist, especially for one who aspires to a position of leadership in a society that gives great value to large feasts and the good fellowship established through generous hospitality. What Monica Wilson says about this problem among the Nyakyusa may be taken as fairly typical:

> The pagans jibe at the Christians for being inhospitable because (as the Christians themselves admit) they entertain their neighbors less

than the pagans do. . . . The Christians are very conscious of the
difficulties of hospitality in a monogamous household, for a wife
must not only do all the cooking for visitors (and many Nyakyusa
dishes require considerable labour to prepare), but she must also
help to grow the food.[44]

So the monogamist, if he would aspire to one of the highest social
ideals of his community, would have to hire servants, if he can
find them, and if he can afford them.

Where it is believed and seen and felt that polygamous, much
more than monogamous, families produce for their members
greater security, prosperity, and prestige, the women themselves
will be seen to favor the custom of plural marriage. Since the
wives, together with their children, share in all the benefits of
belonging to the polygamous family, they themselves will sometimes pressure their husbands into seeking additional wives.[45]
Some women even regard it as a disgrace to be the only wife of a
man.[46] Among the Kaka people of Cameroon, a wife may pro-
voke her husband to take another wife by ridiculing him and
calling him "a poor man."[47] Women, have, of course, many other
ways of exerting pressure on their husbands.

Still, as Paul Bohannan notes, "polygyny is a state into which
most African men enter with a certain trepidation."[48] Frequently,
husbands are reluctant to seek additional wives because of the
greater burdens and responsibilities that go with management of
polygynous households.[49] In many cases, a man may take a
second or third wife only out of a sense of social obligation, in
response to particular pressures, especially such things as the
need for more children or the need for a male heir. The need for
additional wives may also arise from economic necessity when,
for example, a man inherits livestock that must be cared for or
land that must be utilized. There is also the widespread practice
of "wife inheritance": a man inherits the wife or wives of his
deceased brother.

A common form of plural marriage in Africa is that which arises
from the death of a husband whose wife had not passed the age of
childbearing or when the deceased has not left a surviving male
heir. In such a situation, a brother of the deceased, even though
he himself may be married, is obliged to marry his brother's

widow. Among some peoples, the Nuer and Zulu for example, the brother is required by customary law "to cohabit with the widow in order to raise children, which will be counted, not as his, but as the children of the deceased."[50] In order to maintain the family name and continuity, as well as for reasons of inheritance and security, the widow remains the legal wife of the dead man for whom the brother is a surrogate: a husband in everything but the legal title. Among the ancient Jews this was known as the levirate marriage (cf. Gen. 38:8–10; Deut. 25:5–10).

The true levirate marriage is, in effect, very similar to the system of widow inheritance that is found in many other societies.[51] In this situation, a man simply inherits as his own, together with all the conjugal rights and duties, the widow or widows of his deceased brother. Sometimes it is a son who so inherits the wives of his deceased father—but without prejudice to the incest taboos respecting his own biological mother.[52] All such marriages of inheritance normally involve the obligation of bearing children, plus all the other implications of family life. The customary laws governing these situations are clearly aimed at safeguarding all the ideals of family life, the very heart of the social system. So all these customary forms of plural marriage may be seen as "continuations or renewals of the existing structure of social relationship."[53] This is a matter of singular importance for a correct understanding of the custom of widow inheritance or the practice of the levirate marriage. Briefly and clearly, Paul Bohannan explains it in these words:

> If the widow has several children and her children are members of her late husband's kinship group, she has an important position within that kinship group. . . . Her position in life, indeed, may depend upon her children—thus underscoring the hard fate of a barren woman. Her natal group has little obligation to her after her initial marriage—ultimately none. As some Africans put it, "your wife of longstanding becomes your sister." A woman's status derives from her being a mother of lineage members. Therefore, it is only sensible for her to remarry into that group. . . . American and Western European society does not cope very well with widows. They are an anomaly. They occupy an insecure position, are to be pitied, particularly if they have children; they are not quite to be trusted. . . . African societies cope well with . . . widows—getting

them back into families quickly and simply. Loneliness is not an indigenous African problem.[54]

Divorce is usually recognized as legally possible under various fixed conditions. Female infertility, for example, provides socially sanctioned grounds for divorce in many societies. But the whole conception of family life, and the extended relationships established through marriage, work in favor of permanence in marriage.[55] Divorce is usually such a complicated affair, involving the interests of three different conjugal families (the family of the two immediately concerned, and their respective families of origin), that the more favorable solution to the problem of an infertile wife is simultaneous polygamy. To all concerned, this is normally preferable to divorce, where social life is structured on the assumption that all marriages should be permanent, and every woman (fertile or not) should have a husband.[56]

The permanence of a marriage in a polygamous household often depends more on the quality of the relationships between co-wives than it does on the relationships between the husband and the particular wife. A woman may get along perfectly well with her husband, but not at all well with her co-wives; so divorce may be the only way out of an unbearable family situation. On the other hand, in spite of great personal difficulties with her husband, the question of divorce may never arise where the relationships between co-wives are congenial. In any case, the general ideals and practical arrangements of the polygamous family are "such that harmony among co-wives is possible," and often just as rewarding for the wives as for the husbands.[57] So this system tends to support the permanence of marriage.

SEXUAL REGULATION AND FAMILY PLANNING

As already noted, sex is not the only force that draws men and women together into the universally recognized arrangement known as marriage.[58] Since, however, the connection between sexual activity and family planning is rather fundamental, we may ask whether, and to what extent, plural marriage functions in behalf of sexual control and family planning.

In traditional African societies, polygamy provides husbands with a socially accepted way of fulfilling their sexual needs during the periods of prolonged female continence following pregnancy and during lactation.[59] Where this form of marriage is preferential, prostitution is seldom institutionalized. It is, in fact, quite foreign to the traditions of many African peoples.[60] Moreover, polygamy helps to maintain a moderate and stable rate of birth. In some of these traditional societies, notes Claude Levi-Strauss, "the marriage rules, though varied, reveal to the eye of the demographer a common function, namely to set the fertility rate very low and to keep it constant."[61] While living within their indigenous socio-cultural situations, as Paul Bohannan says, "African women do not . . . bear more than one child every two and a half to three years."[62] This spacing is achieved by female continence and by prolonging the periods of lactation, a practice that usually inhibits ovulation and, thus, provides a substantial degree of infertility at least until weaning is commenced.[63]

Although a family may desire as many children as possible, a measure of control over the rate of birth is dictated by the traditional cultural pattern. The determining interest here is doubtless a concern for the health of the mother and the existing child in an economic situation where food supplies are apt to be relatively short and sometimes precarious. There is here a form of family planning that is socially patterned and biologically based, and the practice of polygamy plays a positive role in maintaining a kind of balance between fertility rates and sexual activity. Where monogamy is preferential, however, the period between births tends to be shorter; so the general birthrate is higher in monogamous societies than it is in polygamous societies.[64] Although a man begets more children in a polygamous marriage, a woman does not bear more than she would in a monogamous union: she bears fewer, in fact, as the wife of a polygamist. Hence, as Paul Bohannan points out:

> The moment that enforced monogamy comes into the African situation, the birthrate always soars (although monogamy is not the only factor—enforced monogamy is always accompanied by many other factors which change the way people live).[65]

While the available statistics indicate that the general rate of fertility is lower among polygynously married women than among monogamously married women, there is some disagreement among demographers when it comes to interpreting the data. It seems fairly well established that the significance of venereal disease, as a differential factor, has been exaggerated. The lower fertility rate among polygamously married women should rather be attributed to their less frequent coital performances and to the older average age of their husbands, plus other selective factors.[66]

A soaring birthrate is not the only problematical consequence associated with a change over from preferential polygamy to general monogamy, supported and enforced by extrinsic social pressures. Inevitably, the kinship system will also suffer; and, as kin relationships deteriorate, the whole social fabric will progressively lose its traditional cohesiveness. But the institution of marriage itself is apt to be the first thing compromised, at least as regards stability and permanence. Among the Yoruba people of Nigeria, for example, there is an apparent correlation between social change (Westernization) and the high rate of divorce.[67]

Moreover, it is notorious that the introduction of enforced monogamy contributes in no small measure to the establishment and increase of institutionalized prostitution, while it also encourages casual concubinage and adultery. Although some peoples do not even have in their language a word for prostitution,[68] this institution has developed among them side by side with Christianity. Where the custom of sexual abstinence is maintained during the wife's period of pregnancy and lactation, the monogamous husband tends to seek sexual satisfaction with prostitutes, or temporary concubines, or the wives of other men. This behavior in turn increases the chances of introducing venereal disease into monogamous families, thus reducing the fertility rate.[69] On the other hand, as already noted, the fertility rate of the monogamous segments of the population would normally increase when the customary period of sexual abstinence is not observed by lactating mothers.

The system of polygamy has its own inadequacies in this matter of sexual regulation.[70] When men must wait a long time before marriage and younger women are often married to much older men, there is a tendency toward adultery; or there is a tendency to give considerable license to the association of unmarried persons of both sexes.[71] Where both of these sexual outlets are inhibited by strong sanctions, especially when also girls are married off at an early age, the practice of homosexuality is apt to arise among the unmarried males. Monica Wilson's studies suggest that "it is because unmarried girls are so scarce and lustly bachelors so many, that the seduction of the wives of polygynists is frequent, and homosexual practices are general."[72] So, unless we are prepared to take a more tolerant attitude toward prostitution or concubinage or adultery or fornication or homosexuality, we must say that neither the system of monogamy nor the system of polygamy yields a perfectly balanced control of sexual activity.

Romantic love, a dominant feature in the current Western conception of marriage, is not very notable—or at least it is rarely dramatized—in traditional polygynous societies.[73] "The African," according to Radcliffe-Brown, "does not think of marriage as a union based on romantic love although beauty as well as character and health are sought in the choice of a wife."[74] Meaningful interpersonal relationships, however, are not lacking in polygamous households. Radcliffe-Brown continues:

> The strong affection that normally exists after some years of successful marriage is the product of the marriage itself conceived as a process, resulting from living together and co-operating in many activities and particularly in the rearing of children.[75]

Such relationships of friendship and affection are not by their very nature exclusive, and they exist even between co-wives.[76] There is, nevertheless, a great burden on the husband of plural wives. He must discipline himself to an equitable distribution of his love, which is a service to his whole family: not an exclusive affair of personal gratification between two individuals. If interpersonal relationships, and especially the manifestations of conjugal affection, seem to be less intense in polygamous families than in monogamous families, this may be because they are more extensive. Still, it is possible to maintain, as Paul Bohannan does, "that romantic love occurs in an African familial situation about as commonly as it does in a European or American one."[77] There is, however, some difference, according to Bohannan:

The difference is that Westerners have a series of myths which make them simulate romantic love to see them over the time between initial attraction and the regard that sensitive and sensible living together, breeding, and growing together can foster.[78]

As for the children of these families with several mothers, there is no evidence at all to suggest that their psychological development is adversely affected in any way. Each child has his own normal emotional attachment to his own mother by birth or by adoption; and co-wives are normally very solicitous and affectionate toward all the children of their husband.[79] The husband himself, according to the traditional norms of his society, is fully dedicated to the good of his children, who are regarded as the greatest of his achievements and the joy of his life.[80] It might even be said, at least as a tentative hypothesis, that the children of polygamous households, all other things being equal, will generally tend to be both physically and psychologically healthier than the children of monogamous families, insofar as the latter enjoy less security and less prestige. At any rate, in terms of their own social ideals and cultural values, the advantages are with the children of polygamous households.

CONCLUSION

Where polygamy is preferential, even though in fact the majority of marriages are monogamous, the women themselves generally have an uncritical attitude toward the cultural institution of plural marriage. Since childhood, they have regarded this as a normal and desirable form of marriage. It is not the members of polygamous families, but outside observers, who see polygamy as something undignified or even debasing for women. "In this judgment," comments Denise Paulme, "there lurks a hidden assumption: that any divergence from the Western ideal necessarily implies a lower status for women."[81] And Paul Bohannan has this to say on the subject:

> Polygyny has nothing to do with the position of women in society. African women, by and large, have a high social position. . . . Women in Africa are not, in short, a deprived group as they were in the nineteenth-century Western world.[82]

That is a man's opinion. Denise Paulme goes even further: in her opinion, the status of African wives is actually "higher" than that of the average wife in Western society today.[83]

However, considering the wide variety of marital systems, their vast differences as social phenomena, and the long historico-cultural experiences that led to these differences, it is no easy matter to make a comparative analysis of Western monogamy and African polygamy. It is clear enough that both systems work in their own social contexts, while both systems have their own built-in advantages and disadvantages.[84] A changeover from customary plural marriage to mandatory monogamy involves both loss and gain.

To avoid making *a priori* judgments from our own ethnocentric premises, it is necessary to see the social institutions of other peoples, not as scattered fragments, but as functional elements within concretely livable totalities. As a humanizing socio-economic institution, polygamy can and does work well among most of the peoples of sub-Saharan Africa; and it is a dubious hypothesis that monogamy will work better. This much is clear from the evidence of ethnology.[85]

As most African societies are still going through a period of extensive cultural change, and some of them are just beginning to re-identify themselves consciously with traditions that were regarded as embarrassments during the colonial period of Westernization, it is still too soon to make any definitive generalizations about the positive and negative implications, as well as the future prospects, of the prevailing marriage systems in the different areas. However, there is enough evidence, as we have just seen, to suggest that the traditional systems of plural marriage are still widespread and still in harmony with the prevailing attitude of African peoples. In the words of John Mbiti:

> Getting married to two or more wives is a custom found all over Africa, though in some societies it is less common than in others. The custom fits well into the thinking of the people, serving many useful purposes.[86]

NOTES

1. Cf. Robin Fox, *Kinship and Marriage* (Baltimore: Penguin Books, 1967), pp. 27–31.

2. *Ibid.*, p. 30. See also William Howells, *Back of History* (Garden City, N.Y.: Doubleday Anchor Books, and the American Museum of Natural History, 1963), p. 226: "Kinship is not simply blood ties and marriage relationship. A female baboon knows who her husband of the moment is, and who her own child is. Kinship is rather a cultural pattern, based on these things, but not the same from culture to culture and usually more complex than you might think if you were judging only by your own. . . . But whatever the complications and whatever the variety, there are certain things all such systems (of kinship) do: they provide you with relatives who are considered important, and they govern the behavior that you should hold toward them and they toward you. . . . In other words, kinship enlarges your resources in people. This may be the last thing you think you need, but you (living in the West) are exceptional."

3. C. Jaime Snoek, "Marriage and the Institutionalization of Sexual Relations," trans. Paul Burns, in *The Future of Marriage as Institution*, ed. Franz Böckle, Concilium 55 (New York: Herder and Herder, 1970), p. 116.

4. See Fox, *Kinship and Marriage*, p. 18. Speaking of the "naive" speculations of some of the early evolutionists, Fox makes this important observation: "The data they used was poor and their conclusions about the 'history of mankind' quite staggeringly without foundation. What they failed to realize was that kinship systems are not subject to *cumulative* evolution in the way that, say, technology is. Kinship systems, unlike technological inventions, cannot be ranked as better or worse, higher or lower; they simply represent alternative ways of doing things. Also the evolutionists failed to see that the *whole* of mankind need not have gone through the same series of stages—that there were alternative possible routes. Because they insisted on universal evolution, they regarded any contemporary tribe that showed 'archaic' traits as somehow retarded—a kind of fossil. They overlooked the fact that this tribe itself was the end product of an evolutionary process." For more on this, see also our Chapter Two.

5. Snoek, "Marriage and the Institutionalization of Sexual Relations," p. 116.

6. See George P. Murdock, *Social Structure* (London: Collier-Macmillan, 1949; New York: The Free Press, 1965), pp. 3–10; and Snoek, "Marriage and the Institutionalization," pp. 115–116.

7. See Murdock, *Social Structure*, pp. 8–10; Fox, *Kinship and Marriage*, pp. 37–40; and William J. Goode, "A Deviant Case: Illegitimacy in the Caribbean," in *The Family: Its Structure and Functions*, ed. Rose L. Coser (New York: St. Martin's Press, 1964), p. 20: "It seems safe enough to claim at least that all societies have family systems and that possibly a sociological father is required everywhere."

8. Howells, *Back of History*, p. 229.

9. Paul Bohannan, *Africa and Africans*, (Garden City, N.Y.: Doubleday and The Natural History Press, 1964), p. 159. See also Coser, "Introduction," in *The Family: Its Structure and Functions*, p. xiv: "From the point of view of society the family is a mediator of social values. As Erich Fromm has aptly stated: 'In spite of individual differences that exist in different families (of the same society), the family represents primarily the content of the society; the most important social function of the family is to transmit this content, not only through the formation of opinions and points of view but through the creation of socially desirable attitudinal structure.' (E. Fromm, "Sozialpsychologischer Teil," in *Autoritaet und Familie*, ed. Max Horkheimer, Paris: Alcan, 1936, p.87)."

10. Fox, *Kinship and Marriage*, p. 33.

11. *Ibid.*, p. 25. See also William J. Goode, "The Theoretical Importance of Love," in *The Family: Its Structure and Functions*, p. 211: "Kinfolk or immediate family can disregard the question of who marries whom, only if marriage is not seen as a link between kin lines, only if no property, power, lineage honor, totemic relationships, and the like are believed to flow from the kin lines through the spouses to their offspring. Mate choice thus has consequences for the social structure."

12. See A.R. Radcliffe-Brown, "Introduction," in *African Systems of Kinship and Marriage*, ed. A.R. Radcliffe Brown and Daryll Forde (London, New York, Toronto: Oxford University Press, 1950), p. 43: "There are innumerable social activities that can only be efficiently carried out by means of corporate groups, so that where, as in so many non-literate societies, the chief source of social cohesion is the recognition of kinship, corporate kin groups tend to become the most important feature of social structure." See also William B. Schwab, "Urbanism, Corporate Groups and Culture Change in Africa Below the Sahara," *Anthropological Quarterly* 43 (July 1970) 190: "To an African his village and his kin group are the major factors controlling his behavior." And John Mbiti, *African Religions and Philosophy* (New York and Washington: Praeger, 1969), p. 145: "The elaborate kinship system [in an African society] acts like an insurance policy covering both the physical and metaphysical dimensions of human life."

13. Bernard Lonergan, *Insight: A Study of Human Understanding* (New

York: Philosophical Library: London: Longmans, 1957), pp. 213–214.

14. *Ibid.*, p. 213.

15. See Paul Spencer, *The Samburu* (London: Routledge and Kegan Paul, 1965) pp. 134–135.

16. See Jomo Kenyatta, *Facing Mount Kenya: The Tribal Life of the Gikuyu* (London: Secker and Warburg, 1938), p. 115: "In the Gikuyu community there is no really individual affair, for everything has a moral and social reference." See also Josef Franz Thiel, "The Institution of Marriage: An Anthropological Perspective," trans. John Griffiths, in *The Future of Marriage as Institution*, ed. Franz Böckle, Concilium 55 (New York: Herder and Herder, 1970), p. 23: "Among the [African] ethnic groups examined in this article, the individual exists not for his own sake but for the sake of the kinship group. Marriage is not only his personal concern but above all that of his group."

17. Kenyatta, *Facing Mount Kenya*, p. 118: "No doubt educational philosophy can make a higher synthesis in which these two great truths are one, but the fact remains that while the Europeans place the emphasis on one side the Africans place it on the other."

18. See C.J. Snoek, "Marriage and the Institutionalization," p. 116: "The personalist view which, since Doms, has corrected the naturalist view of scholasticism, does not escape, for its part, from a certain unilateralism. It sees only the 'I' and the 'thou'. And yet for sexuality to be fully human and salvific it is not enough for the 'I' to be torn from his solitude by a 'thou'; the two then have to have the courage to insert themselves into the history of their people." See also Robert Hughes, and others, "The American Family: Future Uncertain," *Time*, December 28, 1970, pp. 41, 42: "As Americans became more mobile, the kinfolk have been gradually left behind. As a result, the typical family has evolved into an isolated 'nuclear' family. . . . Says Dr. John Platt, associate director of the University of Michigan's Mental Health Research Institute: 'All sorts of roles now have to be played by the husband and wife, whereas in the older, extended family they had all sorts of help—psychological support, financial advice, and so on. The pressures of these multiple roles are partially responsible for the high rates of divorce, alcoholism, tranquilizers, etc.' . . . Edward Westermarck observed that 'marriage rests in the family and not the family in marriage.' The corollary used to be that the family existed for many practical purposes beyond love. To base it so heavily on love—including the variable pleasures of sexual love—is to weaken its stability."

19. See Hughes, and others, "The American Family," p. 40: "One in every four U.S. marriages eventually ends in divorce. The rate is rising dramatically for marriages made in the past several years, and in some densely-populated West Coast communities is running as high as 70%.

The birth rate has declined from 30.1 births per thousand in 1910 to 17.7 in 1969. . . . Each year, an estimated half-million teen-agers run away from home."

20. See J. Hajnal, "European Marriage Patterns in Perspective," in *Population in History: Essays in Historical Demography*, ed. D.V. Glass and D.E.C. Eversley (Chicago: Aldine, and Edward Arnold Ltd., 1965), pp. 101, 106: "The marriage pattern of most of Europe as it existed for at least two centuries up to 1940 was, so far as we can tell, unique in the world. There is no known example of a population of non-European civilization which has had a similar pattern. . . . Europeans have married very much later than others and far more of them have remained unmarried throughout life. In non-European civilizations there are scarcely any single women over 25. It is not, of course, intended to suggest that non-European civilizations do not show wide variations in the pattern of their marriage rates. But all of the varieties that exist are separated by a distinct gap from the European pattern."

21. Radcliffe-Brown, *African Systems*, p. 3.

22. *Ibid.*

23. See Robert F. Gray and P.H. Gulliver, *The Family Estate in Africa: Studies in the Role of Property in Family Structure and Lineage Continuity* (London: Routledge and Kegan Paul, 1964), p. 26; and William D. Reyburn, "Polygamy, Economy, and Christianity in Eastern Cameroun," in *Readings in Missionary Anthropology*, ed. William A. Smalley (Tarrytown, N.Y.: Practical Anthropology, 1967), pp. 66–67.

24. For this and the following paragraph, see John C. Caldwell, "Introduction," in *The Population of Tropical Africa*, ed. John C. Caldwell and Chukuku Okonjo (New York: Columbia University Press, 1968), p. 11; Ansley J. Coale, "Estimates of Fertility and Mortality in Tropical Africa," *ibid.*, p. 106; also A.J. Coale, and F. Lorimer, "Summary of Estimates of Fertility and Mortality," in *The Demography of Tropical Africa*, ed. William Brass (Princeton: Princeton University Press, 1968), pp. 157–161: and John Bryant, *Health and the Developing World* (Ithaca and London: Cornell University Press, 1969), pp. 35–36, 50–52.

25. See *Time*, April 6, 1970, p. 48: "Sociologist de Vise cites another dismal statistic: 5% of Chicago's black ghetto infants die before reaching their first birthday—a higher death rate than in any of the fifty states or any civilized nation. As for doctors, he says the ghetto has one physician for every 10,000 blacks, as compared to one physician for every 700 whites." On the number of physicians for African populations, see John Bryant, *Health and the Developing World*, pp. 50–51: Malawi has one physician for every 148,000; Nigeria has one for every 50,000. Senegal has one doctor for 19,000 people: a total of about 164 doctors for a whole nation of some 3.14 million people. However, in the capital city alone

there are 103 doctors, which means one doctor for every 4,270 people
(the city population is 0.44 million). For the rest of the country (the
remaining population of some 2.7 million) there are 61 doctors, which
means one doctor for every 44,300 people.

26. See Bryant, *Health and The Developing World*, p. 51.

27. *Ibid.*, p. 35.

28. *Ibid.*

29. Kenyatta, *Facing Mount Kenya*, p. 3.

30. See Reinhold Niebuhr, *The Structure of Nations and Empires* (New
York: Charles Scribner's Sons, 1959), p. 149: "The forces of cohesion for
the integral community which are most potent are: common language
and a sense of ethnic kinship, geographic unity and contiguity, a common historical experience and frame of political thought, a common area
of economic mutuality, and, sometimes, the fear of a common foe."

31. Lonergan, *Insight*, p. 212.

32. See Kenyatta, *Facing Mount Kenya*, pp. 15–17.

33. R.M. Janssen, "Religious Encounter and the 'Jamaa'," *Heythrop
Journal* 8 (April 1967) 141.

34. See Kenyatta, *Facing Mount Kenya*, p. 15; and John Mbiti, *African
Religions*, p. 142: "If the philosophical or theological attitude towards
marriage and procreation is that these are an aid towards the partial
recapture or attainment of the lost immortality, the more wives a man
has the more children he is likely to have, and the more children the
stronger the power of 'immortality' in the family. He who has many
descendants has the strongest possible manifestation of 'immortality',
he is 'reborn' in the multitude of his descendants, and there are many
who 'remember' him after he has died physically."

35. See Gray and Gulliver, *The Family Estate in Africa; Studies in the Role
of Property in Family Structure and Lineage*, pp. 26–27; Monica Wilson, *Good
Company: A Study of Nyakyusa Age-Villages* (London, New York, Toronto:
Oxford University Press, 1951), p. 14; and Stanislas Bushayija, *Le mariage
coutumier au Rwanda* (Brussels: Ferdinand Larcier, 1966), pp. 136–138.

36. See Rose L. Coser, "Introduction," in *The Family: Its Structure and
Functions*, pp. xiii–xiv.

37. See Robin Fox, *Kinship and Marriage*, pp. 23, 220–221, 228–229.

38. See Kenyatta, *Facing Mount Kenya*, p. 168.

39. John Mbiti, *African Religions*, p. 142: "To be productive, in terms of
having children, is one of the essential attributes of being human. The
more productive a person is, the more he contributes to the existence of
society at large."

40. *Ibid.*, p. 134.

41. The same would be done for a wife whose children had died. The

wives who have several children seem to regard this practice as quite normal; and they would expect the same consideration had they themselves not been blessed with living children.

42. See Bronislaw Malinowski, "Parenthood, the Basis of Social Structure," in *The Family: Its Structure and Functions*, p. 12: This kind of substitution of one maternity for another, "proves undoubtedly that cultural parenthood can override the biological basis, but it does not introduce anything remotely like group-maternity. In fact the severance of one bond before another is established is a further proof of the individuality and exclusiveness of motherhood. . . . Motherhood is always individual. It is never allowed to remain a mere biological fact. These influences are so strong that in the case of adoption they may override the biological tie and substitute a cultural one for it."

43. Wilson, *Good Company*, p. 15.

44. *Ibid.*, pp. 71–72.

45. See Kenyatta, *Facing Mount Kenya*, p. 169; Gerald R. Leslie, *The Family in Social Context* (New York, Toronto: Oxford University Press, 1967), p. 27; E.A. Ayandele, *The Missionary Impact on Modern Nigeria 1842–1914: A Political and Social Analysis* (London: Longmans, Green 1966), p. 336; and Mbiti, *African Religions*, pp. 142–143: "When a family is made up of several wives with their households, it means that in time of need there will always be someone around to help. This is corporate existence. For example, when one wife gives birth, there are other wives to nurse her and care for her children during the time she is regaining her vitality. If one wife dies, there are others to take over the care of her children. In case of sickness, other wives will fetch water from the river, cut firewood, cook and do other jobs for the family. If one wife is barren, others bear children for the family, so that the torch of life is not extinguished. Where peasant farming is the means of livelihood, the many children in a polygamous family are an economic asset—even if they also must eat plenty of food."

46. See Harvey J. Currens, "Polygamy in the Church in Native Africa" (unpublished paper, Chicago Lutheran Theological Seminary, January 1950), p. 42.

47. See Reyburn, "Polygamy, Economy, and Christianity," pp. 66, 76.

48. Bohannan, *Africa and Africans*, p. 146.

49. See Robert F. Gray, *The Sonjo of Tanganyika* (London: Oxford University Press, 1963), p. 69; and N.P. Kipengele, "Marriage Celebrations Among Wamatumbi," *Studia Missionalia, Ethnologie Religieuse* 14 (1964) 84.

50. Radcliffe-Brown, *African Systems*, p. 64. See also Bohannan, *Africa and Africans*, p. 168.

51. See Radcliffe-Brown, *African Systems*, pp. 64–65.

52. See Wilson, *Good Company*, p. 161; and Bohannan, *Africa and Africans*, pp. 166–167: "Rights in women are considered, in most African societies, to be inherited." Since all rights involve obligations, a man may inherit the obligations of his father (or of his brother) with respect to the widow or widows of his father (or of his brother).

53. Radcliffe-Brown, *African Systems*, p. 64.

54. Bohannan, *Africa and Africans*, pp. 167–168.

55. See Marie-André du Sacré-Coeur, *The Household Stands Firm: Family Life in West Africa* (Milwaukee: Bruce, 1962), p. 110.

56. See Ralph E.S. Tanner, *Transition in African Beliefs* (Maryknoll, N.Y.: Maryknoll Publications, 1967), pp. 95, 106. See also Hajnal, "European Marriage Patterns," p. 126: In societies where every woman is expected, or required, to be married the system of polygyny provides a proper place also for women whose defects (blind, deaf, spastic, epileptic, lame, retarded) would otherwise make it impossible for them to find husbands, and thus a place in a family and in society. In monogamous societies such handicapped women may perhaps constitute the bulk of those who never marry. "No one," according to Hajnal, "seems to have discussed this problem."

57. Bohannan, *Africa and Africans*, p. 163: "If they have separate quarters and a pronounced code of behavior known to everyone, it is possible for co-wives not only to live next door, but to share their husband and even become quite fond of one another. They have a great deal in common. . . . At the same time, in many African languages, the word for co-wife springs from the same root as the word for jealousy. The situation is fraught with difficulty—but are not all family relationships fraught with difficulty: the husband-wife relationship in monogamy? The parent-child relationship everywhere? The polygynous family is more complex than the monogamous family, and there are certain difficulties built into it. But the rewards may be great. See also Monica Wilson, "Nyakyusa Kinship," in *African Systems of Kinship and Marriage*, p. 113; and John Mbiti, *African Religions and Philosophy*, pp. 143–144: "There are problems connected with polygamy and it would be utterly wrong to pretend that everything runs smoothly in polygamous families. . . . On the other hand, it needs to be pointed out that the problems of polygamous families are human problems and are not necessarily created by polygamy as such; nor have they been solved or avoided in monogamous families either in Africa or Europe and America."

58. See Murdock, *Social Structure*, pp. 4–7, 260–283.

59. See *ibid.*, p. 37; Bohannan, *Africa and Africans*, pp. 161–162; and Daryll Forde, "Double Descent Among the Yako," in *African Systems of*

Kinship and Marriage, p. 290: "There is a particular inducement to take a second wife very shortly after the first if the latter has borne a child, for a child is normally suckled for two years during which intercourse between the parents is forbidden."

60. See Kenyatta, *Facing Mount Kenya,* pp. 167–168: "The custom [polygyny] also provides that all women must be under the protection of men; and that in order to avoid prostitution . . . all women must be married in their 'teens,' i.e. fifteen to twenty." See also Mbiti, *African Religions and Philosophy,* p. 143: "Polygamy helps to prevent or reduce unfaithfulness and prostitution, especially on the part of the husband."

61. Claude Levi-Strauss, *The Scope of Anthropology,* trans. S.O. Paul and R.A. Paul (London: Jonathan Cape, 1967), p. 47. See Bohannan, *Africa and Africans,* p. 161: "The birth rate in a polygynous situation is never higher than the birth rate in a monogamous situation. It is usually lower. A man may beget more children in polygyny than in monogamy. A woman does not bear any more."

62. Bohannan, *Africa and Africans,* p. 161.

63. See M. Bonte and H. van Balen, "Prolonged Lactation and Family Spacing in Rwanda," *Journal of Biosocial Science* 1 (April 1969) 97–100. In this study of a society with no traditional restriction of intercourse after delivery, it was found that the contraceptive effect of lactation is present for 27 months after delivery: the effect is maximal during the first 9 months; conception is delayed in the majority of cases for a period of 15 months; and the effectiveness thereafter diminishes steadily until the conception rate of lactating women equals that of nonlactating women in the 27th month *post partum.*

64. See Vernon A. Dorjahn, "The Factor of Polygyny in African Demography," in *Continuity and Change in African Cultures,* ed. William R. Bascom and Melville J. Herskovits (Chicago: University of Chicago Press, 1959), pp. 109–112; and Etienne van de Walle, "Marriage in African Censuses and Inquiries," in *The Demography of Tropical Africa,* (Princeton N.J.: Princeton University Press, 1968), pp. 229–230.

65. Bohannan, *Africa and Africans,* p. 161.

66. See A. Romaniuk, "Infertility in Tropical Africa," in *The Population of Tropical Africa,* p. 217.

67. See P.C. Lloyd, "Osifekune of Ijebu," in *Africa Remembered,* ed. P.D. Curtin (Madison and Milwaukee: University of Wisconsin Press, 1969), p. 259.

68. See note 60, above.

69. See Dorjahn, "The Factor of Polygyny in African Demography," p. 111; P.V. Ottenburg, "The Changing Economic Position of Women among the Afikpo Ibo," in *Continuity and Change in African Cultures,* p. 221; J.B. Christensen, "The Adoptive Function of the Fanti Priest-

hood," *ibid.*, p. 269; and F.W. Wellbourn, *East African Rebels: A Study of Some Independent Churches* (London: SCM Press, 1961), p. 183.

70. See Murdock, *Social Structure*, pp. 260–283.

71. It is not always and everywhere the case in polygamous societies that young men must wait a long time before they are permitted to marry. See, for example, Daryll Forde in *African Systems of Kinship and Marriage*, p. 290: Among the Yako people of Nigeria "young men usually marry girls of their own age in the first instance. . . . In later marriages men often take women who differ widely from them in age, and the general tendency is to marry younger women."

72. Wilson, *Good Company*, p. 161.

73. See Goode, "The Theoretical Importance of Love," in *The Family: Its Structure and Function*, pp. 210–211: "Perhaps only the following cultures possess the romantic love value complex: modern urban United States, Northwestern Europe, Polynesia, and the European nobility of the eleventh and twelfth centuries. Certainly, it is to be found in no other major civilization. On the other hand, the *love pattern*, which views love as a basis for the final decision to marry, may be relatively common."

74. Radcliffe-Brown in *African Systems of Kinship and Marriage*, p. 46.

75. *Ibid.*

76. See Kenyatta, *Facing Mount Kenya*, p. 172; Reyburn, "Polygamy, Economy, and Christianity," p. 77; and Solange Falade, "Women of Dakar and the Surrounding Urban Area," in *Women in Tropical Africa*, ed. Denise Paulme, trans. H.M. Wright (London: Routledge and Kegan Paul, 1963), p. 226.

77. Bohannan, *Africa and Africans*, p. 165.

78. *Ibid.*

79. See note 42, above; and also Remi Clignet, *Many Wives, Many Powers: Authority and Power in Polygynous Families* (Evanston: Northwestern University Press, 1970), pp. 154–156. In societies which accept polygamy the child-rearing practices and attitudes are basically the same in both monogamous and polygamous families. According to Clignet (p. 156), "plural marriage does not seem to affect the nature of the bond interwoven between mothers and children."

80. The average polygynist father in Africa probably spends more time with his children than does the average monogamist father in North America. For the observations of another missionary on this particular point, see Adrian Edwards, "Marriage and Mysterion: Reflections of a Bush Theologian," *New Blackfriars* 51 (August 1970) 382–383.

81. Denise Paulme, "Introduction," *Women in Tropical Africa*, p. 4.

82. Bohannan, *Africa and Africans*, pp. 163–164. In societies which accept polygamy, and in which monogamous unions are potentially

polygamous, the husband-wife relationships are essentially the same in both polygamous and monogamous marriages. This relationship, and hence the position of women, is determined not so much by the type of marriage as by the dominant understanding of marriage within a particular cultural complex. As Clignet says (in *Many Wives, Many Powers*, p. 356), "Polygyny is just a mechanism to facilitate the realization of cultural expectations." Thus, for example, the position of women might be influenced or determined far more by the type of lineage system followed in their society than by the presence or absence of polygamy.

83. Paulme, *Women in Tropical Africa*, p. 4. See also David B. Barrett, *Schism and Renewal in Africa*, (Nairobi, Addis Ababa, Lusaka: Oxford University Press, 1968), p. 146.

84. See Kenyatta, *Facing Mount Kenya*, pp. 171–176; Solange Falade, "Women of Dakar," p. 226; Bohannan, *Africa and Africans*, pp. 161–168; and Paul Spencer, *The Samburu*, pp. 57, 67, 133.

85. See Murdock, *Social Structure*, p. 30.

86. Mbiti, *African Religions and Philosophy*, p. 142.

CHAPTER V

POLYGAMY AND THE BIBLE

> *The great evil . . . was not really polygamy as such, but so-called "successive" polygamy —a husband was able to annul his marriage, send his wife away, and enter into a new marriage.*
>
> EDWARD SCHILLEBEECKX

The biblical texts that are usually cited to show the incompatibility of polygamy with Christianity are concerned specifically with other matters. This can be seen just by re-reading the relevant passages, while keeping in mind at the same time the exact meaning of simultaneous polygyny which, unlike consecutive plural marriage (or serial monogamy), involves neither divorce nor remarriage. As Karl Barth says, "we can hardly point with certainty to a single text (of the New Testament) in which polygamy is expressly forbidden and monogamy universally decreed."[1] According to John L. McKenzie, "the teaching of Jesus on marriage is limited to his affirmations of its indissolubility."[2] Polygamy is simply not treated directly and explicitly by the New Testament writers who, quite naturally, under the cultural ethos of their particular time and place in history, accepted monogamy as a normal point of departure for any discussion of marriage.[3]

Adultery, divorce, polyandry, and consecutive polygyny (serial monogamy while the first wife is still living) are manifestly repudiated in the New Testament (cf. Matt. 5:27–32; Mark 10:2–12; Rom. 7:2–3; 1 Cor. 7:2–16; Eph. 5:22–33). But simultaneous polygamy is not considered at all in these passages, although the New Testament writers certainly must have known that this customary form of marriage existed among their Jewish contemporaries, even as it existed during the time of Jesus.[4]

It is, moreover, demonstrable that all of the positive values urged in these same texts—love, faithfulness, indissolubility, and mutual respect for conjugal rights—are capable of realization within the plural marriage system found throughout sub-Saharan Africa. To recognize this is not to deny that the same values may also be realized, and perhaps even more fully, in a monogamous union. The point here is that, while the New Testament explicitly repudiates any number of practices—including also fornication, prostitution, and homosexuality (cf. Rom. 1:24–27; 1 Cor. 6:9, 12–18; Eph. 4:19)—which compormise the Christian ideal of marriage, there is no prohibition against simultaneous polygyny. So, with Edward Schillebeeckx, we may say at least this much:

> Nowhere in the New Testament is there any explicit commandment that marriage should be monogamous or any explicit commandment forbidding polygamy.[5]

Nevertheless, Christian scholars throughout the ages, with very few exceptions, have persistenly affirmed the absolute incompatibility of simultaneous polygamy with the Christian way of life. This view, as already noted, is traditional; and it has been canonized in the discipline of most Christian churches. The reasoning behind this position, which is allegedly based upon the clear teaching of the Bible, is outlined briefly in the following three paragraphs.

Although God permitted polygamy in former times, a careful reading of the Old Testament reveals a gradual evolution, away from this ancient Jewish custom, toward monogamy. Because of this progressive development in the history of salvation, monogamy emerges as the properly human and divinely willed form of marriage. It is, of course, taken as self-evident that the Genesis accounts of creation, and of life in the garden, depict monogamy as something intended by God from the beginning. What the New Testament says about marriage is then seen as a clear confirmation of the monogamy hypothesis. So it is assumed that, so far as Christians are concerned, polygamy was finally "abolished by Christ."[6]

"It is obvious," says Otto Piper, "that what Jesus says about marriage implies monogamy."[7] By implication there is now a divine prohibition against polygamy. The argument, as summarized by W.T. O'Shea, is this:

> The end of marriage is stated in different ways in the two accounts of the creation of man in the book of Genesis. In Gen. 1, 27ff., its stated purpose is that man should "multiply and fill the earth," whereas in 2:18–25, it is conceived as a union in which the woman is the helpmate of the man, for "it is not good that the man should be alone." The implication is that the ideal union of the sexes is a monogamous one, an implication which Christ will make explicit in his discussion with the Pharisees.[8]

Although most theologians would agree that Jesus restored marriage to "its pristine purity" by insisting upon monogamy as well as indissolubility, some would argue more confidently from the relevant Pauline passages.[9] Thus, Jean Jacques von Allmen says:

> Marriage is strictly monogamous, for Jesus has and can have only one bride. In this sense, Christian marriage, in advance of the reign of the law, restores the original will of God.[10]

The common ground for this long-standing interpretation of God's intention is the Gospel account of the Lord's debate with some Pharisees on the question of divorce and remarriage (cf. Matt. 19:3–9; Mark 10:2–12), the Genesis story of "a man" and "his wife" becoming "one flesh" in the beginning (cf. Gen. 2:18–25), and the Pauline analogy between human marriage and the union of Christ with the Church (cf. Eph. 5:21–33). A number of additional texts are usually cited by way of corroboration.

However, the method of interpretation is rather suspect. The whole biblical case against the practice of polygamy is developed only by inferences, and it hinges on a number of assumptions which can no longer be taken as self-evident. Is it possible that our theologians have merely searched the Scriptures for evidence of a divinely revealed conception of marriage that is really just Greco-Roman: not strictly biblical, certainly, and not even clearly in the mainstream of the Jewish cultural tradition? "The system of literary interpretation applied to biblical texts in the pre-scientific period," as Joseph Blenkinsopp reminds us, "allowed both Jew and Christian to find . . . almost anything they wished to find."[11]

"Without really realizing it," says Claus Westermann, "we have become accustomed to listen to [the Bible] in the light of a particular type of interpretation."[12] Surely it is the Western cultural tradition, far more than the Bible, that has provided Christians with their basic notions about marriage.[13] For it has been just too easy in the past for theologians and churchmen to read into the Bible what they expected to find there. Considering the pre-scientific methods of biblical exegesis used in earlier decades, it is reasonable to suppose, therefore, that our traditional Christian theology of marriage derives more from the history of biblical interpretation than from what the Bible actually says on the subject. Some of our past certitudes, submitted to the fresh scrutiny of a more scientific methodology, have become mere probabilities—or less. For the sciences of history, archeology, anthropology, as also the study of ancient Near Eastern languages, have enormously augmented our knowledge and understanding of the Bible. As Robert Springer puts it:

> What the exegetes have done is twofold. First, they transcended the limits of Western thought patterns which had inevitably influenced Western minds interpreting the sacred texts. Necessarily this had involved interpolating meanings and nuances of thought into divine revelation which were not there. We need only recall the impact of literary *genre* on what were thought to be historical passages of Old and New Testaments. This transcultural view of Scripture involved at the same time breaking through into oriental thought patterns which had long kept secret the meaning of words and phrases.[14]

It is only when we begin to take seriously the different cultural conceptions and social institutions of other peoples that some of our traditional, and hitherto unquestioned biblical interpretations are apt to be queried, challenged, and critically reexamined. So it is that the Christian encounter with the cultures of Africa compels us now to take a closer and more critical look at the biblical interpretations that have led the Christian churches to impose the law of monogamy, as though this were an absolutely universal law revealed by God.

Without going into an exhaustive exegesis of the relevant passages and without pretending that polygamy appears as an ideal any place in the Bible, the aim of this chapter is simply to raise some new questions and to cast some doubt on the validity of the retrospective biblical reasons that are usually adduced in support of the traditional Christian stand against the African custom of simultaneous polygamy.

A TENDENCY TOWARD MONOGAMY

A number of scholars have noted a progressive tendency toward monogamy throughout the pages of the Old Testament; and this is presented by them as background for a proper understanding of the divine intention, allegedly expressed in clearer terms in the New Testament, regarding monogamy and polygamy.[15] While no single passage of the Bible stands alone as a clear proof of God's intention in this matter, an impressive number of texts may be cited as indications of a positive inclination toward monogamy. The Damascus Document of Qumran may also be cited as extrabiblical support for this viewpoint.

It is simply taken as self-evident that the Yahwist account of creation (cf. Gen. 2:18–25), with some corroboration from the later Priestly account (cf. Gen. 1:27), depicts marriage as monogamous in the beginning and that these selected verses constitute a formal teaching on the essential nature and ethical structure of marriage. It is pointed out that, while many of the great biblical figures were monogamists, the first recorded plural marriage occured among the reprobate descendents of Cain (cf. Gen. 4:19, 23); so polygamy is somehow tainted from its inception. In Deuteronomy the admonition against multiplying wives, although this is combined with warnings against also acquiring an excessive number of horses as well as too much gold and silver, is used as an apologetic argument in behalf of monogamy (cf. Deut. 17:16–17).

The suggestion is sometimes made that polygamy is problematical even in the Old Testament, because it somehow implies adultery. Particular attention is drawn to the frequent use of the imagery of monogamy in describing the covenant relationship between Yahweh and his people (cf., for example, Isa. 50:1; 54:6–7; 62:4–5; Jer. 2:2; Ezek. 16; Hosea *passim*). In contrast to the values of the earlier period of the patriarchs and kings, the more recent wisdom literature is said to reflect a growing appreciation of monogamy (cf., for example, Prov. 5:15–19; 31:10–31; Eccles. 9:9; Tob. 8:6–7; Ps. 45:9–11; 128:3). Even the Song of Songs, although this is surely one of the most difficult and controversial areas of biblical criticism, is sometimes cited as evidence of the Bible's progressively developing esteem for monogamy.[16]

Thus, by accumulating enough of the right sort of texts, by relating them to each other, and by interpreting them with little regard for their respective historico-cultural contexts, this hypothesis becomes plausible: that the Old Testament was gradually revealing God's preference for monogamy, although the "definitive step" in this evolutionary process is found only in the New Testament.[17] Difficulties arise, however, as soon as we recognize that each of the passages cited can be interpreted, if one really wishes to do so, in such a way as not to exclude polygamy. The interpretation one chooses is all too easily determined by one's presuppositions: what one expects to find or wishes to prove. Many of these texts, as Roland de Vaux observes, "yield a better meaning against the background of a strictly monogamous family."[18] Is this "background" perhaps a postulate consciously or unconsciously present in the minds of most Christians as they read the Bible?

The historically conditioned values and ideals that shaped the Old Testament understanding of marriage are not the traditional values and ideals that Western man has used in making his judgments about what marriage is or should be; and they are very far, indeed, from the modern values and ideals that are having such profound influence today on the Western Christian conception of marriage. So it is important to recall that the real background to marriage in ancient Israel, the background against which the biblical passages on marriage are to be seen, was the larger community of the family and the clan.[19] Marriage was not understood primarily in terms of the husband-wife relationship, and certainly not in terms of an exclusive relationship between only two persons.[20]

The conception was much broader and more complex. Marriage was regarded as a social instrument required for the preservation and continuation of families and clans. Through daughters being married into different families, there was a mutual strengthening of kinship bonds—each family giving its own flesh and blood to other families. The definitive ratification of marriage was achieved neither in sexual intercourse, nor through mutually fulfilling interpersonal relationships, but by the birth of a child. Marriage was mainly a social function with the emphasis on fertility.[21] Fertility was the greatest of God's blessings upon a family, and barrenness was the worst of calamities. Without children, especially a son, the family name was "blotted out of Israel" (cf. Deut. 25:6). Marriage in the Old Testament is never understood without this instrumental significance, and its meaning is always presented within the framework of patriarchal values and social structures.

Such a conception of marriage was congenial to the custom of having more than one wife at the same time. In the Mosaic law polygamy is clearly regarded as a normal and licit practice (cf. Exod. 21:10; Lev. 18:18; Deut. 21:15–17), although among the common people it was probably never very widespread and sometimes even quite rare.[22] Nowhere in the Old Testament is this form of marriage called into question. The one and only admonition against the acquisition of too many wives (Deut. 17:17) is not an attack upon the institution of polygamy; it is, if we take account of the context, simply a warning against an abuse —against the king's taking *too many* wives, *foreign* wives specifically, because they would turn his heart toward their foreign gods (cf. 1 Kings 11:1–8). The meaning of the admonition is even more uncertain, and is no argument at all against the custom of polygamy, if Carlos Santin is correct in suggesting that the Hebrew word *nashim* (wives or women) in verse 17 is a mistake.[23]

It would be wrong, moreover, to suggest that simultaneous polygyny is somehow associated with the biblical problem of divorce. These two practices are not necessarily connected. By its very nature, simultaneous polygyny tends to exclude divorce; or, at least, it does not lead to divorce any more than does monogamy. So the various biblical reactions to abuses that occurred under the existing marriage laws of different periods should not be construed as revealing a divine preference for monogamy.

The recurring affirmations of marital indissolubility say nothing against polygamy which can be just as permanent as monogamy. As Schillebeeckx points out, with particular reference to the postexilic period, "the great evil . . . was not really polygamy as such, but so-called 'successive' polygamy—a husband was able to annul his marriage, send his wife away, and enter into a new marriage."[24] This particular abuse was, at times, a great threat to the integrity and solidarity of the whole people, especially when Jewish wives were sent away (divorce) and replaced by foreign wives (remarriage).

Nor does simultaneous polygyny, in a society which accepts this as normal and licit, imply adultery.[25] According to the biblical understanding of this sin, adultery could be committed only between persons who were not validly and licitly married to each other; and, of course, polygamous marriage was no less valid and licit than monogamous marriage. The Mosaic law gave equal recognition to both types of marriage and usually made no distinction between the two. Indeed, monogamous unions were all potentially polygamous according to the law. Some faults peculiar to polygamy are recorded in Scripture; but these faults are never equated with adultery, which a monogamist could commit just as easily as a polygamist. One could even imagine that a monogamist might, more frequently than a polygamist, be tempted to adultery. Although there were severe penalties for adultery (cf. Lev. 20:10; Deut. 22:22–23), it is nowhere suggested in the Bible that there were any sanctions against Jewish polygamy.

While it is true that many personages of the Old Testament were monogamists, it can be shown that many others were polygamists. So we will get nowhere by compiling and comparing lists of names. However, it may be interesting to recall that the marriage of Elkanah and Hannah is singled out in the Bible as a deep and affectionate expression of conjugal love, although Elkanah, at the same time, had another wife (cf. 1 Sam. 1:2–8). More significant still is the polygamy of Jacob. He had two wives at the same time, as well as two concubines (cf. Gen. 29:15–30; 30;1–9). Yet the Church is not ashamed to hold up one of these wives as a model to be imitated by newly married Christian women. Is there some inconsistency here? The nuptial blessing of the Roman rite before the recent revision (the second prayer after the "Our Father" in the nuptial mass) contained this supplication: "Let her ever follow the model of holy women; let her be dear to her husband like Rachel." Was this really incompatible with what followed? "Let her be true to one wedlock." This certainly "yields a better meaning" when it is taken as a reference to indissolubility: a reference to the exclusion of consecutive polygamy, not simultaneous polygamy.

The Bible frequently describes Yahweh's love for his people in terms of a husband's love for his wife; and this use of the singular, "wife," is supposed to hint at God's preference for monogamy. But what happens to this hypothesis when we notice that both Jeremiah and Ezekiel picture Yahweh also as the husband of more than one wife at the same time (cf. Jer. 3:6–10; 31:31–32; Ezek. 23:2–4)?

With equal ease, as it suits the historical circumstances, the biblical writers are able to depict Yahweh either as a monogamist or a polygamist. What revealed truth is suggested here? Surely, this literalistic method of interpreting some highly figurative language, if applied consistently instead of selectively to all the imagery of the passages in question, would yield some curious notions about God and his interest in man.

It should be noted, moreover, that marriage is not the only image used to describe the love of Yahweh for his people. The same point is made, also, through the imagery of parent and child, shepherd and flock, vinedresser and vine (cf. Deut. 32:18; Hos. 11:1–4; Jer. 3:19; Isa. 5:1–2; 40:11; Ps. 95:7; 80:8–9). Yet these relationships are not exclusive in the same way that a husband and wife are related in a monogamous marriage.

In the descriptions of the covenant relationship between God and his people, the image of the wife, in the singular, might be better understood in terms of "corporate personality." This is a familiar Semitic thought-category and biblical manner of speaking, in which a singular (the individual) may stand for and signify a plural (the collective): in the way, for example, that Adam stands for all men.[26] So the use of the singular, "wife," in reference to God's love for his people need not be understood literalistically, as though these passages intended to say something about the question of monogamy and polygamy. Both of these types of marriage are used as images to illustrate the same point: that God's people should be faithful to him, just as a man's wife (or wives) should be faithful to him. Such imagery is quite appropriate in a society that accepts both monogamy and polygamy as equally valid and licit forms of marriage, and such imagery might be expected in literature that is hardly intelligible without reference to the notion of "corporate personality."[27] Besides, God's people is a plurality.

Even if it were perfectly clear that the sacred writings reflected a progressively developing preference for monogamy, this would not have to be interpreted as a denigration of customary plural marriage. Given the ancient Hebrew understanding of marriage and family life, it might make more sense to say that any real tendency toward monogamy among these people in the course of their history was probably due to nothing more than practical socio-economic considerations. This is the view presented by Hermann Ringeling, in the article previously cited: economic and cultural factors, rather than religious and ethical considerations, were responsible for any inclination toward monogamy in biblical times.[28]

Why should we feel the need to find here some meaning that is deeper and less secular? There is nothing very special in the fact that the image of monogamy occurs frequently in the Bible. From an anthropological point of view this is just what might be expected. Monogamy is, after all, the most commonly experienced form of marriage under the old dispensation as well as under the new; and it is the only available form of marriage for most men, even in societies that esteem polygamy as an ideal.

Those who may still feel that the Old Testament contains a religiously or ethically significant inclination toward monogamy, and some implied teaching against polygamy, may pursue the matter further by reading not only the article by Ringeling, but also the careful analysis of this very question by Werner Plautz.[29] In a far more detailed study than what we have just presented, Plautz reaches this conclusion:

> The Old Testament reports of marriage with one, two, or several women. There is no fundamental questioning of polygamy, at most

only a qualification. Concerning the spread of the various forms of marriage it may be established that polygamy in the grand style was possible only for very few Israelites, and therefore did not frequently occur; that monogamy and bigamy were normal. A general tendency toward monogamy is not traceable in the Old Testament and is also not very probable on the basis of ethnology.[30]

MARRIAGE IN THE BEGINNING

It is widely believed that the Genesis accounts of mankind's origin (cf. Gen. 1:26–28; 2:7–25) contain an evident teaching on marriage: that in the beginning it was, and therefore should be, monogamous. The fact that Jesus, during a discussion about marriage laws, actually quoted some of these verses, is taken as a sign of the divine will that marriage should be monogamous (cf. Matt. 19:3–9; Mark 10:2–12). This viewpoint is expressed typically by Piet Schoonenberg:

> The writer of the story of Eden places the institution of marriage at the beginning of mankind and he depicts it as monogamous. . . . Christ refers to that text and He makes it even more explicit, for instead of "they" He says "the two" and connects it with the words of Genesis 1:27, concerning the creation of the two sexes: "Have you not read that the Creator, from the beginning, made them male and female and said: 'For this cause a man shall leave his father and mother, and cleave to his wife, and the two shall become one flesh'? Therefore now they are no longer two, but one flesh."[31]

Before examining this alleged teaching of Jesus, we must first try to find out just what Genesis really does, and does not, say about the structure of marriage in the beginning. The usual facile interpretation—that monogamy is here presented as the original and divinely willed form of marriage—might give the impression that exegetes have encountered no difficulties at all with the meaning of these passages. It is almost a unanimous opinion that "monogamy is implicit in the story of Adam and Eve, since God created only one wife for Adam."[32] Indeed, this traditional exegesis of God's intention is probably the only example of an interpretation that has remained constant, in spite of all the advances in biblical scholarship, since the earliest of the Church Fathers wrote their first commentaries on Scripture.

The method of interpretation, which yields a clear revelation regarding monogamy, has been altogether too literalistic and focused too exclusively upon selected words. Instead of allowing these words to speak only as parts of a whole story, they have been lifted out of their proper contexts and analyzed with reference to an exclusively monogamous ideal of marriage which is, as we have seen, foreign to the socio-cultural ethos of the Old Testament. Thus the use of the singular, when referring to the female ("a helper," "a woman," "his wife"), is cited as evidence of the monogamous nature of marriage in the beginning and as evidence that the Bible is here teaching us that marriage should be monogamous (cf. Gen. 1:27; 2:18, 20, 22–25).

What happens if the same literalistic method is used for interpreting the significance of the other singulars and plurals in the same passages? Then, for example, we would find a clear revelation that the first human being was an androgyne: "God created man in his own image, in the image of God he created him, male and female he created them" (Gen. 1:27; cf. Gen. 5:2). In reference to this text of Genesis, it is possible that Jesus, while discussing marriage according to the contemporary understanding of those who questioned him (cf. Mark. 10:6), alluded to a rabbinic argument against divorce: an argument based on the belief that the nature of the first man was originally androgynous.[33] According to also to the Yahwist tradition, this creature was alone for quite some time, while the whole vegetable and animal kingdoms were coming into existence, before there emerged from him (or from them) a separate "she-man"; so, in the very beginning, it would seem literally that the two partners were one being (cf. Gen. 2:7–23). Many early commentators saw this androgynous creature in Genesis just as clearly as they saw monogamy there.[34] Moreover, if a return to monogamy is proposed in these verses of Genesis, then the same way of reading the texts should suggest also a return to nakedness, since this seems to have been mankind's pristine style, just as monogamy seems to have been the original form of marriage. Such conclusions become possible only when we forget the narrative character of the literature under discussion.

If we accept it as divinely revealed truth that our species started from only one pair of human beings, then certainly the original marriage must have been monogamous. This interpretation, however, leaves no room for the theory of polygenesis, which is based on the modern sciences of biology and paleontology, and accepted by an ever-increasing number of biblical scholars and theologians. According to this evolutionary understanding of human origins, primitive man must have had animal parents, and mankind emerged gradually from a population: not from a single pair. "The unit of evolution," says Ernst Mayr, "was not the individual but the population ."[35] Scientifically, this makes sense, and it cannot be ignored by theologians when they speculate about human existence in the beginning.

Karl Rahner had initially produced a tedious defense of monogenism.[36] However, he has since changed his mind, because "the great majority of scientists today accept the evolutionary process of homonization and, with it, the theory of polygenesis."[37] The theory, as Rahner explains it, is this:

> It is a general principle of biology that true, *concrete*, genetic unity is not found in the individual but in the population within which alone many individuals can exist in the same biotope (organisms of the same genetic constitution). Only within such a situation can evolution come about, since selection can only exercise its pressure within such a population and not in isolated individuals. . . . This biological-historical unity can also describe the state of mankind at its origin . . . without limiting it to a single couple. Therefore, *mankind remains a biological-historical unity, even in terms of polygenism, because*. . . . [38]

Rahner then goes on to list five reasons (each with a few subreasons) why such a unity of mankind should be regarded as a real unity: a unity "based on real factors and not on a process of abstraction."

If primitive mankind came into existence, as a gradually developing group, and not simply as two original individuals who had to find each other among all of their contemporary "prehumans," then the original human group would very probably have been polygamous both during the transitional period from "prehuman" to human, and during the earliest ages of the human species. "Polygyny is more or less developed in nearly all anthropoid apes," observes Ernst Mayr; and "there are good reasons for postulating that it was characteristic of the primitive hominids."[39] So the theory of polygenesis not only allows for the possiblity, but even suggests the likelihood, of plural marriage in the beginning. Primitive polygamy would have greatly influenced the evolutionary rate of the species, as Mayr points out:

> What effect on evolutionary rate would polygyny have? If the leader of a group has several wives (perhaps even all the mature females of the family group), he will contribute a far greater than average share to the genetic composition of the next generation of his group. Such tremendous reproductive advantage of a leader in a self-contained family group or tribe would favor the very characteristics that have made man what he is.[40]

Theologians who favor the theory of polygenesis—that a group, and not just two individuals, was the basic genetic unit in the beginning—are not consistent when, on the basis of a literalistic interpretation of selected verses, they assure us that monogamy was the form of marriage intended by God from the beginning. If Genesis gives no scientific account of human origins, neither does it provide a sociological description of human behavior in the beginning.

The monogamy hypothesis, if it is to hold together, requires also that the common Hebrew expression "one flesh" (Gen. 2:24) should be understood in a quite restricted manner so that it will dovetail with a distinctly non-Hebrew conception of marriage as an exclusive partnership between two persons only. In the context of the creation narrative, however, this expression certainly can have the much broader and more likely meaning of kinship union or family-making community. "Flesh," says John L. McKenzie, "designates kindred [in a very concrete sense; all the members of a single kinship] group have one flesh, which is conceived as a collective reality possessed by all."[41] One may refer to a kinsman, therefore, as one's own "flesh." In the words of Edward Schillebeeckx:

The idea of "one flesh" provides an answer to the question: How can the division of the old clans and the foundation of new clans be justified? "A man leaves his father and his mother" (Gen. 2:24) in order to found a new clan, a "new house," or a new "one flesh."[42]

This wider meaning is found frequently in the Old Testament (cf. Gen. 29:14; 37:27; Lev. 18:6; Judg. 9:2; 2 Sam. 5:1; 19:12–13; Neh. 5:5; Isa. 58:7). In this broader social sense, a wife may be regarded as becoming "one flesh" with her husband. Through marriage she becomes a member of his kinship group. Hence, it is possible for several wives to be at the same time "one flesh" with the kinship group of the same husband. The observations of Gordon R. Dunstan are very much to the point:

> The Bible applies the phrase "one flesh" to marriage in this sense: a man leaves the kinship group of his father and mother (with whom he was of "one flesh") and enters into a covenant with ("cleaves to") his wife, so creating another such group, within which the same mutual obligations will obtain. This covenant-making is a ready-made model for teaching in symbol the covenant-marriage of Yahweh with Israel, and of Christ with the Church.[43]

It seems therefore, unlikely that the Yahwist author of Genesis 2:24, by his use of the expression "one flesh," would have intended to exclude or to derogate the customary polygamy permitted by the Mosaic law, thus, departing substantially from the traditional Judaic conception of marriage. If such a radical change is implied here, then, according to the same literalistic reading of the same verse, we should also see here a proposed departure from the traditional patriarchal style of family organization in which consanguineous groups follow the practice of viri-local or patri-local residence:[44] "Therefore a man leaves his father and his mother and cleaves to his wife."

But, of course, Western scholars have never read the Bible with the expectation of finding there any antipatriarchal tendencies. How, then, can we be so sure that the expression "one flesh" implies a departure from the customary plural marriage of the ancient Jewish people? It was not this traditional form of marriage, but consecutive polygamy (serial monogamy) and the taking of foreign wives, that was regarded as an abuse, especially after the exile.[45]

In the biblical account of human origins, therefore, if "flesh" and "bone" (cf. Gen. 2:23–24) signify community of species, then, surely, it can be said that "one flesh" signifies community of kinship based on marriage. Each husband-wife relationship, whether in a monogamous or a polygamous marriage, is for the Jews of the Old Testament a foundation for new kinship bonds which bind and extend families and clans into a unified people. This would suggest that the expression "one flesh," insofar as it relates to the structure of marriage, refers to the contemporary problem of indissolubility—not the problem of customary polygamy.[46] Even this may, however, be suggesting too much: that there is a clear reference to indissolubility.

In this retrospective theological reflection on the meaning of the mutual attraction between the sexes, the biblical narrative simply takes for granted the traditional Jewish conception and structure of marriage. "One must emphasize," with Gerhard von Rad, "that our narrative is concerned not with legal custom but with a natural drive."[47] The story is entirely etiological: "It was told to answer a quite definite question."[48] Neither the question nor the answer is concerned directly with the cultural conception and social structure of marriage. According to von Rad, the whole point is this:

> A fact needs explanation, namely, the extremely powerful drive of the sexes to each other. Whence comes this love "strong as death" (Song of Sol. 8:6) and stronger than the tie to one's own parents, whence this inner clinging to each other, this drive towards each other which does not rest until it again becomes one flesh in the child?
>
> It comes from the fact that God took woman from man, that they actually were originally *one* flesh. Therefore they must come together again and thus by destiny they belong to each other. The recognition of this narrative as etiological is theologically important. Its point of departure, the thing to be explained, is for the narrator something in existence, present, not something "paradisical" and thus lost.[49]

The garden situation should also be understood within this same etiological perspective. Then it will be seen that there is here no picture of a romantic Elysium of human perfection and delight. "Our word 'Paradise' as a proper name (which the Old Testa-

ment text does not know) for a state *sui generis* contains a myth-
ical objectification and goes beyond the strict reticence of the
Biblical narrative."[50] The Yahwistic narrator is not trying to tell us
how things were, and therefore ought to be, in an ideal human
condition. There is no teaching here about the ethically perfect
marital behavior of an orginal human couple.

"Under no circumstances," according to Hermann Ringeling,
"is it permissible to interpret the creation accounts as proofs of a
direct monogamous tendency" in the Old Testament.[51] At least
this much may, perhaps, be concluded from the foregoing reflections on what Genesis says, and does not say, about marriage in
the beginning.

THE TEACHING OF JESUS

It is commonly believed that the teaching of Jesus on the permanence (indissolubility) of marriage (cf. Matt. 5:31–32; 19:3–9;
Mark 10:2–12; Luke 16:18) amounts, at least implicitly, to a repudiation of simultaneous polygyny. A quite representative
statement of this position is provided by Pierre Grelot:

> To cast light on the question of marriage, Jesus refers his hearers to
> the original prototype presented in the Creation narrative (Gen. 1:27
> and 2:24): in the kingdom of God, which he is inaugurating, the
> institution of marriage regains the perfection which the consequen-
> ces of sin in human history caused it to lose (Matt. 19:1–9).
>
> The latitude permitted by the ancient Law in this respect was "to
> suit their hard hearts" (19:8); but once the kingdom has been
> founded, once the economy of grace has been introduced into
> history, the human couple must return to its primitive rules of
> conduct, which alone conform to the fundamental intention of the
> Creator.
>
> No reference is made to the problem of polygamy; the authority of
> Genesis is taken as being sufficient to dismiss the possibility: the
> two are to become one flesh. From this point of view, the evolution
> of Jewish customs has already attained a standard which Christ
> consecrates for all time. There remains the problem of divorce.[52]

Since the Lord himself makes no explicit reference to "the problem of polygamy," this whole argument hinges decisively upon
the following assumptions: that Genesis evidently depicts
monogamy as divinely willed from the beginning and that simul-

taneous polygyny (customary Jewish polygamy) is intrinsically
bound up with divorce and remarriage—hence, also, with
adultery.[53] Such assumptions, as we have already seen in this
chapter, are highly dubious. Here, therefore, it should suffice to
emphasize that the Lord's reply to the Pharisees (cf. Matt. 19:3–9)
is limited to the scope of their questions. We need not expect to
find here the answer to a question that was not asked.

First, however, it should be noted that, even though Jesus
addressed himself directly and explicitly to the question of divorce and remarriage, the meaning and intent of his words have
not been easy to grasp; they are still being debated among Christians. "This passage about divorce," according to one respected
New Testament exegete, "is so difficult, and there have been so
many diverse interpretations given by individual scholars and
different sections of the Christian Church, that a commentator
may well feel reluctant to express any opinion at all about it, lest
he should be guilty of adding to the exegetical and ecclesiastical
confusion."[54]

A similar view is expressed in a recent survey of the various
interpretations of the Lord's teaching on marriage: "There can be
little doubt," writes Anthony Kosnik, "that the precise meaning
and interpretation of these passages remains one of the most
vexing and controversial problems of modern biblical
exegesis."[55] To explain the meaning of just one clause, the famous "exceptive clause" of Matthew 19:9, there are some half-
dozen respectable theories; and, according to Rudolf Schnackenburg, each of these theories is hedged with perplexing and unresolved difficulties.[56] Kosnik's survey is instructive, and so is his
conclusion:

> Modern biblical scholarship has given considerable attention to the
> scriptual texts underlying the claims to the absolute indissolubility
> of marriage. A few call into question the authenticity of several key
> passages. Others challenge the usual interpretation and particularly
> the conclusions regarding the permanence of Christian marriage
> that are drawn on the basis of these texts. Even where it is admitted
> that the words do support an interpretation favoring indissolubility,
> there are serious scholars who would see Christ's injunction not as
> imposing a categorical imperative or casuistic absolute but rather as
> exhorting to an ideal. There are even those who find in the texts of

Matthew and Paul regarding marriage an adaptation of the ideal of indissolubility to meet the particular problem arising in the early Christian community. . . .

In the light of this controversy engaged in by serious and competent men, it is difficult to find in the scriptural evidence a sufficiently solid basis for imposing the absolute indissolubility, as formulated in present Church law, upon every consummated marriage that takes place between Christians. In a word, there is good reason for believing that the canonical indissolubility as formulated in Church law is not necessarily identical with the evangelical indissolubility proclaimed in the Scriptures.[57]

It is remarkable, therefore, that some of the scholars, for whom the meaning of indissolubility is an open question, are, nevertheless, able to affirm without any hesitation that the question of simultaneous polygamy is settled by the words of Matthew 19:3–9 and its parallels. Indeed, it could be only by some exegitical sleight of hand that a question, which is neither mentioned explicitly in this passage nor even implied in the historical context, is somehow answered definitively, while the question of divorce and remarriage, which is dealt with explicitly here, remains open for further discussion.

To clarify the polygamy question, some further probing into the Lord's teaching on marriage is surely called for now. In the following exegetical reflections, however, there is no pretense of being either comprehensive or definitive. This is simply an effort to further disclose the problematical character of the absolute prohibition of polygamy, which may have been too easily attributed to the Bible.

The questions put to Jesus by the Pharisees were precisely formulated for the purpose of leading him into a trap: "Is it lawful to divorce one's wife for any cause?"; and "Why then did Moses command one to give a certificate of divorce, and to put her away?" (Matt. 19:3, 7). These questions were asked against the background of a well-known controversy that was raging at the time between the rival rabbinical schools of Hillel and Shammai. They were divided over the exegesis of Deuteronomy 24:1–4 (cf. Jer. 3:8; Matt. 19:9).

According to the law, "some indecent thing" may be a reason for a man's divorcing his wife.[58] Those who followed the liberal tradition of Hillel—and this was the more popular school at the time—interpreted this particular rule as allowing divorce for quite trivial reasons. The school of Shammai, on the other hand, taught that the only "indecent thing" that might justify divorce was unchastity or adultery. According to Bruce Vawter, "the legitimacy of divorce itself, sanctioned by the law of Moses, was not a point at issue."[59] Was simultaneous polygamy a point at issue?

In a "new interpretation" of the exceptive clause of Matthew 19:9, Leonard Ramaroson suggests that simultaneous polygamy was indeed a point at issue.[60] Ramaroson sees here, not only a clear affirmation of marital indissolubility, but—precisely on the basis of the much-disputed meaning of "some indecent thing" (*porneia*)—he proposes the hypothesis that the text speaks against both successive and simultaneous polygamy. Since both divorce and remarriage are obviously under discussion in this passage of Matthew, there is really nothing new in the suggestion that there is here a teaching against successive polygamy, as this particular form of plural marriage necessarily involves divorce and remarriage. Such an interpretation finds support also in various other passages of the New Testament. What is really new, and finds little or no support elsewhere in the New Testament, is the proposal that the exceptive clause somehow amounts to a teaching against the Jewish custom of simultaneous polygamy, even when this form of marriage is dictated by the levirate law (cf. Deut. 25:5).

Ramaroson's basic argument, presented by him in a brief form and in a tentative manner, is that the Septuagint translation of the Old Testament (c. 250 B.C.) uses the Greek word *porneia* to render the meaning of the Hebrew *zenuth* and *zonah*, while these same Hebrew terms are used in the Essenes' Damascus Document (probably a century before Christ) and in the Talmud (quoting a second-century source) with specific reference to plural marriage. The connection between these documents and the teaching of Jesus is made by observing that these documents cite Genesis 1:27 as evidence that marriage should be monogamous; and, of course, Matthew 19:5 refers explicitly to this same text of Genesis. Thus, the argument for this "new interpretation" rests upon the analysis of two Hebrew terms which are "sometimes" used, in two extrabiblical Jewish documents, to identify polygamy with "some indecent thing" (*porneia*).

In Ramaroson's presentation there is, moreover, a tacit assumption that successive and simultaneous polygamy may be regarded as morally the same thing. Indeed, both of these forms of marriage involve the taking of another wife while the first wife is still living. But there is a very real moral, sociological, and psychological difference arising from the fact that successive polygamy necessarily involves divorce and remarriage, while simultaneous polygamy does not. The difference between these two forms of marriage is greater than the difference between dissolubility and indissolubility.

Even if the hypothesis were accepted, that the word *porneia* in the exceptive clause refers to simultaneous polygamy, it would not follow that there is necessarily a teaching against this form of polygamy: it would not follow that a polygamous husband must or should send away all but one of his wives. Rather, if *porneia* really has the meaning suggested by Ramaroson, the lawfulness of simultaneous polygamy would seem to be presupposed in the text. The whole point of the exceptive clause would then be that a real distinction is explicitly recognized between the two kinds of polygamy, with the clear implication that simultaneous polygamy as such is no part of the discussion concerning adultery as a consequence of divorce.

Whatever one may think about the meaning of the exceptive clause, it is by no means evident that simultaneous polygamy came under discussion at all, as it was not part of the controversy into which the Pharisees were attempting to draw Jesus. Aside from some of the Jewish sects, there is in the mainstream of traditional rabbinical literature a fairly consistent recognition of polygamy as a valid form of marriage sanctioned by the Law of Moses.[61] The particular divorce regulation, proposed for discussion by the Pharisees, could apply to all Hebrew marriages, whether monogamous or polygamous.

Elsewhere in Deuteronomy, the singular, "wife," is used in laws that could apply to cases either of monogamy or polygamy (cf. Deut. 22:13, 22); and "wives" appears only in regulations which could not apply to monogamy (cf. Deut. 21:15–17), while other rules of behavior simply take polygamy for granted (cf. Exod. 21:10; Lev. 18:18).

So the questions put to Jesus prescind from whether or not the husband is a monogamist or a polygamist. No matter how many wives a husband may have, the action of divorce is normally directed against only one "wife" at a time. The fact that Jesus spoke of the "wife" in the singluar is, therefore, just what might be expected in a discussion about divorce according to the law of Moses. It is surely too much to construe this use of the singular as an argument, a teaching, or a statement against simultaneous polygamy.

The questioners were hostile. "The Pharisees," says Schillebeeckx, "wanted to force Christ to choose between these two schools (Hillel and Shammai) so that on the basis of his answer they could accuse him either of laxity or of shortsighted and narrow rigorism and, thus, inflame the people against him."[62] Hence, the Lord's response is circumspect, and his conclusions are carefully introduced: "So then" (Matt. 19:6) and "Now I say to you" (v. 9). Even the famous exceptive clause which has occasioned so much disagreement among scholars, whatever its real significance may be, was perhaps added here in verse 9 for the sake of greater precision: it does, anyway, indicate the limited scope of the discussion; and it reminds us that exegetes are still wondering not only what Jesus meant here, but also what he really said. The other addition in Matthew, "for any cause" (v. 3) is a further indication that the whole context is dominated by the contemporary controversy, between the rival schools of Hillel and Shammai, over the correct interpretation of Deuteronomy's divorce rule.[63]

Jesus knew all about the casuistry and the debating methods of the rabbinical schools; so he was not about to fall into any trap. In replying to the first question, he affirmed, as a basic principle, the indissolubility of marriage. Thus, it is clear from his teaching that men may not divide what God has joined (cf. Matt. 19:6). The preceding reference to the unity of "two" in "one flesh" is a kind of premise from which the principle of marital permanence flows.

As previously explained, "one flesh" has the obvious and quite unavoidable connotation of family unity and kinship solidarity.[64] For consanguinity, real and fictive, is based on marriage which is normally expected to be permanent (whether it is a monogamous or a polygamous marriage) for the social stability and security of the family and also the clan, the tribe, and the people. For example, Jacob belonged to the "flesh" of his mother's brother (cf. Gen. 29:14). If Jacob could be called "my flesh" by Laban, then Esau could also be regarded as "one flesh" with both Laban and Jacob, and with any number of other relatives for that matter, including even the two wives of Jacob; for they were all members of the same kinship group.[65] There is signified here a unity in "one flesh."

If "one flesh" in Genesis says nothing against polygamy, then the Lord's reference to this expression in Genesis, during the course of a debate with some Pharisees, need not be taken as a condemnation of polygamy. Must we believe that Jesus, while rejecting the legalism of the Pharisaical approach to human behavior, was here promulgating an entirely new rule for the legal validity of marriage? Instead of interpreting the words of Jesus as a part of a new Christian legal code, it might be more in keeping with the whole spirit of the New Testament to see in the Lord's response to the Pharisees what George Vass describes as "a reassertion of the holiness of marriage as an indissoluble union which was implied in God's creative will."[66] So the Mosaic law is not here contradicted by Jesus whose purpose, after all, was, not to multiply new laws in place of old ones, but to encourage new attitudes.

According to Vass and a number of contemporary scholars cited by him, "the point of the discussion between Jesus and the Pharisees is the exact meaning of Deut. 24:1–4."[67] Since these verses are concerned only with divorce and remarriage—neither of which is implied in simultaneous polygamy—there is no question here of a new teaching or a new regulation regarding polygamy. What is reprehensible in the sight of Jesus is the attitude or the intention of a husband who would *dismiss his wife and marry another.* Adultery is a consequence of this attitude or intention, for divorce and remarriage are contrary to the permanence or indissolubility implied in the Jewish notion of "one flesh." But polygamy is quite compatible with the Jewish understanding of "one flesh," permanence or indissolubility.

To avoid the sharp edge of the second question asked by the Pharisees, Jesus turned the discussion upon a possible reason for the permissive attitude of Moses toward divorce: because of the hardness of men's hearts (cf. Matt 19:8). This retort, while pointing to a renewed attitude toward the permanence of marriage, involves no patent contradiction of the Mosaic law. The exceptive clause found in Matthew's Gospel (19:9) might suggest that the Pharisees, followers of Shammai, must have been further confounded to hear their own viewpoint reflected by Jesus. The very next verse indicates that even the disciples were perplexed by the words of their Master: "The disciples said to him, 'If such is the case of a man with his wife, it is not expedient to marry.'" (19:10).

If Jesus placed polygamy in the same category with divorce —something previously tolerated because of the hardness of men's hearts—this is not self-evident from the words of the passage under consideration. The Lord's reply to the second question, as to the first, is an affirmation of indissolubility and a repudiation of divorce—not a condemnation of polygamy, which is quite compatible with marital indissolubility. The Lord's conclusions were concerned with divorce and indissolubility:

> What therefore God has joined together, let no man put asunder. . . . For your hardness of hearts, Moses allowed you to divorce your wives, but from the beginning it was not so. And I say to you: whoever divorces his wife, except for unchastity, and marries another, commits adultery (Matt. 19:6, 8–9).

If the teaching of Jesus is limited to his affirmations of the indissolubility of marriage, if polygamous marriage can be quite as indissoluble as monogamous marriage, and if adultery follows from an attitude or intention to divorce a spouse and marry another, is it really possible to hold that the words of Jesus somehow say that simultaneous polygamy is a form of adultery—and to hold this view in spite of all that has been said in this chapter?

Dominic Crossan rightly recognizes that Matthew 5:31–32 says nothing at all in favor of monogamy or against polygamy.[68] What is repudiated by the Lord is divorce and remarriage; for adultery occurs when a husband divorces his wife and then marries another, when a divorced woman is married by another man, or when either married partner is simply unfaithful in attitude or intention or fact. Simultaneous polygamy, as understood by Jesus and his Jewish contemporaries, did not by itself imply divorce, remarriage, or unfaithfulness.

However, when Crossan relates Luke 16:18 and Matthew 19:3–9, it becomes "clear" to him "that monogamy is being presumed at the same time that divorce and remarriage for either party is being prohibited."[69] Is it so clear? Not if we recall the ideas already presented on what is signified, or what is not signified, by the biblical use of the singular "wife." Not if we consider the very tenuous inference which suggests that polygamy is also prohibited. The isolated logion of Luke mentions adultery only when this is a consequence of divorce, but polygamy does not necessarily involve divorce. Moreover, if Jesus wished to avoid the trap set for him by the Pharisees, it is hardly likely that he would have gone out of his way to contradict the Mosaic permissiveness toward polygamy and, thus, allow himself to be ensnared by an issue which was not even raised by his learned adversaries.

The Lord certainly must have known that polygamy still existed among his Jewish contemporaries.[70] If his teaching on marriage was intentionally incompatible with this immemorial custom, we might expect to find some clear statement of his against the permissiveness of the Mosaic law. We might expect to find at least a clear hint of disapproval in the one passage where Jesus actually discussed the practice of levirate marriage (cf. Matt. 22:23–30, and parallels). This practice frequently, perhaps even more often than not, involved polygamy. For marriage was so highly esteemed among the Jews that men, as well as women, normally married at an early age (usually just after puberty), and bachelors must have been very rare indeed.[71] So it may be assumed that levirate marriages must very frequently have been polygamous.

"This duty [levirate] was enjoined by the law," says Bernard Häring, "even in cases where the brother-in-law of the widow

was already married."[72] The sin of Onan, for which he was
punished with death by God, was not masturbation; it was his
refusal to perform the levirate duty of taking his brother's widow
and raising up offspring for his deceased brother (cf. Gen.
38:8–10).[73] Even in Deuteronomy the formulation of this law
—considering, also, the fact that celibacy was rare and men
married young—suggests a polygamous situation:

> If brothers dwell together, and one of them dies and has no son, the
> wife of the dead shall not be married outside the family to a stranger;
> her husband's brother shall go to her, and take her as his wife, and
> perform the duty of a husband's brother to her (Deut. 25:5).

Jesus discussed the levirate law only because it was basic to the
hypothetical case proposed to him by the Sadducees, who were
actually testing his views on another matter—the resurrection (cf.
Matt. 23–30). But it may be of some significance that the Gospel
story of this encounter contains no reservations at all about the
polygamous implications of the levirate law. There is not even a
hint, here or elsewhere in the teaching of Jesus, that there may be
something wrong with this kind of legally prescribed and socially
accepted marriage, which certainly existed among the Jews at
that time.[74]

THE TEACHING OF ST. PAUL

Several Pauline passages are usually cited as corroborating evidence by those who hold that polygamy was merely tolerated by
Moses and finally repudiated by Christ. In various places Paul (or
"the author," as may be the case with some of the Epistles)
speaks of the husband-wife relationship in the singular; he uses
the Old Testament expression "one flesh" with reference to conjugal unity; and he depicts the love of Christ for the Church in
monogamous terms. These alleged indications of monogamy are
combined in the Epistle to the Ephesians and presented there
very concisely in the last three verses of the fifth chapter. As most
of this ground has just been covered, these three points may now
be considered briefly.

The use of the singular in discussing the husband-wife relationship should come as no surprise in the writings of Saint Paul.

As we have aleady seen, this is a normal biblical way of talking about marriage which, in the socio-cultural context of the Jewish people, could be either monogamous or polygamous. Additionally, Paul's understanding of marriage was developed in a context of pastoral concern for Christians in a Greco-Roman world where monogamy was the socially determined form of marriage, while polygamy was legally proscribed.

Moreover, Paul's understanding of marriage was usually articulated by him in the form of practical directives for concrete problems presented to him. Although polygamy still existed in Jewish communities and the Roman authorities were generally tolerant of this custom among the Jews, the incidence was surely much less than in former times; and, indeed, polygamy would have been especially rare among the Hellenized Jews with whom Paul was more in contact. Hence, it would seem appropriate that Paul should speak of marriage in monogamous terms. But this does not necessarily amount to a teaching against polygamy.

Paul probably did not think much, if anything, about this particular pastoral problem—unless perhaps he had polygamists in mind, among others, when he gave this ruling about newcomers into the Christian community:

> To the rest I say, not the Lord, that if any brother has a wife who is an unbeliever, and she consents to live with him, he should not divorce her. . . . Only, let every one lead the life which the Lord has assigned to him, and in which God has called him. . . . Was any one at the time of his call already circumcised? Let him not seek to remove the marks of circumcision. . . . For neither circumcision counts for anything nor uncircumcision, but keeping the commandments of God. Every one should remain in the state in which he was called (1 Cor. 7:12, 17–20).

This rule applied to "every one" in "whatever state each was called" (cf. 1 Cor. 7:20, 24); so the rule concerned not only freedom and slavery as states in life, but also the marriage status of new Christians, whether single or married according to gentile or Jewish law. Those who were married or unmarried, circumcised or uncircumcised (under the Mosaic law or not), did not have to change their status in order to live as Christians. And, if slaves were even to "remain" as they were, then presumably slave-owners could also continue as they were before being called to the new life in Christ. Indeed, the owners were not required to free their slaves; they were urged merely to treat them with kindness (cf. Eph. 6:5, 9).

It is certainly possible that there may also have been called to the faith at that time some Jewish families that were polygamous before being called: new Christians "already circumcised" and living by the law of Moses. Would Paul's rule have applied to them and to their marital status? Would a Jewish polygamist have been required, before answering the call to Christian faith, to divorce all but one of the mothers of his own children? The answer to this question would have to be no, if Schillebeeckx was right when he observed that "the Jews who became Christians continued to follow the Jewish laws of marriage, while the Gentiles who were converted to Christianity kept the Greco-Roman laws of marriage."[75]

In this connection, Saint Jerome's comments on the "one wife" passages of the Pastoral Epistles (cf. 1 Tim. 3:2, 12; Titus 1:6) are very enlightening:

> The text quoted by the objector, "a bishop must be the husband of one wife," admits of quite another explanation. The apostle came of the Jews and the primitive Christian church was gathered out of the remnants of Israel. Paul knew that the Law allowed men to have children by several wives, and was aware that the example of the patriarchs had made polygamy familiar to the people. Even the very priests might at their own discretion enjoy the same license. He gave commandment therefore that the priests of the church should not claim this liberty, that they should not take two wives or three together, but that they should each have but one wife at one time.[76]

Saint Chrysostom gives a similar explanation of the "one wife" passages.[77] So, also, does Theodoret of Cyr.[78] Much later the same interpretation found a vigorous echo in the words of Cardinal Cajetan. Commenting on 1 Timothy 3:2, Cajetan says that the "one wife" rule was given because at that time many men, following the example of the Old Testament fathers, had several wives.[79] Even today this is regarded as one of several possible ways of interpreting the "one wife" passages of the Pastoral Epistles.[80] Such an interpretation suggests that polygamy may not have been regarded as absolutely incompatible with the

Christian way of life, although it appears that official functionaries of the Church (bishops and deacons, anyway) were expected to have no more than one wife at the same time.

Perhaps this "one wife" rule came from nothing more than the young Church's need to accommodate itself to the ways of the Greco-Roman world, which saw polygamy as an objectionable foreign custom: something forbidden to Roman citizens, hence inappropriate for Church leaders in the Roman world. Or was it just a matter of ecclesiastical economy? A bishop with only one wife would be less of a financial burden on the Christian community than a bishop with two or three wives.

So the question comes back again: Were Jewish polygamists, who were subsequently called to the new life of Christian faith, permitted to participate in the sacramental life of the Church while remaining in the marital state in which they were at the time of their calling? In spite of the early Church's gradual accommodation to the ways of the Greco-Roman world (much to the discomfort of the Judaizers), there may be some likelihood that the Church leaders, even following the example of the Roman civil authorities, tolerated polygamy among Jewish converts to Christianity, while excluding such persons merely from holding the offices of deacon and bishop.

Now what about Saint Paul's intriguing use of the expression "one flesh?" Far from being a certain revelation concerning monogamy, the Pauline usage would illustrate rather the broadness and flexibility of this Old Testament expression.[81] For Paul this unity in the "flesh" is not confined to the conjugal union of one husband and one wife, nor is it limited to the bonds of kinship. Even a man who joins himself to a prostitute becomes "one flesh" with her: "for, as it is written, 'The two become one' " (1 Cor. 6:16–17). This kind of unity is obviously not exclusive in the way that a monogamous union is supposed to be, for a man can become "one flesh" with any number of prostitutes. According to this use of the expression, it would follow also that a man becomes "one flesh" with more than one wife in a society which accepts this form of marriage. Even where monogamy is the rule, a man becomes "one flesh" with more than one wife, consecutively, when the previous wife dies.

The carnal and kinship unity thus signified by the expression, "one flesh," is not confined exclusively to only two persons. According to this usage we may say, therefore, that the several children of one mother are "one flesh" with her, by reason of their unity in generation and in maternal love. The relationship between the mother and each child, respectively, may even be regarded as a union of "two" in "one flesh," without thereby excluding the other children from this same relationship with their mother. So, by reason of a socially valid polygamous marriage, a man may be conjugally united with each of his wives, respectively, as "two" in "one flesh"—both in a carnal sense and in terms of kinship.

The relationship between Christ and the Church is supposed to be reflected in Christian marriage, which derives its sacramental symbolism from this likeness. The Church is the bride of Christ (cf. 2 Cor. 11:2; Eph. 5:22–33). "Marriage," says von Allmen, "is strictly monogamous, for Jesus has and can have only one bride."[82] Further questions arise contrary to this hypothesis, however, as soon as we note that, while the Church is pictured as the bride of Christ (not the brides), Saint Paul in the very same breath describes the Church as a plurality of persons: a husband must love his wife, "as Christ does the church, because *we are members* of his body" (cf. Eph. 5:28–33; 1 Cor. 5:15; 12:27).

This reference to the Church, as one wife, need not be understood in a rigidly literalistic manner; and, indeed, it should not be so understood. What we have here is the familiar biblical notion of corporate personality: the singular (bride, wife) standing symbolically for the plural (we, the members), the individual representing the collective.[83]

Is it possible that the union between Christ and the Church can be symbolized in a simultaneously polygamous marriage? Christ, standing for the husband, is one; and the Church, as his spouse, is plural. For, in actual historical fact, God's beloved people is a plurality of persons.

The Old Testament, which recognized the authenticity of both monogamy and polygamy (often without making any distinction between the two), provided the groundwork for the New Testament notion and image of sacramental marriage.[84] The sacramental symbolism is originally based on the covenant union of Yahweh's love for his chosen people, who were many different persons, clans, and tribes—yet one bride, one family, one flesh, one body. The covenant union, as described by Jeremiah in terms of a polygamous marriage, may have little meaning for Christians in the Western world; but perhaps these words signify much to the majority of the peoples in Africa south of the Sahara:

> "Behold, the days are coming, says the Lord, when I will make a new covenant with the house of Israel and the house of Judah, not like the covenant which I made with their fathers when I took them by the hand to bring them out of the land of Egypt, my covenant which they broke, though *I was their husband*, says the Lord." (Jer. 31:31–32).

NOTES

1. Karl Barth, *Church Dogmatics*, III-4, ed. G.W. Romiley, trans. G.T. Thompson and H. Knight; (Edinburgh: T. & T. Clark, 1961), p. 199. See also George Crespy, "The Grace of Marriage," in *Marriage and Christian Tradition*, ed. by George Crespy, Paul Evdokimov, Christian Duquoc, trans. Agnes Cunningham (Techny, Ill.: Divine Word Publications, 1968), p. 19: "It has not been pointed out often enough that there is not one word in the Bible against polygamy."

2. John L. McKenzie, *Dictionary of the Bible* (Milwaukee: Bruce, 1965), pp. 505–506.

3. Edward Schillebeeckx, *Marriage: Secular Reality and Saving Mystery*, 2 vols., trans. N.D. Smith (London: Sheed and Ward, 1965), I, p. 284.

4. On the existence of polygamy in those days, see Joachim Jeremias, *Jerusalem in the Time of Jesus*, trans. F.H. and C.H. Cave (London: SCM Press, 1969), pp. 93–94, 370–372; Bruce Vawter, *The Four Gospels* (Garden City, N.Y.: Doubleday, 1967), p. 315; L.W. Barnard, *Justin Martyr: His Life and Thought* (London and New York: Cambridge University Press, 1967), p. 46; Salo Wittmayer Baron, *A Social and Religious History of the Jews*, 2nd ed., rev. (New York and London: Columbia University Press, 1937, 1952, 1962), II, pp. 223–229; and George Hayward Joyce, *Christian Marriage: An Historical and Doctrinal Study* (London and New York: Sheed and Ward, 1933), pp. 570–571.

5. Schillebeeckx, *Marriage: Secular Reality and Saving Mystery*, I, p. 284.

6. Karl Rahner and Herbert Vorgrimler, *Theological Dictionary*, ed.

Cornelius Earnst, trans. Richard Strachan (New York: Herder and Herder, 1965), p. 361. Elsewhere, however, Vorgrimler takes the opposite view: that the New Testament does not expressly forbid polygamy and that it gives no norms to follow in the case of newly converted polygamous peoples. See H. Vorgrimler, "Polygamie," in *Lexicon für Theologie und Kirche*, ed. Michael Buchberger, Josef Höfer, and Karl Rahner, 10 vols. (Freiburg: Herder, 1957–1965), VIII, col. 595.

7. Otto Piper, *The Biblical View of Sex and Marriage* (New York: Scribner's 1960), p. 149.

8. W.T. O'Shea, "Marriage and Divorce: The Biblical Evidence," *The Australasian Catholic Record*, 168 (1970) 90. See also J.S. Wright and J.T. Thompson, "Marriage," in *The New Bible Dictionary*, ed. J.D. Douglas (London: The Inter-Varsity Fellowship, 1962), p. 787: "Monogamy is implied in the story of Adam and Eve, since God created only one wife for Adam. . . . It would seem that God left it to man to discover by experience that this original institution of monogamy was the proper relationship."

9. Cf. A.H. van Vliet and C.G. Breed, *Marriage and Canon Law: A Concise and Complete Account* (London: Burns and Oates, 1964), p. 7: "Jesus Christ, restoring marriage to its pristine purity, made its unity and indissolubility a law obligatory on all, both the baptized and the unbaptized (Matt. 5:31–32; 19:3–9; Mark 10:11–12; Luke 16:18; cf. 1 Cor. 7:10; Rom. 7:2 ff.)."

10. Jean Jacques von Allmen, "Marriage," in *A Companion to the Bible*, ed. J.J. von Allmen, trans. P.J. Allcock and others (New York: Oxford University Press, 1958), p. 257.

11. Joseph Blenkinsopp, *Sexuality and the Christian Tradition* (Dayton: Pflaum Press, 1969), p. 46. Blenkinsopp finds so many misinterpretations of what the Bible says in relation to sexuality that "we might be tempted to conclude that an interpretation of these writings as authoritative and normative has, on balance, done more harm than good" (p. 45).

12. Claus Westermann, *The Genesis Accounts of Creation*, trans. Norman E. Wagner (Philadelphia: Fortress Press, 1964), p. 1: "We have some extremely deeply rooted notions regarding the creation of the world and of man, which . . . do not really come from the text of the Bible, but from the history of interpretation. By formulating our questions in certain ways, we have led ourselves up blind alleys."

13. For more on this point, see Chapter One.

14. Robert H. Springer, "Conscience, Behavioral Science and Absolutes," in *Absolutes in Moral Theology?*, ed. Charles E. Curran (Washington and Cleveland: Corpus Books, 1968), pp. 33–34.

15. See Pierre Grelot, *Man and Wife in Scripture*, trans. Rosaleen Bren-

nan (London: Burns and Oates, 1964), *passim*; Schillebeeckx, *Marriage: Secular Reality and Saving Mystery*, I, pp. 136–140; Piet Schoonenberg, *God's World in the Making*, trans. Walter van de Putte (Pittsburgh: Duquesne University Press, 1964), pp. 107–112; P.E. Herrell, *Divorce and Re-Marriage in the Early Church* (Austin, Texas: R.B. Sweet, Co., 1967), pp. 53–54; G.N. Vollebregt, *The Bible and Marriage*, trans. R.A. Downie (London: Sheed and Ward, 1965), pp. 82–83; and Roland de Vaux, *Ancient Israel: Its Life and Institutions*, trans. John McHugh (New York: McGraw-Hill, 1961), pp. 24–26.

16. Cf. Grelot, *Man and Wife in Scripture*, p. 76.

17. Cf. Schoonenberg, *God's World in the Making*, p. 108.

18. R. de Vaux, *Ancient Israel*, p. 25.

19. For the Old Testament ethos of marriage, see Schillebeeckx, *Mariage: Secular Reality and Saving Mystery*, I, pp. 127–152; R. de Vaux, *Ancient Israel*, pp. 19–23, 26–28; Donald W. Shaner, *A Christian View of Divorce* (Leiden: Brill, 1969), p. 31; Hermann Ringeling, "Die biblische Begründung der Monogamie," *Zeitschrift für Evangelische Ethik* 10 (Jaunuary 1966), p. 83–86; I. Mendelsohn, "The Family in the Ancient Near East," *The Biblical Archeologist* 11 (February 1948) 25; Waldemar Molinski, "Marriage: Institution and Sacrament," in *Sacramentum Mundi: An Encyclopedia of Theology*, ed. Karl Rahner with Cornelius Ernst, Kevin Smyth, and others (New York: Herder and Herder, 1969), III, pp. 381–392: "Marriage primarily figures in the OT tradition as an institution for the preservation of the husband's clan. The idea is not to found a new family but to continue one that already exists. . . . The structure of marriage is altogether determined by the needs of the clan, which quite overshadow the interests of the partners. For the sake of the race, and in view of social and economic conditions, certain forms of polygamy and of concubinage with slaves are allowed."

20. See Schillebeeckx, *Marriage: Secular Reality and Saving Mystery*, I, pp. 132–133; The Old Testament does indeed reflect the existence of faithful and intimate love relationships between married partners, but this was not the dominant characteristic of marriage in that particular historico-cultural setting; and "in the ancient Near East nothing like what we in nineteenth and twentieth century Western society might call an intimate 'communion of souls' existed between man and woman in marriage."

21. *Ibid.*, p. 139: "The idea that the woman was there 'to bear children' was, in this type of society, and certainly in the ideology of the people, of overriding importance."

22. See R. de Vaux, *Ancient Israel*, p. 25.

23. See Carlos Santin, "The Law of the Kings: A Study of Deu-

172   POLYGAMY RECONSIDERED

teronomy XVII: 14–20," (Master's thesis, Baptist Theological Seminary, Ruschlikon-Zurich, April 1969), pp. 46–52: After pointing out the
numerous problems associated with the word *nashim* . . . in verse 17,
when this is taken to mean "women" or "wives," Santin argues that a
more likely translation would be "tributes," or "exactions" of tribute.
Although it has not yet appeared, Santin's thesis has been accepted for
publication in the series *Beihefte zur Zeitschrift für die alttestamentliche
Wissenschaft.*

24. Schillebeeckx, *Marriage: Secular Reality and Saving Mystery*, I, pp.
139–140; and on p. 46, n. 1, Schillebeeckx says explicitly that, while
reactions against polygamy as a sign of wealth and power may be found
in Deuteronomy, in the Priestly tradition, and in the wisdom literature,
this reaction was "not directed against polygamy as such, but against the
taking of foreign wives." According to the Damascus Document (iv), it
seems that all forms of plural marriage were opposed at least by the
Qumran sect; but this is still a moot question, as we see in Yigael Yadin's
"L'attitude essénienne envers la polygamie et le divorce," and the response by Jerome Murphy-O'Connor, *Revue Biblique* 29 (January 1972)
98–100.

25. For this paragraph, see Robert Holst, "Polygamy and the Bible,"
International Review of Mission 56 (April 1967) 209–210; and R. de Vaux,
Ancient Israel, pp. 36–37.

26. See H. Wheeler Robinson, *Corporate Personality in Ancient Israel*
(Philadelphia: Fortress Press, 1964), *passim;* Jean de Fraine, *Adam and the
Family of Man*, trans. Daniel Raible (Staten Island, N.Y.: Alba House,
165), pp. 24, 272.

27. See De Fraine, *Adam*, p. 273: "Even if we experience a certain
difficulty in accepting as our own this Semitic or Oriental mode of
thought, rather than reject it, we should adapt ourselves to this scriptural category in which the divine Word has been clothed."

28. See Ringeling, *Begründung der Monogamie*, p. 87, n. 1; and also, for
a defense of the traditional interpretation, see Pierre Grelot, "The Institution of Marriage: Its Evolution in the Old Testament," trans. Lancelot Sheppard, in *The Future of Marriage as Institution*, ed. Franz Böckle,
Concilium 55 (New York: Herder and Herder, 1970), pp. 44–45. However, Grelot does qualify the traditional interpretation by admitting here
that "the 'Yahwist' account of creation (Gen. 2, and probably tenth
century) makes no claim to provide a definite theory of primitive
monogamy of the human race on a par with archaic societies."

29. Werner Plautz, "Monogamie und Polygynie im Alten Testament,"
Zeitschrift für die Alttestamentliche Wissenschaft, 75, new vol. 34 (1963)
1–27.

30. *Ibid.*, pp. 26–27.

31. Schoonenberg, *God's World*, p. 111.

32. J.S. Wright and J.T. Thompson, "Marriage," p. 787.

33. Cf. Krister Stendahl, *The Bible and the Role of Women*, trans. Emilie T. Sander (Philadelphia: Fortress Press, 1966), pp. 26–27; and David Daube, *The New Testament and Rabbinic Judaism*, (London: Athlone Press, 1956), pp. 71–73.

34. Cf. Von Allmen, "Marriage," p. 250; and E. Schillebeeckx, *Marriage: Secular Reality and Saving Mystery*, I, pp. 267–270, where it is shown that St. Paul also reflects this androcentric conception which considerably influenced his understanding of marriage and provided a theological rationale for the subordination of women in the socio-cultural ethos of that time (cf. 1 Cor. 11:3, 7–9, Eph. 5:23; Rom. 7:2).

35. Ernst Mayr, *Animal Species and Evolution* (Cambridge: Harvard University Press, 1966), p. 651.

36. Karl Rahner, *God, Christ, Mary and Grace*, Theological Investigations, vol. 1, trans. Cornelius Ernst (London: Darton, Longman and Todd, 1966), pp. 229–296.

37. Karl Rahner, "Evolution and Original Sin," trans. Theodore L. Westow in *The Evolving World and Theology*, ed. Johannes Metz, Concilium 26 (New York: Paulist Press, 1967) p. 31.

38. *Ibid.*, p. 32.

39. Mayr, *Animal Species*, p. 651. Mayr adds this note: "It [polygyny] may still be an original condition in a few living primitive tribes. Most cases of polygyny among contemporary people were, however, secondarily derived from a preceding monogamy."

40. *Ibid.*, and Mayr continues (pp. 651–652): "However, the condition described for primitive hominids is completely different from the situation in . . . other organisms in which the favored male does not contribute in any manner to the survival of his offspring. Reproductive advantage in the primitive hominid society, we may speculate, was not a matter of any bizarre secondary sex characters, but one of special position within the group which depended on definite qualities, physical as well as mental. These in turn depended to a considerable extent on the genetic endowment of the individual. In this case, then, reproductive advantage results in a maximal contribution to the fitness of the entire group."

41. McKenzie, *Dictionary of the Bible*, p. 280. See also Henricus Renckens, *Israel's Conception of the Beginnings*, trans. by Charles Napier (New York: Herder and Herder, 1964), p. 228; and Gordon R. Dunston, "Hard Sayings—V," *Theology* 66 (December 1963) 491–492: "The phrase 'one flesh' in the Bible must be interpreted in the light of current Semitic

usage (see T. W. Manson, *Ethics and the Gospel*, p. 16). . . . It meant to the Jew very much what being 'one body' with Christ means to the Christian, namely membership in a kinship group bound together by the strongest sense of mutual obligation. It is this similarity—'one flesh' and 'one body'—which enabled St. Paul to pass so easily from one to the other in Eph. 5:30–32; and which enabled his early copyist to gloss the words 'we are members of Christ's body' in verse 30 with 'of his flesh and his bones' (as in A.V.)."

42. Schillebeeckx, *Marriage: Secular Reality and Saving Mystery*, I, p. 45. Because the Samaritan Pentateuch and the Septuagint "translated the Hebrew 'and they became one flesh' interpretatively as 'and these two became one flesh' (Gen. 2:24)," Schillebeeckx (p. 49) sees here "a deliberately pointed reference to monogamous marriage." But, then, he immediately qualifies this in a footnote indicating that what we have here is a reaction, not against customary Jewish polygamy as such, but against the taking of foreign wives. However, it should be noted also, as Roger Le Deaut pointed out to me, that the Septuagint, the Vulgate, the Syriac Peshitta, and the Aramaic Targum, suppose "the two" to be in the original Hebrew: see *Biblia Hebraica*, ed. Rudolf Kittel (Stuttgart, Privilegierte Wurttembergische Bibelanstalt, 1929), p. 4, footnote 24a.

43. Gordon R. Dunston, "Hard Sayings—V," *Theology* 66 (December 1963) 492.

44. For the significance and implications of rules of residence, matrilocal, and patri-local, see George P. Murdock, *Social Structure* (London: Collier-Macmillan, 1949; New York: The Free Press, 1965), pp. 16–20, 31, and p. 144: "Non-sororal polygyny . . . is very highly associated with patri-local residence, patrilineal descent, and the types of kin groups that depend upon these rules."

45. See Note 24, above; and also McKenzie, *Dictionary of the Bible*, p. 549.

46. See Holst, "Polygamy and the Bible," p. 207: "To be one flesh means that the man and the woman who were before marriage unrelated are now a new family unit. This phrase indicates the absolute indissolubility of marriage—not that it is of necessity monogamous. The correctness of the preceding interpretation is indicated by the manner in which Jesus used Genesis 2:24 (Matt. 19:3–9; Mark 10:2–12)." Thus Holst concludes (in his footnote 1, p. 207) that "there is no limit to the number of people who can be 'blood-relatives.' In the case of a man married to two wives, these 'three' would be 'one flesh.'" See also Rudolf Schnackenburg, *The Moral Teaching of the New Testament*, trans. J. Holland-Smith and W.J. O'Hara (New York: Herder and Herder, 2nd ed., 1964), pp. 79, 84–85, 135–137, and 249: "The early Church took its stand, as Jesus had

done, on the account of creation, in which it saw the primordial will of God. The text of Gen. 2:24 'they shall be two in one flesh' was the foundation of the early Christian ethic of marriage. . . . Jesus' exegesis and precept bound it strictly to maintain the indissolubility of marriage (1 Cor. 7:10), although difficulties quickly arose, especially in mixed marriages between Christians and pagans." Schnackenburg says nothing in this discussion about any exegesis or precept by Jesus regarding polygamy.

47. Gerhard von Rad, *Genesis: A Commentary*, trans. John H. Marks (London: SCM Press; Philadelphia: Westminster Press, 1961), p. 83.

48. *Ibid.*, p. 82.

49. *Ibid.*, pp. 42–43.

50. *Ibid.*, p. 78.

51. Ringeling, "Bergründing der Monogamie," p. 87. See also Crespy, "The Grace of Marriage," p. 20: "If polygamy had appeared odious in itself to the authors of the Bible, they would certainly have let some hint of this be apparent in their manner of relating patriarchal history. The fact that the Patriarchs were polygamous seems neither to have shocked nor scandalized the biblical writers. This seems to indicate that the monogamous character of marriage was not, in their eyes, the unique and inevitable consequence of what they had discovered in the Genesis account regarding the union of man and woman. For centuries, men who had learned from a reliable source that God made man and woman to be a *single* flesh had practiced polygamy and concubinage without any embarrassment. How is this phenomenon to be understood?"

52. Grelot, *Man and Wife in Scripture*, p. 86. See also Vollebregt, *The Bible and Marriage*, pp. 82–83; and, for some additional references, see above: Notes 6, 7, 8, 9, and 10.

53. For the opinion that polygamy amounts to adultery, see Willard Burce, "Polygamy and the Church," *Concordia Theological Monthly* 34 (1963) 227–228; E.G. Parrinder, *The Bible and Polygamy* (London: SPCK, 1950), p. 48; and Pope Innocent III, excerpt from his letter "Gaudemus in Domino," to the Bishop of Tiberius in the beginning of 1201, in Heinrich Denzinger, ed., *The Sources of the Catholic Faith*, trans. Roy J. Deferrari from Denzinger's *Enchiridion Symbolorum*, edition 30 (St. Louis: B. Herder, 1957), no. 408, pp. 159–160. See also the response to this opinion by Holst, "Polygamy and the Bible" pp. 207–210: "There is no indication in Scripture that polygamy can be equated with adultery."

54. R.V.G. Tasker, *The Gospel According to St. Matthew: An Introduction and Commentary* (Grand Rapids, Mich.: Eerdmans, 1961), p. 179.

55. Anthony Kosnik, "The Pastoral Care of Those in Canonically Invalid Marriages," *The Jurist* 30 (January 1970) 36.

56. See Schnackenburg, *Moral Teachings*, pp. 137–141.

57. Kosnick, "Pastoral Care," p. 36.

58. See Jeremias, *Jerusalem*, p. 370; Schillebeeckx, *Marriage: Secular Reality and Saving Mystery*, I, pp. 140–143.

59. Bruce Vawter, *The Four Gospels*, p. 274. See also Vincent Taylor, *The Gospel According to St. Mark* (London: Macmillan; New York: St. Martin's Press, 1966), pp. 415, 418.

60. Leonard Ramaroson, "Une nouvelle interprétation de la 'clausule' du Mt. 19:9," *Science et Esprit* 23 (May-September 1971) 247–251. For more on this, see Leopold Sabourin, "Notes and Views: The Divorce Clauses," *Biblical Theology Bulletin* 2 (February 1972) 80–86; and Bruce Malina: "Does *Porneia* Mean Fornication?" *Novum Testamentum* 14 (1972) 10–17.

61. See S. Lowy, "The Extent of Jewish Polygamy in Talmudic Times," *Journal of Jewish Studies*, 9 (1958), pp. 130–131, 134; and Ze'ev W. Falk, *Jewish Matrimonial Law in the Middle Ages* (London: Oxford University Press, 1966), pp. 1–3, 9.

62. Schillebeeckx, *Marriage: Secular Reality and Saving Mystery*, I, p. 206.

63. See Taylor, *The Gospel According to St. Mark*, p. 415; and Schillebeeckx, *Marriage: Secular Reality and Saving Mystery*, I, p. 214.

64. See Paul Hoffmann, "Jesus' Saying about Divorce and Its Interpretation in the New Testament Tradition," in *The Future of Marriage as Institution*, ed. Franz Böckle, trans. J.T. Swann, Concilium 55 (New York: Herder and Herder, 1970), p. 55. Hoffmann points out that Jesus quotes Genesis 2:24, according to the Septuagint: "and the *two* shall become one flesh"; while the Hebrew text says "*they* shall become one flesh." For an interesting comment on the English translation of this verse in the Revised Standard Version of the Bible, and also in the New American Bible, see Paul Ramsey, *Fabricated Man: The Ethics of Genetic Control* (New Haven and London: Yale University Press, 1970), p. 132: "I am reminded of that strange translation . . . (to which Roger Shinn recently drew my attention). There, where Jesus quotes Genesis on marriage: 'The two shall become *one flesh*,' the RSV reads 'the two shall become *one*' (Matt. 19:5). The translators drop a footnote which says 'Greek *one flesh*' (*not* 'Some ancient authorities,' or 'Some manuscripts say *one flesh*')! The neutral word 'one' permitting, the modern mind completes the sentence by saying 'one person,' or one in the personal realm." Such an understanding would contrast sharply with the ancient Semitic connotations of the expression "one flesh." On the biblical meaning of "one flesh," see also notes 41–43, above.

65. See Holst, "Polygamy and the Bible," pp. 206–208; and Dunstan, "Hard Sayings—V," pp. 491–492.

66. George Vass, "Divorce and Remarriage in the Light of Recent Publications," *Heythrop Journal* 11 (1970) 259–260.

67. *Ibid.*, p. 259.

68. See Dominic Crossan, "Divorce and Remarriage," in *The Bond of Marriage*, ed. William W. Bassett (Notre Dame and London: University of Notre Dame Press, 1968), p. 10; and David Daube, *The New Testament and Rabbinic Judaism*, pp. 76, 81, 83, 84: "There is in the New Testament no opposition to polygamy but that based on the teaching of the androgynous Adam. Moreover, there was a tendency among the Jewish New Testament authors—i.e. a tendency not shared by Luke—to suppress this opposition as they forgot about, or came to disapprove of, its base. . . . The subsequent private discussion between Jesus and his disciples, in Matthew (19:10–12), does not concern divorce or polygamy at all, but the question of whether marriage as such is a good thing."

69. Crossan, "Divorce and Remarriage," pp. 11, 13.

70. See Note 4, above.

71. See R. de Vaux, *Ancient Israel*, p. 29; Baron, *Social and Religious History*, II, pp. 218–220; and E. Neufeld, *Ancient Hebrew Marriage Laws* (London and New York: Longmans, Green, 1944), p. 139.

72. Bernard Häring, *A Theology of Protest* (New York: Farrar, Straus and Giroux, 1970), p. 147.

73. For this interpretation of Onan's sin, see Grelot, *Man and Wife in Scripture*, p. 43; Joseph Chaine, *Le livre de la Genèse* (Paris: Editions du Cerf, 1948), pp. 385–386. *The Jerusalem Bible*, ed. and trans. Alexander Jones and others (London: Darton, Longman and Todd, 1966), p. 61, footnote c. For an older and rather different interpretation, that Onan's sin and punishment had to do primarily with contraception, see Johannes B. Schaumberger, "Propter quale peccatum morte punitus sit Onan?" *Biblica*, 8 (1927) 212; and C.F. De Vine, "The Sin of Onan," *Catholic Biblical Quarterly* 4 (1942) 340.

74. See Note 4, above.

75. Schillebeeckx, *Marriage: Secular Reality and Saving Mystery*, I, p. 212.

76. St. Jerome, "To Oceanus" (Letter No. 69), in *A Selected Library of Nicene and Post-Nicene Fathers of the Christian Church*, ed. P. Schaff and others (Oxford, 1890–1900), VI, p. 144; in P.L. 22, cols. 657–658.

77. See John Chrysostom, "Homily X (1 Tim. 3:1–4)," in *A Selected Library of Nicene and Post-Nicene Fathers of the Christian Church*, ed. P. Schaff and others (Grand Rapids, Mich.: Eerdmans, 1956), XIII, p. 438.

78. See Theodoret of Cyr, "Omnia Opera Theodoreti Episcopi Cyrensis," in *Patrologia graeca*, ed. J.P. Migne (Paris, 1857–1866), 82, cols. 804–805.

79. See Cajetan, as quoted by Dennis Doherty, *The Sexual Doctrine of Cardinal Cajetan* (Regensburg: Varlag Fredrich Pustet, 1966), p. 205, footnote 78: "Et dixit hoc (1 Tim. 3:2) quia tunc temporis multi plures uxores habebant imitantes patres Veteris Testamenti: quum nullibi legamus hoc prohibitum."

80. See Holst, "Polygamy and the Bible," pp. 210–212; Anthony Tyrrell Hanson, "The Pastoral Letters: Commentary on the First and Second Letters to Timothy and the Letter to Titus, in *The Cambridge Bible Commentary*, ed. P.R. Ackroyd, A.R.C. Leaney, and J.W. Packer (London and New York: Cambridge Uniersity Press, 1966), p. 41: " . . . 'married to one wife' is quite possible because polygamy . . . was still practiced among Jews at this time, and the Church of the author's day was still in close touch with Judaism." See also Roy S. Nicholson, "The Pastoral Epistles," in *The Wesleyan Bible Commentary*, ed. Charles W. Carter and others (Grand Rapids, Michigan: Eerdmanns, 1965), V, p. 587; and George A. Denzer, "The Pastoral Letters," in *The Jerome Biblical Commentary*, ed. Raymond E. Brown, Joseph A. Fitzmyer and Roland Murphy (Englewood Cliffs, N.J.: Prentice-Hall, 1968), II, p. 354: "Clearly it is not only polygamy that Paul means to exclude but also a second marriage, . . . that would take place either in the case of conversion from paganism . . . or after the death of the first wife."

81. On the Pauline usage of "one flesh," see Rudolf Bultmann, *Theology of the New Testament*, trans. Kendrick Grobel (New York: Charles Scribner's Sons, 1951), I, pp. 192–200.

82. Von Allmen, *loc. cit.*, in Note 10, above.

83. For references on the notion of corporate personality, see Note 26, above.

84. See Louis Bouyer, *Dictionary of Theology*, trans. Charles U. Quinn (New York: Desclée, 1965), 292.

CHAPTER VI

THE REASONING OF THEOLOGIANS

Situations can and do arise . . . in which it
would be sheer brutality for the Christian
Church to confront men with a choice between
baptism and institutional polygamy.
KARL BARTH

From the biblical texts cited in the previous chapter, theologians inside the boundaries of ancient Christendom concluded that the New Testament forbids absolutely the practice of simultaneous polygamy among Christians. This, as we have seen, is largely a matter of interpretation. It now appears that many of the earlier exegetes, perhaps overly influenced by their own Western cultural tradition of mandatory monogamy, may have deduced more that is warranted by their biblical premises.

It is significant that the traditional interpretation of the relevant biblical texts, and the usual ecclesiastical discipline regarding polygamy, must be buttressed by a variety of purely rational arguments: appeals to a natural law theory, to a cultural-progress hypothesis, and to sociological conjecture. Then, as the ultimate means of disposing of any remaining objections against the traditional ecclesiastical discipline, the danger of scandal is apt to be mentioned. A critical look at these rational grounds, or extrabiblical reasons, for rejecting polygamy is now in order.

Attention will also be given to the views of some modern theologians who argue that a change in the traditional approach to polygamy is dictated by a wise and compassionate assessment of the theological, missionary, pastoral, and human implications of this whole problem. From these reflections some conclusions will be drawn: proposals for a different policy and a new approach.

A NATURAL LAW THEORY

Following the opinion of Saint Augustine and Saint Thomas Aquinas, the majority of Christian theologians have taught that simultaneous polygamy is not in itself evil, since it was clearly permitted by God under the Old Testament revelation and since it also conforms with the natural purpose of procreation within the permanent bonds of marriage. Augustine's view, already mentioned in Chapter 1, was set forth in the form of an apologia for the polygamy of Jacob and the other Old Testament heroes who had more than one wife at the same time. In the words of Augustine himself:

> Again, Jacob the son of Isaac is charged with having committed a great crime because he had four wives. But here there is no ground for a criminal accusation: for a plurality of wives was no crime when it was the custom; and it is a crime now, because it is no longer the custom. There are sins against nature, and sins against custom, and sins against the laws. In which, then, of these senses did Jacob sin in having a plurality of wives? As regards nature, he used the women not for sensual gratification, but for the procreation of children. For custom, this was the common practice at that time in those countries. And for the laws, no prohibition existed. The only reason of its being a crime now to do this, is because custom and the laws forbid it. In the present altered state of customs and laws, men can have no pleasure in a plurality of wives, except from an excess of lust; and so the mistake arises of supposing that no one could ever have had many wives but from sensuality and the vehemence of sinful desires.[1]

Elsewhere, while pointing out that polyandry was never permitted in former times for any reason, Augustine says explicitly—in the course of astonishingly quaint argument—that polygamy is contrary neither to the law of nature nor to the nature of marriage:

> For by a secret law of nature, things that stand chief love to be singular; but things that are subject are set under, not only one under one, but, if the system of nature or society allow, even several under one, not without becoming beauty. For neither hath one slave

so several masters, in the way that several slaves have one master. Thus we read not that any of the holy women served two or more living husbands: but we read that many females served one husband, when the social state of that nation allowed it, and the purpose of the time persuaded it: for neither is it contrary to the nature of marriage. For several females can conceive from one man: but one female cannot from several, (such is the power of things principal:) as many souls are rightly made subject unto one God.[2]

Saint Thomas in his time also gave some careful consideration to polygamy as an abstract apologetical question—not, however, as a concrete missionary or pastoral problem. He came to the conclusion, from his theory of the primary and secondary precepts of the natural law, that simultaneous polygamy was not always and everywhere prohibited.[3] Prohibitions proceeding from the secondary precepts of the natural law were not regarded as absolute; they were always relative to the circumstances of historical time and place. In the words of Thomas himself:

> A plurality of wives is said to be against the natural law, not as regards its first precepts, but as regards the secondary precepts, which like conclusions are drawn from its first precepts. Since, however, human acts must needs vary according to the various conditions of persons, times, and other circumstances, the aforesaid conclusions do not proceed from the first precepts of the natural law, so as to be binding in all cases, but only in the majority.[4]

Polygamy belongs, therefore, to this problematical category of relative and dispensable prohibitions, since the principal end of marriage (the good of offspring, or the procreation and education of children) can obviously be realized in a polygamous union. What are apt to be compromised are the secondary ends of marriage: mutual love and/or remedy for desires, household tranquillity, and the sacramental significance of marriage as a sign of Christ's union with the Church. In this Thomistic theory, these secondary goods may be disregarded for a time, when the principal end of marriage may so require, as, for example, "when it behooved the aforesaid precept (the monogamy rule) not to be observed, in order to ensure the multiplication of offspring."[5] In this matter, however, God alone could grant a dispensation for the nonobservance of the precept.

Dispensations from the secondary prohibitions of the natural law (e.g. the indissolubility rule) were normally left to the good judgment of the appropriate authority.[6] But in the particular case of polygamy—and probably only because Thomas had to harmonize his theory with the teaching of Pope Innocent III —nothing less than a divine dispensation would be required. Innocent had taken a firm stand on the *deus ex machina* notion that a dispensation from the monogamy rule was possible only "by a divine revelation."[7] Nevertheless, Thomas notably modified Innocent's teaching when he affirmed that "a dispensation in this matter could be granted . . . through an internal inspiration."[8]

A number of reputable scholastic theologians later took the view, as did some of the Reformers, that polygamy is not at all contrary to the natural law.[9] While there seems always to have been some room for debate, the more common view of the scholastics during the past centuries—and this was also the view of Calvin—was that monogamy is prescribed by natural law.[10] As expressed even today in a standard Roman Catholic commentary on canon law, polygamy is "directly opposed to the secondary end (of marriage) in as much as it hinders domestic peace and reduces each of the wives to a condition of too great inferiority; and indirectly tends also to prejudice the child's education."[11] While the major objection is that polygamy compromises the secondary ends of marriage, there is also a hint that it tends to compromise some aspects of the principal end of marriage. This same argument is found also in the *New Catholic Encyclopedia*, published in 1967:

> Wherever polygamy is practiced, the wife is no more than chattel or at least is only a servant to be used and enjoyed. Without dignity she is treated as an inferior, never as an equal. Her children are bound to suffer as they grow aware of the degraded position of their mother and receiving only a share of the divided attention of their father.[12]

Such generalized allegations provide a good example of ethnocentric moralizing, and they reveal a vast ignorance of the socio-cultural reality of African polygamy. In this or that particular society it may, or it may not, be true that the dignity of women is compromised and that their children suffer from a lack of paternal attention because of the custom of polygamy. If women are abused and children are neglected in some polygamous families or societies, must it be assumed that this same abuse and neglect are due specifically to the practice of polygamy? Have women always been treated as equals, and not as inferiors, in monogamous societies? Is it always and only among polygamists that women are degraded and children neglected?

From the available literature dealing with peoples who practice polygamy, this same argument about realizing or not realizing the ends of marriage could be completely turned around, and a quite respectable brief could be presented for plural marriage under certain historico-cultural and socio-economic conditions. It could even be demonstrated that in certain societies today the women and children of polygamous households fare much better generally than do those of monogamous households. Indeed, this whole manner of argument concerning the end of marriage could even be turned against monogamy. In some cases of monogamy, for example the primary end of marriage (procreation) cannot actually be achieved; so there follows a strong tendency toward adultery, divorce, and remarriage. But this fact would hardly justify the conclusion that monogamy works against the nature of marriage. Again, the fact that polygamy seems to serve the purpose of procreation more efficiently than monogamy would hardly warrant the conclusion that polygamy is, therefore, more in accord with the nature of marriage, hence more in conformity with the natural law.[13]

What we are indicating here is, of course, the peculiar weakness of many arguments based on the natural law. Theologians tend to take as universally natural, and therefore normative, the ways and values of their own particular time and place in history, while the unfamiliar ways and values of other peoples in different times and places tend to be seen as unnatural. The methodological errors are then compounded by what Bernard Häring calls "a rationalistic natural law philosophy that draws its logical conclusions from formulas, without first studying the phenomenon of men."[14] In his critical analysis of this same nonhistorical and culture-bound natural law moralizing, Josef Fuchs tells us that this "preceptive understanding of natural law as a summary of precepts conformable to nature" is not even in keeping with the authentic traditional concept of the natural law.[15]

It may be instructive to recall, at this point, that for many centuries the greatest theologians of Christendom, including Saint Thomas, taught that the Western socio-economic institution of slavery was in accord with the law of nature. In the view of St. Thomas, slavery was as natural as old age:

> Slavery is contrary to the first intention of nature. Yet it is not contrary to the second, because natural reason has this inclination, and nature has this desire—that everyone should be good; but from the fact that a person sins, nature has an inclination that he should be punished for his sin, and thus slavery was brought in as a punishment of sin. . . .
>
> The natural law requires punishment to be inflicted for guilt, and that no one should be punished who is not guilty; but the appointing of the punishment according to the circumstances of person and guilt belongs to positive law. Hence slavery which is a definite punishment is of positive law, and arises out of natural law, as the determinate from that which is indeterminate.[16]

The demise of slavery in the Western world was not due to the preceptiveness of moral theologians with their traditional natural law rationale. "The church," says Reinhold Niebuhr, "left the institution of slavery undisturbed until economic forces transmuted it into the serfdom of the Middle Ages."[17] And how did the Christian theological tradition address itself to the large-scale enslavement of Africans? In 1727 the Bishop of London addressed these words to slave owners in the British colonies:

> Christianity and the embracing of the Gospel does not make the least alteration in civil property or in any of the duties which belong to civil relations; but in all these respects it continues persons just in the same state as it found them. The freedom which Christianity gives is freedom from the bondage of sin and Satan and from the Dominion of Man's Lusts and Passions and inordinate Desires; but as to their outward condition, whatever that was before, whether bond or free, their being baptized and becoming Christians, makes no manner of change in them.[18]

Even as the nineteenth-century abolitionist movement was gaining ground everywhere, and several secular states had already repudiated slavery, many churchmen—drawing upon the traditional teaching of the majority of Christian moralists—found ways of compromising with slavery in Africa and in North America. The Roman Catholic Bishops in the Southern United States, according to a series of letters written in 1840 by Bishop John England of Charleston, were able to "justify" the continuation of slavery by making a convenient distinction between the "slave trade" and "domestic slavery."[19] They argued, from the words of certain papal documents, that the transatlantic slave trade was morally wrong, while the domestic slave trade was permissible.

As late as 1866, the *Inquisitores Generales* of the Holy Office in Rome were still teaching officially that, according to the "approved theologians and interpretors of the sacred canons,"it is "not contrary to natural and divine law for slaves to be sold, bought, exchanged or given." Therefore, "Christians may lawfully buy slaves, and accept them in payment of a debt or as a gift." However, Christians were permitted to engage in such business only "as long as they have moral certainty that those slaves have not been taken away from their lawful owner nor unjustly kidnapped into slavery."[20] The *Inquisitores*, with their astonishing respect for the sacredness of private property, carefully pointed out that it would be morally wrong for Christians to buy or accept slaves "who had been stolen from their lawful owner," because "it is wrong to buy property taken by theft."

So much for the abstract natural law moralizing that takes no account of what is actually happening in the real world of living persons.[21]

THE CULTURAL-PROGRESS HYPOTHESIS

Another curious argument, which frequently appears when Western theologians and churchmen discuss the non-Western form of plural marriage, is based on the cultural-progress hypothesis already mentioned in Chapter 2. In this hypothesis the Western experience, especially the socio-psychological experience of the past one hundred years, is taken as normative for the whole of humanity. It is assumed, and this assumption is not always and only tacit, that Western peoples are superior (higher, more civilized, more mature, more human) in the realm of social behavior as well as in technology and that non-Western peoples are progressive (civilized, mature, human) to the extent that they approximate Western ways and values. A sample of this kind of thinking is provided by Vittorio Bartoccetti, sometime Secretary of the Supreme Tribunal of the Apostolic Signature in the Roman Curia: "Monogamy is an accepted principle in the civil codes of the more progressive nations."[22] Popular Western psychology lends support to this view. Thus, for example, Marc Oraison confidently assures us that "the practice of polygamy in a society is always a sign of psychological immaturity."[23] Ignace Lepp confirms this in a very revealing passage:

Erotic love establishes a direct bond between two persons. They give themselves to each other totally. It is difficult therefore for the majority of men, and psychologically impossible for most women, to love several persons simultaneously. Polygamy and polyandry are conceivable only within human groups in which sexual possession is not yet intrinsically linked to love. There was no need for a law to require the civilized Moslems of North Africa, Egypt and elsewhere to renounce polygamy. It passed away of its own accord as soon as their psychological maturity had attained to a sufficiently high level for them to look not only for the pleasure of the senses from a woman but also, and primarily, for spiritual communion with her.[24]

Helmut Thielicke offers another example of this same Western ethnocentrism. In a philosophical reflection on the psychology of sex, starting from some insights provided by Greco-Teutonic mythology (Plato, Aeschylus, Goethe, Schopenhauer), Thielicke finds that men tend toward a polygamous style of sexual self-realization, while women are monogamously oriented.[25] If women are to be properly respected, then men must learn to conform to the monogamous pattern. Besides, masculinity itself is a relational thing: one is a man only in relation to a woman. "The woman cannot live polygamously without damage to the very substance of her nature." So, according to Thielicke, "the man cannot do so either."[26] Only in an exclusive union is it possible for two persons to really go out of themselves and, thus, to live for the other. This is true love (*agape*).

The same Western philosophical and emotional presuppositions, concerning the nature of personhood and the psychology of love, are reflected also in Bernard Häring's earlier writings, especially in the reasons he educes for the inappropriateness of polygamy:

> Sexual love between man and woman, if it is in the fullest sense human and in accord with human dignity, tends of its inner nature to exclusiveness. . . . The love of spouses is naturally so exclusive that it can only exist in absolute honesty if both partners give themselves to one another, wholly and unconditionally. To put it in other words, simultaneous or consecutive polygamy may be marriage-like unions, but in no sense are they valid realizations of conjugal love.[27]

From this highly individualistic and typically Western conception of love it follows that "a society which accepts polygamy as normal is . . . on a lower plane than one which outlaws it."[28] Is this an *ad hominem* type of apologetics? Even the most obvious objection to this culturally conditioned notion of conjugal love is apt to be anticipated with a confident show of logic. Thus, for example, Otto Piper tells us this:

> The fact that some people are able to love more than one person at the same time does not prove that polygamy is as valuable as monogamy but that love can become shallow.[29]

Must we conclude, therefore, that the marriage union of Elkanah and Hannah, or the union of Jacob and Rachel, was less than valid, not in accord with human dignity, and a manifestation of shallow love? Not if we recall all that was said in Chapter 2 about the meaning of culture and the significance of cultural differences among peoples. For a number of complex socio-economic and historico-cultural reasons it may well be, as Denis O'Callaghan points out, that in this or that particular society "polygamy may happen to be the marriage structure which best safeguards . . . the basic values in human sexual relationship."[30] This, of course, is very apt to be the case "where the man's role is that of patriarch, *pater familias*, father-leader of an extended family, where he tends to marry late in life, where the woman is in need of protection from an early age and where the only available

protection is marriage into a plural family unit"—or at least
where the plural family unit offers the best opportunities for a
secure and dignified existence, and where all women are expected to find their fulfillment in marriage.

So we must face honestly the perceptive questions of the African theologian, Manas Buthelezi:

> The matter of testing the hypothesis that it is only in monogamy that
> love between a man and a woman can be best expressed in its ideal
> form, should rather be left to the sociologists. We can only raise
> questions. What universal norm do we have for testing the ideal
> expression of love between husband and wife? Can it be established
> empirically that in those countries where monogamy is a general
> social practice, there is a higher level of family stability than in
> polygamous societies? If this is possible, can it also be established
> that the number of wives is the determining factor in that stability? Is
> the rate of divorce lower in monogamous societies than in polygam-
> ous ones?[31]

It is by no means self-evident that the contemporary Western
conception of conjugal love, at least as it is often idealized in
rather abstract terms, and as it is frequently pursued in relative
isolation from the larger communities of kinship, is higher and
more fully human than the broader conception of conjugal love in
polygamous families. Indeed, there is some evidence to suggest
that family life in the Western world is deteriorating today precisely because of this late Western idea that marriage is based
primarily upon a mutually fulfilling interpersonal relationship
which is totally self-giving and exclusive. While such love may be
a desirable fruit of marriage, it is surely too fragile a hope to serve
as the only foundation for the stability of marriage.[32] Still, it is
quite natural that Western thinkers should have worked out, on
the basis of their own culturally conditioned psychology of love, a
philosophical proof that monogamy is the ideal form of marriage.
For them, because of their culture, it is the ideal. At the same time
there are also many other peoples who are no less convinced,
because of their different experience and mythology, that
polygamy is the ideal.

One's conception of the ideal marriage is determined by the
values that are emphasized in one's own culture. Where procre-

ation is no longer the primary purpose of marriage, because of changed economic conditions and the lower mortality rate among children, greater emphasis may be given to the purpose of mutual love between husband and wife, so much so that this love aspect may even become detached from the family-making aspect of marriage. The exclusive love union of two partners, with little or no reference to offspring or to the kinship bonds established through marriage, occurs only in, and perhaps only as a concomitant of, certain well known socio-economic conditions in modern industrial-consumer-mercantile societies.

Under vastly different conditions in some other societies, polygamy makes sense, especially where the idea of marriage is almost interchangeable with the idea of the extended family, and where a strong sense of community is all-pervading. In a society that has no place for unmarried women, where marriage alone offers women the security and dignity required for their normal self-realization, and where economic forces prevent men from marrying at an early age, polygamy is apt to be both a social necessity and a positive social value. In such a society the right that every woman has to marriage and the society's need for legitimate progeny is actually well served by the system of polygamy; hence the system is widely supported and encouraged by women themselves.

Do the mass of African women accept polygamy as an ideal form of marriage, simply because they do not know any better? Are they so dull that they do not know what is good for them? Perhaps this is another example of an oppressed group having internalized the consciousness of the ruling group, in the same way that many slaves in former times acquiesced in their condition and served their masters with genuine loyalty.

If this is true, then a minority of African women, especially those who have become "Westernized" through schools and churches, would seem to be in the vanguard of African womanhood "come of age." Again: the movement from immaturity to maturity, backwardness to advancement, by imitating Western social behavior! This would certainly be the view of many older missionaries and even of older African Christians. But an hypothesis is not verified simply by affirming that it is so.

Indeed, this very hypothesis seems to be established by projecting the attitudes and values of one group upon another group whose experience has given them some very different attitudes and values. Are the needs and interests, hence the attitudes and values, of both groups the same: the minority who have been "Westernized," and the masses who have not? May we assume, anyway, that the attitudes and values of the African masses in the future will be identical with the attitudes and values of a contemporary minority?

The nature of man, and also his sense of human dignity, is reflected in the institution of marriage. But the nature of man is not merely biological and psychological; it is also historical and, therefore, always being reshaped and conditioned by changing and differing socio-economic situations. What is normal behavior among one people may be abnormal among another people. But this does not mean that the ways of one of these peoples are less human than the ways of the other. "It is evident," as Leonhard Weber says, "that economic revolutions are closely bound up with social changes within marriage and that they often determine the actual form of marriage to a greater extent than ethical and religious considerations. The axiom *'primum vivere, deinde philosophari'* is clearly applicable here."[33] What many of our Western theologians and churchmen have not yet fully recognized is that "in mankind as a whole there must be many different, complementary, and reciprocally stimulating expressions of married life."[34]

SOCIOLOGICAL CONJECTURE

As a supplementary reason for maintaining the traditional discipline in the face of polygamists who would become Christians, appeals are sometimes made to sociological conjecture. It is uncritically affirmed that, no matter how problematical the traditional insistence on monogamy may seen to be, the practice of polygamy is rapidly vanishing in Africa anyway. Various strong Westernizing tendencies are clearly working against the custom: the schooling of girls, for example, and especially the changing economic conditions and the new values of the urban elites. If we just wait a little longer, the problem will solve itself: the problem-people will no longer be there.

Although polygamy is diminishing notably in some regions of Africa, it is also on the increase in other regions—even in urban areas and in the more sophisticated and prosperous segments of the population. So it is by no means certain that the custom will vanish in the foreseeable future. The relevant demographic, sociological, and anthropological data are presented in Chapters 3 and 4, so there is no need to go over all of this ground once again. However, it should be noted just one more time that the needs and interests and expectations of a minority group, even a prophetical minority that feels a sense of mission, are not necessarily the real needs and interests and expectations of the majority. Does history indicate that such minorities lead always and only to better ways of living and that the masses inevitably follow the paths opened to them by creative minorities? Nor should we assume that the perspective of a contemporary minority in Africa will be the perspective of the generations now in schools that are influenced by the postcolonial reaffirmation of ancient African traditions and values.

Even if polygamists were few and diminishing, the same basic missionary and pastoral question would still deserve the attention of theologians and church leaders. This point may be exemplified by mentioning just two parallel moral issues.

The fact that a government may be working honestly, and with a measure of success, to eliminate poverty among its citizens would not excuse Christians in that country from facing the moral implications of poverty in their midst, even if the poor were only a small minority of the population. Another example: The fact that only a relatively small number of soldiers and civilians may be dying daily in a particular war does not diminish the essential seriousness of the moral questions raised by such human wastage, even if the end of the conflict may be in sight. It would be irresponsible to take the attitude that, if we just wait a little longer without thinking too much about it, the moral questions will vanish.

THE DANGER OF SCANDAL

Now what about the danger of scandal among monogamously married Christians if the Church's discipline were modified for the sake of the polygamist who might wish to become a Christian without first having to divorce all but one of his wives? This question of scandal is like a two-edged sword. The greater scandal would surely be in the Church's reluctance to change, if it were shown clearly that the traditional discipline is ill-founded and unjust. It would be the worst kind of scandal to maintain a legalistic improvization based on an archaic anthropology and on dubious methods of biblical interpretation and moral theologizing. Was there nothing scandalous in the traditional teaching of the approved theologians and canonists on the matter of slavery? No doubt, some Christians took scandal from the novel teaching of a minority of theologians who insisted that the traditional teaching of the "approved authors" was wrong.[35]

Is there nothing scandalous now in the practice of requiring a polygamist to divorce the mothers of his own children and to do this in the name of the Christian ideal of indissoluble marriage and stable family life? Such questions are valid and point to the need for more reflection on the part of theologians before any final answer can be given one way or another. The Christian pilgrimage is hard enough in its essential demands. So moral theologians must heed the New Testament warning against binding heavy and oppressive burdens on the backs of men (cf. Matt. 23:4, 15). It is therefore a fair question, which all teachers of the law must ask themselves continuously: Do we traverse land and sea with a liberating message that summons Christ's disciples from among the nations—and then make their last condition worse than the first?

What might happen in the Christian communities of Africa, if the traditional discipline regarding polygamy were altered, may be reasonably ascertained by considering what actually did happen when the Lutheran Church in Liberia adopted the new policy of admitting to baptism and communion polygamists who had been married before encountering the gospel message. This policy, after it had been followed for fourteen years, was evaluated in 1965. The Christian community during this time was "not inundated with polygamists," nor was there "any indication that the Church's teaching on monogamy as the standard of Christian marriage is compromised by baptizing those who had previously entered into polygamy."[36] Some other pertinent findings were these:

> Well over 90 percent of the church members are identified with the traditional Christian standard of monogamous marriage. . . . It is unlikely that the proportion of polygamous to monogamous Christians will increase appreciably. . . . It is highly significant that almost all (over 90 percent) of the men baptized as polygamists are heads of Christian families, that is, wives and children are also members of the church.
>
> Men with more than one wife have usually attained to a position of some means and influence in the community. Such a Christian home can be an effective witness to non-Christian neighbors in several ways: the stability of the marriage relationship, the harmony and unity of the home, the Christian upbringing of the children.
>
> The church's position with respect to a Christian man marrying a second wife or a Christian woman marrying a man with one or more wives is generally known and accepted. . . . The real problem with respect to the monogamous Christian is not his entering subsequently into a polygamous marriage, but rather the committing of adultery.
>
> If anything, the policy of baptizing polygamists is a strong testimony to the sanctity of the marriage bond and supportive of the stability of the home, influences which are not to be regarded lightly in a culture where the marriage relationship is subjected to the same destructive forces as other institutions of society.
>
> In practice, some congregations have elected as members of the church council men and women who are polygamists. The gifts of leadership, Christian piety and zeal do not appear to be restricted to monogamists.
>
> This policy is a vivid witness to the gracious God who meets men where they are and accepts them as they are, and then by His Spirit transforms their lives.
>
> The more disturbing problem with respect to Christian marriage and family life is not with the polygamists, but with the over 90 percent of the church's membership identified with monogamy. The real issue confronting the church is not the fact of plural mar-

riage, but rather how to deal with the vast grey area of unresolved difficulties in the relationship between men and women who are unmarried or who are so-called monogamists.

It is highly questionable in fact whether 90 percent of the Lutheran Church in Liberia is "monogamous," if by that is meant a marriage union in which the husband and wife are faithful to each other. What does exist among the majority of members are varying degrees of extra-marital liaisons—from casual adultery, or the temporary taking of a lover while the wife is nursing a child, to covert but established concubinage. Such relationships are sanctioned by tribal culture and almost universally practiced in the Westernized segment of society.

The gradual decline of polygamy is not due to Christian influence, but to economic and social factors which militate against it. Correspondingly, as polygamy diminishes, the problem of adultery increases, and that, not only in society as a whole, but within the church as well.[37]

A final word must be added about the dire prognostications of scandal. Assuming that a careful theological reconsideration of this whole polygamy question leads to the conclusion that something like the policy of the Lutheran Church in Liberia should be adopted by other Christian Churches in Africa, what is to be said about the danger of scandal? For a start, this Lutheran experience suggests that such a danger may turn out to be quite unreal. Nevertheless, if we take this danger as an hypothetical possibility, we would first have to recall that there are different kinds of scandal: some kinds are unavoidable, while some, that are avoidable, are also tolerable.[38]

The fact that some men who are already Christians, and who might have desires for more than one wife, might be scandalized by the toleration of polygamy among some new Christians would not be in itself a sufficient reason for withholding the sacraments from the newly evangelized men. Such scandal need not be avoided, as it would generally be only "pharisaic scandal." Even the less likely danger of "scandal of the weak" would be tolerable in this case, by reason of the principle of double effect with reference to the good purpose of the sacraments.[39] The need that the newly evangelized persons have for the sacraments must take priority over the danger of scandal, because participation in the sacraments is considered to be a necessity for the salvation of those who have been truly evangelized.[40]

Another way of looking at this is suggested by Bernard Häring in his preface to this book. If the Church is the sacramental sign of saving peace, inviting all men to participate in the manifestation of this sign, then the sacramental life of the Church, far from being a closed system that admits only those who can fulfill selected legal prescriptions, must be truly open to all men of good will in whatever socio-cultural condition they may be when they first hear the call to Christian faith.

SOME ARGUMENTS FOR CHANGE

A number of modern theologians would favor some modification of the traditional discipline regarding polygamy. Some would not go so far as the Lutheran Church in Liberia has gone, while others would go further in an effort to find a satisfactory solution to this missionary and pastoral problem.

The abandonment of polygamy has become in practice an indispensable element, an essential sign, of conversion to Christianity in Africa. In the popular mind, therefore, the monogamy rule is one of the marks of the Christian Chruch in Africa. According to Lesslie Newbigin, among others, "this is wrong on theological grounds and disastrous in missionary practice."[41] While he believes firmly that "monogamy is God's will for the human family," Newbigin denies vigorously "an absolute identification of conversion with a particular ethical decision in the matter of polygamy." The argument is this:

> All conversion has an ethical content, but conversion is an event which is more than its ethical implications. To deny this is to leave the order of grace and freedom and to go over into the world of legalism and bondage. True goodness, as the Christian understands it, is the fruit of grace, that is to say, of a personal relationship with God, in whom alone is perfect goodness, and who with unwearying patience deals with men—commanding, sustaining, chastening, forgiving, guiding in a continuous and living intercourse of love. To be converted is to be brought into that personal relationship with God who is the author and ground of my being. . . . Simply to identify conversion with a decision to act in a certain way, whether it

be in the matter of polygamy, or slavery, or segregation, is to leave
the realm of grace for the realm of law.[42]

Again, we are reminded that the liberation of their slaves was
never required of slave owners when they were converted to
Christianity or when they wished to participate in the sacramental life of the Church.[43] The practice of polygamy, as it may be
observed today in many African societies, could hardly be regarded as more incompatible with Christianity than was the
institution of slavery. If slavery could be tolerated by the Christian conscience for centuries, then why is it necessary to repudiate immediately the social institution of polygamy which is
not in itself evil, even according to our traditional moral teaching?

Could it be that in particular times and places there are some
deeply rooted institutions which Christianity cannot change, and
perhaps should not even try to change immediately, by the
imposition of foreign rules of social behavior? Such things may,
however, be transformed gradually from inside the society by
indigenous Christians who are supposed to function after the
manner of a leaven within their own respective socio-cultural
situations. Doubtless, the Christian leaven in the Western world
had something to do with the gradual realization of the fact, now
disputed by no one, that Christianity and slavery are incompatible.

Saint Paul, Saint Augustine, and Saint Thomas Aquinas were
unable in their respective times to see the full implications of their
own belief that, on account of Christ, there is no more distinction
between slaves and free men (cf. Gal. 3:28). But it is still expected
that the ideal of monogamy can and should be put into practice
immediately among all those who are just now, for the first time,
turning to the Lord in faith. Christian apologists have repeatedly
taught, with particular reference to slavery, that "the church did
not begin by condemning an institution which she found established, and which as a system of social and economic organization seemed then quite natural, if not necessary, to almost all the
world."[44] The conclusion of this apologetical argument is that
"together with a *de facto* acceptance of the existing social regime
there was brought into being a moral system which undermined

its bases," and thus contributed to the eventual abolition of slavery. Why not, therefore, a *de facto* acceptance of polygamy which would certainly appear to be more tolerable than slavery?

Charles E. Curran also proposes that the polygamy question should be approached in a manner similar to the very gradual and tolerant approach of the early Church to the question of slavery. Because of the well-known historical and cultural complexity of human existence, there is an important and meaningful distinction to be made between objective and subjective morality. "This approach," says Curran, "develops the concept of invincible ignorance and the need for a morality of growth according to which the person here and now for a number of reasons might not be able to do what the fullness of objective morality requires."[45]

It is better understood today than in former times that human behavior is influenced and limited by psychological and sociological elements and forces which make it almost impossible for individuals to realize subjectively some of the objective goals of traditional Christian morality, and that sometimes even the pursuit of certain objective goals may be forbidden by some higher rules of morality. For example, the traditional discipline regarding polygamy has given scant attention to the rights of the wives who are supposed to be sent away in the name of the Christian ideal of marriage; so, for the sake of these women and their children, the objective ideal should not perhaps be pursued in some situations; nor should any valid and just contracts, made previously in good faith between husbands and wives, be violated subsequently because the gospel message has been heard and believed: the message of love, liberation, and justice. There are conditions, therefore, under which "Christians can go along with the prevailing custom of polygamy while working for its ultimate change and abolition."[46] The operative principle in this solution may be formulated in the words of Saint Thomas:

> A thing is not brought to perfection at once from the outset, but through an orderly succession of time; thus one is first a boy and then a man.[47]

Laws imposed on men should also be in keeping with their condition, for as Isidore says (*Etym.* v. 21), law should be "possible both according to nature and according to the custom of the country."[48]

Helmut Thielicke, in a later consideration of the missionary implications of his own earlier teaching about monogamy and polygamy, frankly recognizes the absurdity of the traditional legalistic improvisations by which the acceptance of the monogamy rule becomes a primary and indispensable requirement for admission into the Christian fold. "The task of the mission," writes Thielicke, "is not to preach monogamy but the Gospel." Instead of resorting to legalism and commands, the Church must learn to allow things either "to grow or to wither away under the power of the Gospel."[49] The theological issue, as seen by Thielicke, is this:

> The new life—and also the new order—must arise out of the freedom of the children of God; otherwise what grows out of it will be not children but slaves. And then it could turn out that even the most Christian order would not be expressing the new fellowship between God and man, but would rather infringe upon it and destroy it from within.

To this Thielicke adds a pragmatic consideration:

> It is well known how destructive have been the effects of certain missionary measures which have been carried out without distinguishing between Law and Gospel, and therefore have all too often identified European customs with Christianity itself. This kind of illegitimate and unchristian violence done to native customs usually has to be paid for in the rebellion that comes in the second and third generations.[50]

As a general practical rule, therefore, Thielicke proposes that "existing polygamous marriages may be allowed to continue when a person is baptized and that it must be left to the freedom of the candidate whether and to what extent he can justify the dissolution of his polygamous marriage."[51]

While defending the ideal of monogamy, Karl Barth is also among the small group of theologians who would allow for exceptions under some circumstances. "Situations can and do arise . . . in which," according to Barth, "it would be sheer brutality for the Christian Church to confront men with the choice between baptism and institutional polygamy."[52] What is called for, instead, is a wise and compassionate assessment of the situation:

> Situations can and do arise in which the immediate abolition of polygamy as an institution (for example, the discharge of all but one of a man's existing wives) would bring about not only a cruel but an ethically irresponsible confusion and dissolution of social relationships which may be highly problematical, yet are not senseless and wicked; but are the guarantees of law and order and security and protection, and can no longer be so if there is an abrupt transition to monogamy. . . . The decision of theological ethics in favor of monogamy against polygamy calls for a clear recognition of matter and purpose. . . . There are exceptions. And they will always have to be worked out in accordance with a wise assessment of the situation.[53]

In 1967 a professor of canon law at Gregorian University in Rome told a group of missionaries that, far from being always wrong and completely forbidden, polygamy in some societies is clearly "a good institution."[54] In some situations it would even be morally wrong, because unjust and cruel, to send away the wives of polygamous households. Hence, it would be scandalous to tell husbands that they must, in the name of Christ, repudiate wives who had been married to them in good faith. Here is another way of viewing the scandal that might be involved in a more tolerant attitude toward polygamy. "We," says Professor Buijs, "have created it [the scandal] by preaching a gospel in which monogamy takes the first place as the main precept."[55]

The surprising thing about Buijs's remarks is that they occur in the course of an argument which is very conventional in manner and quite within the framework of traditional Roman Catholic moral theology. Simultaneous polygamy belongs to the category of things that are not always and everywhere forbidden by natural law or divine law. In any conflict of law, in any determination of rights and duties to be followed in actual practice, the higher law of Christian love must always have priority over the lower law of monogamy. So the polygamous husband may not always be required to send away his wives, because this might be unjust and cruel both to the wives and to their children.

Nevertheless, this man may be admitted to baptism (together with all his wives and children), provided that only one of his wives henceforth acts fully as his wife, while the others are wives in everything but the right to have sexual relations with their husband.

This is regarded as a tolerable situation even though it is foreseen that the required sexual abstinence can hardly be observed, in spite of the intentions of all concerned. In the jargon of Roman Catholic moralists, this predicament is called "a necessary proximate occasion of sin." In other words, for serious reasons a situation may be permitted, although it is recognized that in this situation sin—in so far as sin is indicated by the external infringement of a law—can hardly be avoided, while guilt from such sin is mitigated by the circumstances. To illustrate the point, Buijs presents an hypothetical case based on a parallel situation in another part of the world:

> If in Italy, or elsewhere, we find that a housekeeper or a secretary from time to time sins with her employer, the first condition for sacramental absolution would be for the employer to dismiss the woman, and for the woman to look for another job. But supose the employer says, "I cannot dismiss her because my wife is sick, in need of a housekeeper." And suppose the woman herself says, "I cannot quit my job because I look after my mother who lives near by, and I could not look after her if I worked elsewhere." In Europe or in the United States, what would we do in such a case? After a pious exhortation we would give absolution to both the employer and the employee. Instead, with our neophytes in the mission field, we are more severe. Are we not perhaps too severe, too strict?[56]

To be sure, the compromise solution proposed by Buijs may seem much too legalistic, and even bordering on pharisaism. But it is an earnest attempt to meet the problem within the limited terms of a traditional moral system and to stretch that system as far as possible in an effort to take account of the way life really is in man's fallen condition, and to take account of the order of priorities set forth in the New Testament.

Even so, it may be impossible for moralists to find a satisfactory solution to the polygamy problem in Africa until they have first asked themselves a further question concerning the monogamous ideal of Christian marriage: whether this is really *the* Christian ideal, or whether it is simply the Western Christian ideal. It is an *a priori* presupposition of all the innovative theologians just cited that monogamy is *the* ideal which all Christians must accept in intention, if not always in actuality.

Now Josef Fuchs asks, without himself offering a final answer, "whether marriage . . . is to be understood and lived according to the Congolese or Western European style."[57] This leads, in turn, to a series of complex questions with far-reaching implications. Here, however, we would single out only some of the questions asked by Fuchs with particular reference to African polygamy:

> Changes in the data, differences in concepts and experiences—or even interpretation—occur not only in successive cultures, if not in cases of actual pluralism, within the same culture. This is readily understandable if heterogeneous economic, social or political situations admit, respectively, of different modes of behavior. But what if varying experiences and concepts and varying self-images of men in different societies or groups lead to different options and so to a diversity of statements on behavior norms in relation to similar bodies of facts? . . . In many cases a given self-concept and a given viewpoint and form of reality, e.g., marriage in, let us say, a certain African tribe, may not 'in themselves' correspond in all respects to recta ratio. Then . . . the question arises, whether another form of marriage, presupposing another culture, may legitimately be imposed upon men belonging to an endemic culture—by missionaries, for example—provided the indigenous culture itself has not changed by a rather gradual process, and provided it admits of a 'human' form of marriage.[58]

Due to the deep and extensive dissimilarity of the human experience, mankind's self-concept is necessarily heterogeneous, and authentically human behavior must allow for varying options, even though some measure of onesidedness and incompleteness may be expected because of the conditionality without which man *de facto* does not exist. Must we not suppose, therefore, "that the behavioral norms encountered in a particular civilization or cultural area were formulated partly in consideration of just this civilization and culture, hence for them alone?"

And must we not suppose this to be the case, "despite the fact that definitive or generally valid norms of conduct were actually intended, simply because one does not advert to the possibility of other civilizations and cultures?"[59] In other words, we may ask whether the monogamy rule is, after all, universally normative for all Christians; or whether it is normative only among those Christians whose culture gave rise to this rule. Against the accusation of moral relativism, Fuchs has a ready defense and also a word of warning against "an *a priori* universalism." According to Fuchs, the decisive truth which must not be overlooked is this:

> If behavioral norms are to be operative, the entire pertinent reality (including the social factor) has to be taken into account and enter into the judgment. The *a priori*, hence universal, non-historical social ethics that stands opposed to this, that provides norms in advance for every social reality, sacrifices the indispensable objectivity and therefore validity of duly concrete solutions to an *a priori* universalism. The critical question, then, is not one of relativism but of objectivity, or the 'truth' of the action which must be in conformity with the whole concrete reality of man (of society). . . . Our own previous consideration . . . had to do with *moral behavior norms* which men (humanity) 'discover' as being appropriate to their actual civilization, experience, etc. We asked: Is this relativism? And now the correlative question: Is it not rather the necessary connection with concrete human reality to which human behavior must be adapted if it is to be 'objective' and 'true' and so 'right', *secundum rectam rationem?* The demand to be this is absolute.[60]

It is by following this same line of thought that Denis O'Callaghan is able to see polygamy as a system which may best serve and safeguard the basic human values and interests of some societies.[61] While he is more directly concerned with the problem of divorce, O'Callaghan enunciates some fundamental principles which should also contribute notably to the solution of the polygamy problem:

> The structure of marriage is really derived from rational analysis of the over-all human values which it serves in the family-unit and in society. It is not as if there were some pre-existing blueprint written in human nature in a kind of invisible ink which the trained mind can read. Man does not discover by following hidden clues what the

pattern of marriage is. He concludes to what it should be by examining the values which it serves in the person, in the family and in the community. Natural values come before structures; they determine what the structures must be. Analysis of the whole complex of personal relationships in the family community and in the social community indicate the pattern of marriage as institution.[62]

If one is honest in affirming that personal values precede and determine human structures, one must admit that the structure may vary with civilization, with the vastly differing circumstances of man's life across space and time. The critierion which will decide whether a given marriage structure is valid in natural law will be the extent to which it safeguards and promotes the relevant human values to the greatest extent that this is possible in a given civilization or historical situation of mankind.[63]

Anton Morgenroth suggests that a satisfactory solution to the missionary and pastoral problem of African polygamy might be found by accepting polygamous marriages as true and valid, but simply not sacramental or not fully sacramental.[64] Does every Christian's marriage have to be actually, always and everywhere, a full and perfect sign of the loving union between Christ and the Church? Assuming that the monogamy rule is essentially based only upon the sacramental nature of Christian marriage, this approach might very well lead to a satisfactory solution. As already noted in Chapter 5, the union of Christ and the Church can be signified through a polygamous marriage, even as the Old Testament occasionally used the image of polygamy to signify the union of God and his people.[65] After all, Christ is one and the Church is a plurality.

In this connection, it is noteworthy that Thomas Aquinas also understood the sacramentality of marriage in such a way as to allow, at least theoretically, for a plurality of wives. In answering those who felt that "fidelity and the sacrament" could not possibly be maintained when one man is joined to several wives, Saint Thomas affirmed that "fidelity and the sacrament" were not entirely absent in a polygamous union. Although he was not dealing with a really practical and living question of polygamy in his time, the intriguing reply of Aquinas may cast some light on the case of the African polygamist who, because he has heard and believed the essential gospel message, wishes to be baptized and to participate in the Eucharist, without first having to violate the just and valid bonds previously established in good faith between himself and his wives. The words of Saint Thomas:

> Now the faith to be kept with God is of greater import than the faith to be kept with a wife, which is reckoned a marriage good, and than the signification which pertains to the sacrament, since the signification is subordinate to the knowledge of faith. Hence it is not unfitting if something is taken from the two for the sake of the good of offspring. Nor are they entirely done away, since there remains faith towards several wives; and the sacrament remains after a fashion, for though it did not signify the union of Christ with the Chruch as one, nevertheless the plurality of wives signified the distinction of degrees in the Church, which distinction is not only in the Church militant but also in the Church triumphant. Consequently their marriages signified somewhat the union of Christ not only with the Church militant, as some say, but also with the Church triumphant where there are *many mansions* (John 19:2).[66]

Finally, something must be said about the practical solutions worked out by missionaries and pastors in the field. Some, with little theological rationale to support them, simply defer the baptism of polygamous catechumens until they are very old or dying, while others deal with this whole problem in an even more negative manner: they avoid presenting the gospel to polygamists.

The policy of deferring the baptism of evangelized polygamists raises some questions immediately about the meaning and the purpose and the necessity of baptism. If baptism is the outward sign of grace and Christian faith, and not the sign of a particular legal observance, then Peter's question must be answered: "Can anyone forbid water for baptizing these people who have received the Holy Spirit just as we have?" (Acts 10:47). If baptism signifies membership in the historically present community of Christian witness, then what is signified by deferring baptism until one is very old or dying? Implied in this practice is a teaching, which nobody misses, that the polygamists, who are usually among the most respected members of African communities, are really unworthy of full acceptance into the Christian community —the fellowship of the saints.

What is really wrong with this half-way policy is that its point of departure is a law rather than the gospel or faith or the meaning of the sacrament of baptism itself; it leaves the evangelized polygamist in a quasi-Christian limbo which the missionaries themselves have invented as a device for safeguarding the law of monogamy. Moreover, since the leaven of the gospel becomes properly effective among a people only through their active participation in the sacramental life of the Church, and since growth in Christian perfection is supposed to be gradually achieved in the course of a person's whole life, it would seem to be theologically unsound to evangelize polygamists and then to prevent them from participating fully in the Christian fellowship. Such a compromise policy might almost amount to putting people in bad faith. Insistence upon law can nullify the grace of God (cf. Gal. 2:21).

Some missionaries and pastors have, therefore, found themselves practically avoiding the problem by not trying very hard to present the gospel to polygamists. Those wearing the wrong cultural garments are not invited into the Christian fellowship. But, on whose authority is such a decision made—that some persons ought not to hear the gospel message? How do we reconcile this with the final command of the risen Lord? Even before they have been approached by missionaries, the polygamists themselves are apt already to have received the message that admission into the Church depends on the law of monogamy no less than it depends of faith in Jesus Christ. Precisely because this legal condition is both intolerable and incomprehensible to them, polygamists find it hard to listen to the whole Christian message, so they are unable to respond fully to the call of Christ. Since the law of monogamy is often the first thing that people hear about Christianity, many do not care to hear any more. The message of Christian freedom does not liberate them, because it is presented equivocally under the burden of a law (cf. Acts 15:10–11).

FINAL CONCLUSIONS

After the manner of a cumulative argument, the numerous questions raised and the comments offered in the various parts of this

book point to the general conclusion that the traditional ecclesiastical discipline regarding African polygamy is not as well
founded, biblically and theologically, as has been supposed
heretofore. Since the available evidence indicates, moreover, that
this form of plural marriage still sustains important social values
in most African societies and that it will continue to be practiced
widely among African peoples in the foreseeable future, it would
be morally irresponsible for Church leaders and theologians to
simply ignore the missionary and pastoral implications of such a
problematical discipline. Now, with the theological reflections
presented in this chapter, even though every conceivable aspect
of the problem has not been touched upon, the way should be
clear for some new missionary and pastoral approaches, together
with some new theological initiatives.

At the present time, following the reasons given by the reputable theologians cited in this chapter, it should be possible to adopt
at least a new policy of toleration, along the lines already tested
by the Lutheran Church in Liberia. Persons who have previously
entered polygamous marriages, in good faith and according to
the socially accepted practice of their time and place in history,
should not be prevented from participating in the sacramental life
of the Church. As part of their normal instruction in the faith,
however, it should be made clear to them that no additional
polygamous marriages are permissible once they have entered
the Christian community through baptism. As the Lutherans in
Liberia have found, it is possible to safeguard and promote the
ideal of monogamy, as normative, while allowing people of good
will to remain in the polygamous condition in which they were at
the time of their calling to the new life of explicit Christian faith.

After some further study, discussion, and even debate by
competent scholars, a much more radical and positive and
catholic solution might very well emerge: a solution that accepts,
as they are in the real world—not just individual persons of good
will—but also their established socio-economic institutions and
their varied cultural ideals. Indeed, such a solution seems already
contained, at least implicitly, in the contemporary rethinking of
moral theology by men like Josef Fuchs and Denis O'Callaghan,
who urge upon us the importance of seeking answers to moral

questions, not through a series of impersonal and nonhistorical logical inferences, but through insight and understanding, and by first looking to see what authentic human values are supported, or undermined, by the particular social institution under consideration.[67]

Such an approach is possible only for those who have abandoned the classicist view that one culture alone—that of Western man—is universally normative for the whole of humanity.[68] In order to become truly catholic, the Church needs, and is just now beginning to take seriously, all the cultural riches of the peoples who constitute humanity in the extension of different historical times and places and cultural experiences. Marriage, after all, is a pre-Christian social institution universally experienced in a great variety of cultural forms. Most human beings do not live in the Western world and must, therefore, experience and conceptualize and structure marriage in the ways of their respective cultures.

Once we recognize that these non-Western cultural patterns are not less valid than our Western patterns, then we are hard put to prove that the Western concept of marriage, although profoundly influenced by the leaven of the gospel and canonized by the Church in the West, must be taken as the universally absolute ideal or norm for Christians everywhere. "Similar rules for marriage and family in one case generate bliss and in another misery," says Bernard Lonergan who further elaborates the point in these words:

> The family, the state, the law, the economy are not fixed and immutable entities. They adapt to changing circumstances: they can be subjected to revolutionary change. But all such change involves change of meaning—a change of idea or concept, a change of judgment or evaluation, a change of the order or request."[69]

If the historicity and the cultural embeddedness of man are constitutents of human nature, then theologians must make allowances not only for vast changes, but also for great diversity, in the conceptualization and structuring of marriage and family life. Natural law moralizing, in other words, must take account of the necessity and the validity of the varied historico-cultural ways of human existence.[70] This contemporary understanding of the natural law, with particular reference to the variations in the man-woman relationship, is set forth by Fuchs in these terms:

> The true question is one of the natural law. For in different conditions of man and woman, including social conditions, different principles have to be applied. For instance, there are continuous changes in the world of man in regard to the concept of woman's role in society, changes that reflect a different estimation of the relationship between man and woman.
>
> Likewise, social conditions might legitimate a certain way of choosing a marriage partner in certain periods or countries; whereas other social conditions would not so easily allow for the same way of choosing a partner at other times or in other conditions.
>
> Perhaps for many questions there could be, theoretically, an ideal solution. But this ideal solution could be applied to ideal conditions only when they are actualities in a certain time or a certain culture. And if these particular conditions are not realized, then neither could this ideal solution be realized.[71]

So it is still an open question—deserving far more theological attention than it has so far received—whether the marriage institution, canonized by the Church in the West, is in fact only a product of the Western historico-cultural experience and is not, therefore, a universally normative ideal to which the marriages of Christians in the non-Western world must conform: "whether marriage," in the concrete terms used by Fuchs, "is to be understood and lived according to the Congolese or Western Euopean style."[72]

The purpose of these final proposals, and indeed of this whole study, would be badly misconstrued, if they were taken merely as an argument for ignoring the appropriate ecclesiastical authorities and violating the existing ecclesiastical discipline regarding polygamy in Africa. We are, indeed, arguing for change—but only for change which is consequent upon research, reflection, and deliberation by the responsible Church leaders. This kind of change, even in the realm of morality and doctrine, was envisaged by the fathers of Vatical II and encouraged by them.[73] These proposals may, therefore, be seen as a partial contribution to a contemporary theological discussion: a discussion which can no longer be avoided with impunity.

NOTES

1. Augustine, "Contra Faustum Manichaeum," lib. xxii, c. 47, in P.L. 42, col. 428. English translation from *A Selected Library of Nicene and Post-Nicene Fathers of the Christian Church*, ed. Philip Schaff and others, (Grand Rapids, Mich.: William B. Eerdmans, 1956), IV, p. 289.

2. Augustine, "De bono conjugali," lib. i, c. 20 P.L. 40, col. 387). English translation from *A Selected Library of Nicene and Post-Nicene Fathers of the Christian Church*, III, pp. 407–408.

3. Thomas Aquinas, *Summa Theologiae*, Suppl., q. 65, art. 1, respond., ad 7 and 8.

4. *Ibid.*, art. 2, respond. English translation from *Summa Theologica, Literally Translated by the Fathers of the English Dominican Province* (New York: Benziger 1948). See Bruno Schüller, "What Ethical Principles Are Universally Valid?", *Theology Digest* 19 (Spring 1971) 25, 26: "Rather lame reliance has been placed on the 'presumption of a general danger,' whereby polygamy is forbidden absolutely because in most cases it is bad. . . . Why did the theologians never proclaim that the death-penalty could *never* be used, when in fact tyrants so universally misused it?"

5. Thomas Aquinas, *Summa Theologiae*, Suppl., q. 65, art. 2.

6. *Ibid.* For the discussion of this point with regard to the indissolubility rule, see Liam Ryan, "The Indissolubility of Marriage in Natural Law," *Irish Theological Quarterly* 30 (1963) 293–310; and 31 (1964) 62–70, especially pp. 67–68.

7. See Innocent III, quotation from his letter *Gaudemus in Domino*, to the Bishop of Tiberius, in Denzinger, *The Sources of Catholic Dogma*, no. 408, p. 159. See also Denis O'Callaghan, "Theology and Divorce," *Irish Theological Quarterly* 37 (July 1970) 216: "The incidence of polygamy and divorce in the Old Testament made this question very real for St. Thomas. Here, of course, he had the *Deus ex machina* of divine dispensation, the plea that God had dispensed the Patriarchs from the laws of monogamy and indissolubility. But he does seem to use dispensation in a wide sense, not just of an explicit inspiration but of a legitimate interpretation of the facts of the case." See also Schüller, "What ethical Principles Are Universally Valid?" p. 25: "Even sharply-defined cases of the traditional unconditioned prohibition, like marriage with one's sister, polygamy, suicide, murder, were embarrassingly known to have had their exceptions commanded by God in the OT. This is still ex-

plained in manuals as a kind of eminent domain: like the capricious oriental potentate, God can do anything he wants. As exegesis, this is today recognized as pathetic."

8. Thomas Aquinas, *Summa Theologiae*, Suppl., q. 65, art. 2, respond., and also ad 3: "Since the law of nature is imprinted on the heart, it was not necessary for a dispensation from things pertaining to the natural law to be given under the form of a written law, but by internal inspiration." English translation, as cited in note 4, above. See the discussion of this by Ryan, "Indissolubility of Marriage," pp. 67–69.

9. For the names of these theologians, see George H. Joyce, *Christian Marriage: An Historical and Doctrinal Study* (London: Sheed and Ward, 1948), pp. 568–569. For the views of Cardinal Cajetan, Martin Luther, and Philip Melanchthon, the most famous of these theologians, see the Appendix: "Polygamy and the Council of Trent."

10. See Joyce, *Christian Marriage*, pp. 569–572.

11. Timothy L. Bouscaren and A.C. Ellis, *Canon Law: A Text and Commentary* (Milwaukee: Bruce, 1957), p. 448.

12. R.J. Levis, "Marriage (Theology of): The Ends of Marriage," in *New Catholic Encyclopedia* (New York, London, Toronto, Sydney: McGraw-Hill 1969), IX, p. 270. "There is a further reason why polygamy is unnatural. Since there are approximately equal numbers of males and females that survive to adulthood, many men would be forced to remain unmarried because others would already have taken all the available women." This kind of theorizing is possible only when the available sociological data, already presented in Chapters Three and Four, is ignored.

13. A polygamous family may normally expect to have more children than a monogamous family, although polygamous societies do not normally have a greater birth rate than monogamous societies. For more on this, see Chapter Three.

14. Bernard Häring, "Magisterium and Natural Law," *American Journal of Jurisprudence* 14 (1969), p. 95. See also Häring's *Theology of Protest* (New York: Farrar, Straus and Giroux, 1970), p. 142: "Our ethics has not made clear that the proclamation of the Gospel and the joy-giving moral message to other people and to other social classes and other cultures presupposes first of all readiness to listen to these people and to appreciate their culture. We remained unable to say this because we moralists were also infected with this sense of superiority of our European or national culture."

15. Josef Fuchs, "The Absoluteness of Moral Norms," *Gregorianum* 52 (1971) 431, 439, and 453: "In this case [concerning operative norms of action] to defend as a theoretical possibility the complete universality

of ethical statements—perhaps on the basis of an *a priori* metaphysical understanding of determined actions—is to succumb to the utopia of rationalism."

16. Thomas Aquinas, *Summa Theologiae*, Suppl., q. 52, art. 1, ad 2 and 3; and art. 3, respond.: "The positive law arises out of the natural law, and consequently slavery, which is of positive law, cannot be prejudicious to those things that are of natural law." See also I-II, q. 94, art 5, ad 3; and II-II, q. 57, art. 3, ad 2: "Considered absolutely, the fact that this particular man should be a slave rather than another man, is based not on natural reason, but on some resultant utility, in that it is useful to this man to be ruled by a wiser man, and to the latter to be helped by the former. . . . Wherefore, slavery which belongs to the right of nations is natural in the second way but not in the first." English translation, as cited in Note 4, above.

17. Reinhold Niebuhr, *Moral Man and Immoral Society* (New York: Charles Scribner's Sons, 1959), p. 77. See also Karl Kautsky, *Foundations of Christianity*, trans. Henry F. Mins (New York: Russell and Russell, 1953), pp. 122–124. The decline of Roman slavery, according to Kautsky, was not due to Christian moral sensitivity, but to changing socio-economic conditions. It may, however, be assumed that Christianity, wherever it was authentically lived, made for a more humane treatment of slaves. The fact that Christians were not an organized opposition to slavery in all of its historical manifestations can be explained only in terms of the historico-cultural conditions of the various times and places. So it is not for us to reproach the men of different times and places for what now appears to be their lack of moral sensitivity. Rather, this retrospective reflection should suggest our own need to search ourselves with reference to contemporary moral issues.

18. The Bishop of London, as quoted by H.Richard Niebuhr, *The Social Sources of Denominationalism* (Cleveland and New York: World, 1957), p. 249.

19. See John England's several long letters to John Forsyth, United States Secretary of State, in *The Works of John England,* ed. Sebastian G. Messmer (Cleveland: Arthur H. Clark Co., 1908), V. In this extraordinary defence of domestic slavery we are told on page 195 that "slavery . . . is regarded by the church of which the Pope is the presiding officer not to be incompatible with the natural law, to be the result of sin by divine dispensation, to have been established by human legislation, and when the dominion of the slave is justly acquired by the master to be lawful, not only in the sight of the human tribunal but also in the eye of Heaven."

20. Instruction of the Sacred Congregation of the Holy Office, June 20,

1866, to Guillelmus Massaia, Vicar Apostolic among the Galla people, in *Collectanea S. Congregationis De Propaganda Fide* (Rome, 1907), I, p. 719. On the general failure of Christians regarding slavery, see John T. Noonan, Jr. "Making One's Own Act Another's" in *The Catholic Theological Society of America: Proceedings of the 27th Annual Convention* 27 (1972) 32–35: as quoted in our Chapter Two, Notes 6 and 66). See also the extensive biblical and theological arguments presented by Bishop John England in defence of slavery in the United States, *Works*, V, p. 194: "The existence of slavery is considered by our theologians to be as little incompatible with the natural law as is the existence of property. The sole question will be in each case, whether the title on which the dominion is claimed be valid."

21. In the course of the Church's history a number of prophetical voices were indeed raised against slavery; so there is much more to be said on the question of the Christian attitude toward slavery. What we are concerned with here is merely the voices of the "approved theologians and commentators on the sacred canons." For more on all of this, see Augustin Cochin, "L'Abolition de l'Esclavage" (Paris: 1861); *The Results of Slavery*, trans. M.L. Booth (Boston: Walker, Wise and Company, 1863), x+413 pp. Also, among the minority who opposed the views of the "approved authors," was Theodor Meyer, *Institutiones Juris Naturalis* (Freiburg im Breisgau, 1885–1900), II, n. 123 (5).

22. Vittorio Bartoccetti, "Polygamy," in *Dictionary of Moral Theology*, comp. and ed. Franceso Roberti and Pietro Palazzini, trans. H.J. Yannone (Westminister, Md: Newman Press, 1962), p. 921.

23. Marc Oraison, *Learning to Love*, trans. André Humbert (New York: Hawthorn Books, 1955), p. 112.

24. Ignace Lepp, *The Psychology of Loving*, trans. Bernard G. Gilligan (Baltimore: Helicon Press, 1963),pp. 202–203.

25. See Helmut Thielicke, *The Ethics of Sex*, trans. John W. Doberstein (New York: Harper and Row, 1964), pp. 79–98.

26. *Ibid.*, p. 89.

27. Bernard Häring, *Marriage in the Modern World* (Westminster, Md.: Newman Press, 1965), p. 258.

28. *Ibid.*, p. 262.

29. Otto Piper, *The Biblical View of Sex and Marriage*, (New York: Charles Scribner's Sons, 1960), p. 149.

30. O'Callaghan, "Theology and Divorce," p. 215.

31. Manas Buthelezi, "Polygyny in the Light of the New Testament," *Africa Theological Journal* 1 (February 1969), p. 64.

32. See Robert Hughes and others, "The American Family: Future

Uncertain," *Time*, December 28, 1970, pp. 40–45. For some relevant quotations from this article, see Notes 18 and 19 in Chapter Four.

33. Leonhard M. Weber, *On Marriage, Sex and Virginity*, trans. R. Brennan (Freiburg: Herder, 1966), p. 33.

34. *Ibid.*, p. 44.

35. See Note 21, above.

36. G.E. Currens and R.J. Payne, "An Evaluation of the Policy of the Lutheran Church in Liberia on the Baptism of Polygamists," Monrovia, June 1965 (Mimeographed), pp. 2 and 3.

37. *Ibid.*, pp. 2, 3, 4, 6, 7.

38. For a brief explanation of the meaning of scandal, see Karl Rahner and Herbert Vorgrimler, *Theological Dictionary*, ed. Cornelius Ernst, trans. Richard Strachan (New York: Herder and Herder, 1965), p. 426: "Scandal may lie in the person taking offense, that is if a certain action is good in itself but becomes an occasion of sin (scandal) to someone either lacking in judgment and humility (pharisaic scandal) or spiritually immature and of weak character (scandal of the weak). There is no reason to avoid pharisaic scandal, but scandal of the weak should be avoided as far as practicable. . . . In certain circumstances scandal may be tolerated."

39. *Ibid.*, p. 137, for a brief explanation of what is meant by the principle of double effect.

40. *Ibid.*, pp. 309–310, for a brief explanation of the sense in which the sacraments may be considered necessary for the salvation of believers.

41. Lesslie Newbigin, *Honest Religion for Secular Man* (London: SCM Press, 1966), p. 74.

42. *Ibid.*

43. See *Ibid.*, p. 73: "After all, the primitive Church did not attack slavery outright. Paul did not tell Philemon that he could not remain a Christian while he kept Onesimus as a slave. It took many centuries for the Church to see that slavery was intolerable for the Christian conscience. But the question of polygamy was different: that required a decision now." See also Bishop John England, *Works*, V, especially p. 191, where he says that "among the most pious and religious" of the Roman Catholic flock in the Southern States, "are large slaveholders, who are most exact in performing all their Christian duties, and who frequently receive the sacraments."

44. Jacques Zeiller, in *The History of the Primitive Church*, by Jules Lebreton and others, trans. Ernest C. Messenger (New York and London, 1942–1947) I, Bk. 2, p. 510. See also the editor's footnote 30, in *The Works of John England*, V, p. 187: "When slavery presents itself as an existing fact which can be removed only at the great disadvantage of the

slaves and to the detriment of the government, then the Pope declares existing conditions must be tolerated and the slaves held to practice patience and forbearance."

45. Charles E. Curran, "Methodological and Ecclesiological Questions in Moral Theology," *Chicago Studies* 9 (Spring 1970) p. 60.

46. *Ibid.*, p. 61. See also O.'Callaghan, "Theology and Divorce," pp. 214–215: "Moral responsibility means taking account of all the factors of moral significance in a given situation. . . . Responsible moral decisions will sometimes be unable to safeguard all the values—one value may have to be subordinated to another. . . . The values to be taken into account are—the welfare of children (their maintenance, education, happiness, and security); the welfare of the partners (support in prosperity and adversity, security in old age, the living-out of the life-long surrender which their love demands); the welfare of the community (certainly of parenthood or legitimacy where children are concerned, harmony in personal and sexual relationships which a stable institution of marriage secures, the guarantee of equality to all citizens, and concern that the old and the weak are not exploited). In making a judgement on the pattern of marriage one is not confining oneself to the situation of any individual family-unit; one is dealing with an institution in society and so the repercussions of decisions go far beyond the individual case. . . . Only as society develops, the emancipation of woman proceeds and as wider possibilities come into being in their way of life will the monogamous structure become of proximate obligaton, as the structure which achieves the human values which are now realizable for them. A change in the human situation comes before and conditions a change in structure. . . . In primitive tribes one might see polygamy as a more acceptable way of avoiding the hardships which would be caused by divorce. At least the wife and her children are guaranteed security and, where the plural household is an accepted pattern, discord and jealousy are not as great as one would expect."

47. Thomas Aquinas, *Summa Theologiae*, I-II, q. 106, art. 3. English translation from work cited in Note 4, above.

48. *Ibid.*, q. 96, art. 2: "And in like manner many things are permissible to men not perfect in virtue which would be intolerable in a virtuous man."

49. Thielicke, *The Ethics of Sex*, p. 180.

50. *Ibid.*, p. 181.

51. *Ibid.*, pp. 181–182.

52. Karl Barth, *Church Dogmatics*, III-4, ed. G.W. Bromley, trans. G.T. Thompson and H. Knight (Edinburgh: T.&T. Clark, 1961), p. 203.

53. *Ibid.*

54. Louis Buijs, "Polygamy" (paper presented to a group of missionaries at Generalate of Verona Fathers in Rome, April 1967), trans. from Italian by R. Cefalo (typewritten), p. 2: "Any marriage system is intimately connected with a socio-economic system. In the underdeveloped countries, and throughout ancient times, there has never been a place in society for a woman alone: there are no jobs which a woman can do, so she cannot earn a living by herself. Every woman in such a society must be married. For many women in such a society polygamy is a good institution rather than something evil. It is far better to be a second or a third wife than to have no husband at all."

55. *Ibid.*, p. 6.

56. *Ibid.*, pp. 5–56.

57. Fuchs, "The Absoluteness of Moral Terms," p. 423: "The materiality of culturally and ethically right mastery of the concrete reality of life—education, economy, technology, sexuality, etc.—are not directly concerned with salvation, or union with God; only faith and love, *together with the effort* to incarnate this materiality in the 'true' way in the reality of life are concerned. That the material mode of this incarnation can represent only a *secondarium*, already makes it reasonable that within certain limits moral pluralism might well be possible. If, for example, faith and love have to be expressed in the maintenance of the 'right' social position of women, then the concrete expression in the Pauline conception and in the twentieth-century Western European conceptions must [!] be regarded as necessarily differing from each other."

58. *Ibid.*, pp. 437–438. See also, John T. Noonan, Jr., "History and the Values of Christian Marriage," in *Marriage in the Light of Vatican II*, ed. James T. McHugh (Washington, D. C.: Family Life Bureau, 1968) p. 20; and Liam Ryan "The Indissolubility of Marriage," pp. 74–75.

59. Fuchs, "The Absoluteness of Moral Terms," pp. 438–439.

60. *Ibid.*, p. 439.

61. O'Callaghan, "Theology and Divorce," p. 215.

62. *Ibid.*, pp. 213–214.

63. *Ibid.*, p. 215.

64. Professor Morgenroth of Duquesne University in Pittsburgh suggested this to me during a conversation in December 1971.

65. See the last four paragraphs of Chapter Six and also Schüller, "What Ethical Principles Are Universally Valid?", p. 27: "Presumably those who argue from the parallel of marriage to the union of Christ with his Church are forgetting what kind of shattered marriage they are concretely here talking about."

66. Thomas Aquinas, *Summa Theologiae*, Suppl., q. 65, art. 2· ad 5. English translation from work cited in Note 4, above.

67. See Fuchs and O'Callaghan, as cited in this chapter and in the Introduction.

68. See Bernard Lonergan, *Method in Theology* (New York: Herder and Herder,1972), especially pp. 49–51, 78–81, 123–124, 240, 268, 300–302, 326–329; and "Revolution in Catholic Theology," *The Catholic Theological Society of America: Proceedings of the 27th Annual Convention* 27 (1972) 20: "There are not a few writers who assert that the normative view of culture and the universal uniformity it implies derive from Greek thought. . . . A more exact understanding of the normative approach is to be had by turning from the Greek philosophers to the humanists, the orators, the school-teachers, to the men who simplified and watered down philosophic thought and then peddled it to give the slow-witted an exaggerated opinion of their wisdom and knowledge. After all, from a contemporary viewpoint it seems an incredible conceit to suppose that one's own culture is the one and only uniform and universal culture."

69. Lonergan, *Method in Theology,* pp. 49 and 78.

70. Lonergan, "Revolution in Catholic Theology," p. 19: "Cultures are many and varied: they all have their good points and their deficiencies; and the ideal culture is far far rarer than the ideal man. To grasp the empirical notion of culture leads to a grasp of what is meant by a person's historicity. . . . It is the culture as it is historically available that provides the matrix within which persons develop and that supplies the meaning and the values that inform their lives. People cannot help being people of their age, and that mark of time upon them is their historicity."

71. Fuchs, "Theology of the Meaning of Marriage Today," in *Marriage in the Light of Vatican II,* p. 17.

72. See *Ibid.,* p. 20; and Fuchs, "The Absoluteness of Moral Terms," p. 423.

73. See Vatican II, as cited in the Introduction.

APPENDIX

POLYGAMY AND
THE COUNCIL OF TRENT

The safest course for the King [Henry VIII
of England] *is to take a second wife,
while not sending away the first one.*

PHILIP MELANCHTHON

It is the consistent teaching of Roman Catholic officialdom that
polygamy is incompatible with the Christian way of life.[1] Here I
will examine what is generally regarded as the strongest, clearest,
and most definitive of the Church's statements against simultaneous polygamy. This is found in the teaching of the Council of
Trent on the sacrament of matrimony, particularly in the second
canon of the twenty-fourth session of the Council. This is the one
authoritative source most frequently cited by Roman Catholic
theologians and canonists whenever any question arises concerning polygamy; so it may be regarded as their principal argument
from authority or the most representative statement on the matter by the ecclesiastical magisterium.[2] Even Pope Pius XI, in the
Encyclical Letter *Casti Cannubii* (December 31, 1930), cites only
this Council as evidence that "two persons only are to be united
and joined together" in Christian matrimony.[3]

The Council of Trent officially took up the question of simultaneous polygamy on four occasions. Twice it was discussed by a
group of the Council's theologians and twice by the Council
Fathers themselves. A consensus having been previously

reached and some slight modifications having been made on the proposed statement, a final vote was taken in the "solemn session" of November 11, 1563. The Council's opinion, unanimously agreed upon, was formulated thus:

> If anyone says that it is lawful for Christians to have several wives at the same time, and that it is not forbidden by any divine law (Matt. 19:4f): let him be anathema.[4]

The particular question before us, therefore, is this: Are Roman Catholics justified in affirming, without more ado, that the missionary and pastoral problem of African plural marriage was settled, once and for all, some four hundred years ago by the Council of Trent? Is there nothing more to be said?

THE NEED FOR A HERMENEUTICAL APPROACH

At first glance it would, indeed, seem that there is nothing more to be said. For many moralists these words of Trent are so "obvious" in their meaning that there is no need for any further discussion. "Why," asks Piet Fransen, "should theologians be forced to engage in studies which are often very difficult and yet completely useless, since the 'obvious sense' of a text ought to be amply sufficient for the correct reading of a conciliar text?"[5] To this question Fransen himself immediately replies that "there is nothing less certain than the 'obvious sense' of a text. . . . There is no 'obvious sense' apart from a context of thought." To this may be added the slightly polemical but very pertinent remark of Edward Schillebeeckx:

> Authentic orthodoxy is seldom to be found in those who simply repeat what has already been said, with Denzinger in their hands as material to prove their point.[6]

Trent's seventh canon on marriage (dealing with divorce) provides a good example of the difficulties involved in the task of correctly interpreting a conciliar text. This canon has often been understood in a sense "exactly opposite to that intended by the Council of Trent."[7] Thanks, however, to the careful scholarship of men like Fransen, we know now that it would be quite wrong to see in this conciliar text a condemnation of the opposite practice of the Greeks (who traditionally allow divorce on the ground of adultery).[8] Yet, such a condemnation is "obviously" contained in the words of the canon when these words are considered apart from their historical context. Such misunderstandings are inevitable when history is not taken seriously. In the words of Schillebeeckx:

> The answer to questions asked in the thirteenth or the sixteenth century—in other words, the literal repetition of unambiguously dogmatic definitions, such as those of Trent—is not an answer to our contemporary problems in which we are trying to come to an understanding of faith. Without the *Tridentine* answer to *my question now*, I shall not understand what Trent means . . . Anyone who maintains—as some do—that Trent, because it is formulating a dogma, is, in what it explicitly says (*das Gesagte*), *a priori* an answer to my present-day question is radically misconceiving the historicity of man's existence, of human questioning, and of human understanding.[9]

A recognition of the fact that the documents of the magisterium are historically conditioned and culturally formed renders it impossible to maintain some of the facile interpretations that have been accepted in the past, and regarded as somehow transhistorically comprehensive or absolute.[10] What is called for now, according to Yves Congar, is "an entire historical hermeneutic . . . in relation to conciliar documents."[11] Again, the comments of Schillebeeckx are very much to the point:

> A text is a document, the real meaning of which can only be understood beyond its literal meaning because it tells us about something, a "matter", which we too are trying to understand and about which we ask questions in the light of our present day experience. . . . The magisterial statement may in certain cases (according to the subtle distinctions of the First Vatican Council) even be infallible, but the important point is to know precisely what (maybe in an infallible way) is said to me in that statement. *What* precisely is expressed and to what can we and may we bind ourselves in obedience to faith? The fact is that whole volumes of commentary have to be written in order to establish what the Council of Trent, for example, meant."[12]

To date there has been no critical study of Trent's teaching on simultaneous polygamy. What is offered in these pages, therefore, is merely an initial effort to open up for further discussion a question that had previously seemed closed because of the "obvious sense" of the particular conciliar text. Since the canon on polygamy is formulated in rather sweeping terms, it is a matter of some importance—if we wish to understand the intention of the Council Fathers and, thus, the authentic meaning of their teaching on this point—to examine this proposition in its own proper historical context.[13] This means especially that we must try to see the question as it was understood and discussed by theologians in the sixteenth century, and with particular reference to the precisely limited aims of the Council of Trent. This means, also, that we must take a closer look at the connotations of certain technical terms used in the canon on polygamy, with a view to ascertaining whether these terms still convey the same meaning today.

THE HISTORICAL CONTEXT

In April of 1547 a group of the Council's theologians passed judgment on certain positions taken by the Reformers regarding the sacraments of last anointing, holy orders, and matrimony. Here, and in subsequent conciliar discussions on marriage, the main concern was not with the question of polygamy. Indeed, this seems to have been one of the least important matters on the agenda. Even the question of marital indissolubility was given less attention than such things as clerical celibacy, the authority of the Church in marriage cases, and clandestine marriage. It was only on this last issue that any important divergence of opinion was expressed in all of the conciliar deliberations on matrimony. From the record of the first theological discussion on marriage, as also from the work of the theologians who reviewed all of the same propositions again in February of 1563, it appears that this sacrament was considered only in relation to certain positions taken by the Reformers. Polygamy, at the Council of Trent, was considered only within this limited frame of reference.[14]

Some of the Anabaptists—those in Münster—permitted plural marriage in the style of the Old Testament; and, in a much more restricted sense, so did Martin Luther, Philip Melanchthon, and

Martin Bucer. These three, together with a few others, had cautiously but clearly set forth their position in writing; and the Council focused its attention precisely on their words. Already, in his letter of August 1531 to King Henry VIII of England, Melanchthon had expressed his opinion in these terms:

> But what is to be done, if the public welfare renders a new marriage advisable for the sake of the succession, as is the case with the King of England, where the public welfare of the whole kingdom renders a new marriage advisable? Here I reply: if the King wishes to provide for the succession, it is much better to do this without any stigma on the previous marriage. And this can be done, without any danger to the conscience or reputation of anyone, through polygamy. . . . So I hold that the safest course for the King is the first one; for it is certain that polygamy is not forbidden by divine law (*quia certum est polygamiam non esse prohibitam iure divino*), nor is it a thing altogether without precedent. Abraham, David, and other holy men had several wives; hence it is obvious that polygamy is not against divine law (*unde apparet polygamiam non esse contra ius divinum*).[15]

The argument from precedent was further developed in the same letter by pointing out that the Emperor Valentinus legalized simultaneous polygamy, practiced it himself, and thereby obtained his successor—Theodosius. Moreover, Melanchthon noted that popes in former times had granted such permission; and so the present pope could give the same permission to King Henry. The letter concluded with the affirmation that, even without a papal dispensation, the King may by his own right take a second wife, while retaining the first one.

This opinion of the Reformers, whose antipapal rhetoric doubtless caused as much concern as what they actually said, was reiterated eight years later in the form of a pastoral solution to the marital problem of Philip the Landgrave of Hesse. In their letter to Philip, dated December 10, 1539 and signed by seven others besides themselves, Luther and Melanchthon were a little more circumspect.[16] In a lengthy preamble they reaffirmed their belief that monogamy was the normal form of Christian marriage. They were in no sense proposing that polygamy should become a generally accepted practice or norm. They understood "how grievous it would be, if it were charged upon anyone that he had introduced this law into the German nation" where monogamy had been traditional and normative for centuries.[17] Elsewhere, Luther points out the great importance of respecting the historico-cultural significance of monogamy among the Germanic peoples:

> Such a thing (polygamy) is out of order among us, since a man is permitted to have only one wife. This is why Moses' law cannot be valid simply and completely in all respects with us. We have to take into consideration the character and the ways of our land when we want to make or apply laws and rules, because our rules and laws are based on the character of our land and its ways and not on those of the land of Moses, just as Moses' laws are based on the ways and character of his people and not those of ours.[18]

Polygamy, in the view of the Reformers, was to be seen as a solution to marital problems only in rare and exceptional cases and as a dispensation from the general law of monogamy, which was not binding absolutely, always, and under all circumstances. For the Christian gospel neither revoked nor prohibited what the law of Moses permitted with respect to marriage.[19] Besides, the aim of Christianity is not to change outward rules and structures of society, but rather to introduce into daily life the perspective and the leaven of faith.[20]

This teaching of the Reformers would not have been regarded by their contemporaries as a theological novelty, although it was certainly a minority opinion. Other theologians, whose orthodoxy (and loyalty to Rome) were never called into question, had considered the problem of simultaneous polygamy along very similar lines. For centuries the polygamy of the Old Testament patriarchs had been discussed and debated academically, especially by the scholastic theologians and canonists in their treatments of marriage and natural law.[21] According to William Durandus, writing at the beginning of the fourteenth century, there were some theologians who maintained that in certain emergency cases the pope could give a dispensation for the practice of polygamy; but Durandus did not mention their names.[22] However, we do know that there were at least two highly respected scholars who expressed views very much like those of the Reformers.

In 1328 Gerard Odonis, a professor of moral theology at the University of Paris and later "Master General" in the Order of Friars Minor, proposed that simultaneous polygamy might be an acceptable solution for a husband who wished to divorce his adulterous wife and to marry another woman.[23] This solution was offered as an alternative to divorce and remarriage (consecutive polygamy) which the Lord had explicitly forbidden, while never even mentioning simultaneous polygamy. According to Odonis, the unity of matrimony is not based on natural law. Indeed, he saw polygamy as something arising from nature itself in man's present fallen condition. Nor is the unity of matrimony based on any divine law of the New Testament, much less the Old Testament. So Odonis concluded that, since this is merely a matter of man-made law, the pope can give a dispensation for the practice of polygamy.

And there was also Thomas de Vio, better known as Cardinal Cajetan (1469–1534). This most famous of the many commentators on the works of Thomas Aquinas was an advisor to four popes and a major figure in Rome's dealings with Martin Luther. Cajetan's opinion on simultaneous polygamy, unlike that of the Reformers, was not singled out and condemned by the Council of Trent; yet he taught, just as the Reformers did, that this Old Testament form of marriage is neither contrary to natural law nor forbidden in Scripture.[24] In support of his viewpoint, Cajetan points to this passage from Saint Augustine's reply to Faustus:

> For a plurality of wives was no crime when it was the custom; and it is a crime now because it is no longer the custom. . . . This was the common practice at that time in those countries. . . . The only reason of its being a crime now to do this is because custom and laws forbid it. . . . In the present state of altered customs and laws, men can have no pleasure in a plurality of wives, except from an excess of lust; and so the mistake arises of supposing that no one could ever have had many wives but from sensuality and the vehemence of sinful desires. Unable to form an idea of men whose force of mind is beyond their conception, they compare themselves with themselves, as the apostle says (2 Cor. 10:12), and so make mistakes.[25]

In his commentaries on Genesis and Leviticus, Cajetan says without any qualification that "having a plurality of wives is not against the law of nature."[26] As for the divine prohibition which others had found in the New Testament against polygamy, he says in his commentary on Mark that "a law concerning one wife is nowhere written in the canonical books."[27] Regarding the "one wife" passages of the Pastoral Epistles, Cajetan remarks that the author of the first epistle to Timothy mentioned this "because at the time many men, imitating the Fathers of the Old Testament, had plural wives: since we see nowhere that this is forbidden."[28] Nevertheless, Cajetan recognized that the law of monogamy was well founded in ecclesiastical law; and so it was to be maintained. He was certainly not suggesting, any more than were Luther and Melanchthon, that polygamy should be accepted as a general practice among the peoples of Europe.

Although Cajetan's available works contain no explicit mention of this, it would certainly be consistent with his position to regard the pope as having the power to dispense a husband from the law of monogamy so that he could take another wife while also retaining the first one. If we recall the significance of royalty in those days and how political stability and economic security depended largely upon continuity in royal families, it is understandable that simultaneous polygamy should have been considered as a possible solution in the event of a royal wife failing to provide the kingdom with a suitable heir. Since Cajetan was the most eminent of the pope's theological advisors, it is probable that he would have proposed just such a solution to the problem raised by King Henry VIII in his anxiety for a male heir.[29] According to Henry's agents in Rome, Pope Clement VII himself mentioned that a solution might possibly be found through the practice of simultaneous polygamy, and that "a great theologian" had advised the granting of a papal dispensation for this purpose, and to avoid a greater evil. It is certain from the evidence that the pope actually did consider this possibility.[30] Other notable persons at the time, such as the King of France, suggested this same solution.[31] And so did Desiderius Erasmus, proffering his opinion in these words:

> Far be it from me to mix in the affair of Jupiter and Juno, particularly as I know little about it. But I should prefer that he should take two Junos rather than put away one.[32]

As we know, this advice was not followed—doubtless because, according to the more common opinion of theologians and canonists at that time, the pope did not have the power to grant such a dispensation.[33] Indeed, it was believed then that such a dispensation could be granted only through a divine revelation. This more common opinion, which Cajetan did not share, drew its support largely from the authority of a letter written by Pope Innocent III, at the beginning of 1201, to the Bishop of Tiberius. Here the Pope said, "It is never permitted to anyone to have several wives at the same time, except to whom it was granted by divine revelation."[34] Not only did Cajetan take exception to Innocent's point on the necessity of a "divine revelation" for the practice of polygamy, but he argued further that the Pope's whole line of reasoning was erroneous. This, according to Cajetan, was just one of those mistakes that Roman Pontiffs sometimes make in their judgments concerning marriage.[35]

Innocent III, in this much quoted letter, was answering a question about polygamy in a missionary situation. Since the Fathers and theologians of Trent based themselves explicitly upon the arguments contained in this letter and, hence, their own theological reflections on polygamy did not really go beyond the content of this letter, the relevant passages are here presented:

> But since pagans divide their conjugal affection among many women at the same time, it is rightly doubted whether after conversion all or which one of all they can retain. But this [practice] seems to be in disagreement with and inimical to the Christian faith, since in the beginning one rib was changed into one woman, and Divine Scripture testifies that "on account of this, man shall leave father and mother and shall cling to his wife and they shall be two in one flesh" (Eph. 5:31; Gen. 2:24; cf. Matt. 19:5); it does not say "three or more" but *two*; nor did it say "he will cling to wives" but *to a wife*. Never is it permitted to anyone to have several wives at the same time except to whom it was granted by divine revelation. . . .
>
> Certainly this opinion is proved to be true also by the witness of Truth, which testifies in the Gospel: "Whosoever puts away his wife (except) on account of fornication, and marries another commits adultery" (Matt. 19:9; cf. Mark 10:11). If, therefore, when the wife has been dismissed, another cannot be married according to the

law, all the more she herself cannot be retained; through this it
clearly appears that, regarding marriage, plurality in either sex
—since they are not judged unequally—must be condemned.[36]

Although Trent followed the biblical exegesis and the theological
method of Innocent III, the conciliar records show no signs of any
discussion of polygamy with reference to the Church's missionary outreach to the peoples living beyond the cultural sphere of
Western Christendom.[37] In those days the missionary aspects of
the question were already being dealt with under the "privilege
of the faith" regulations of the constitution *Altitudo*, issued by
Pope Paul III in 1537.[38] The aim of the Council, in any case, was
not to solve missionary problems. It was rather a matter of dealing with a variety of concrete and urgent problems among the
Christians in Europe; and many of these problems hinged on the
more basic issue between Trent and the Reformers: the Church's
authority to legislate in a manner that was binding in
conscience.[39] According to Carl Peter, therefore, "no effort was
made to treat all aspects, even important ones, of a doctrine."[40]
As Hubert Jedin puts it: "The Council restricted itself to meeting
the needs of the moment."[41]

The formal teachings of Trent are set forth as definitions in the
canons; and these, as Fransen has shown, were "called forth
solely by the contrary teaching of Luther, Melanchton, and later
(1562–1563) Calvin."[42] Hence, the Tridentine canons on matrimony, far from being a comprehensive treatment of this sacrament, were simply a matter of responding, in rather negative
terms, to the Reformers; and, on the particular issue of
polygamy, the Reformers were especially vulnerable. Their position, as previously noted, appeared to contradict the cultural as
well as the theological tradition of all the European peoples—the
whole Christian world at that time.

So it is no coincidence that Trent's canon on polygamy is
formulated in the terms of the Reformers. Commenting on this
second canon, Karl Rahner tells us that here "the Council deliberately had in mind the Reformers, Luther in particular, in the
case of Philip of Hesse's bigamous marriage."[43] Indeed, one of
the few points made by the Council Fathers in their discussion of
this canon, just before voting on it, was that "the words of the

heretics" should be used in the formulation.[44] Moreover, had the Council intended to do more than respond to the Reformers on this question, then surely they would have pointed out also that there were some others, aside from the Reformers, who maintained that simultaneous polygamy was forbidden neither by the law of nature nor by divine law, but only by the human law of the Church.

THE MEANING OF TRENT'S TERMS

Another area for careful consideration, if we would avoid the mistake of reading into the teaching of Trent something that might not be there at all, is the significance of certain technical terms used in the second canon on marriage. What, it must be asked, was the force then of a conciliar teaching which anathematized those who held to an opposite view? And what was the contemporary understanding of "divine law"?

Surely these terms, "anathema" and "divine law," did not mean to the Fathers of Trent what they came to mean much later in history, especially under the influence of a highly centralized Roman curial theology of infallibility consequent upon the First Vatican Council.[45] Does the Tridentine use of "anathema" and the reference to "divine law" always indicate that a divinely revealed truth is proposed as a dogma, in the sense of this word today, and that it is proposed in an adequate and universally comprehensive manner? If a closer look at these terms does not suggest a purely negative reply, it may at least indicate the highly problematical character of any facile conclusions on the scope of Trent's teaching about polygamy.

The difficulties here are formidable. For we are approaching the words of Trent from a viewpoint that differs profoundly from that of both Trent and Vatican I. We differ, not only historically and culturally in our world view, but also in our methods of theological reflection and biblical exegesis.[46] We are, moreover, greatly influenced in our day by a general ecclesiastical council that hurled anathemas at no one and spoke of divine law only in reference to human dignity, conscience, and religious freedom. Still, it is possible to say something about the meaning of these terms at the time of Trent. From the various studies of the binding character of conciliar teaching, particularly that of Trent, it now seems incontestable that these technical expressions were then much more amorphous in their meaning than they are today.[47]

The recurring formula *anathema sit* has various meanings in the Tridentine documents; but it certainly does not always indicate that a heresy, as we understand it today, is being condemned and a divinely revealed truth is being proposed as something absolutely universal. In those days many things, which are not so regarded today, were counted as heresy.

One example may suffice to show the folly of interpreting the words of Trent in a purely literalistic and nonhistorical way. The Council had anathematized anyone who did not accept the canonical books of the Bible, as they are contained in the Old Latin Vulgate Edition.[48] A literalistic understanding of this teaching led some Roman Catholics to the conclusion that the Old Latin Vulgate Edition was something more than a work of human translation, with the astonishing corollary that even the extant Greek and Hebrew codices should be corrected in the light of the Vulgate.[49] It was not until the appearance of the Encyclical Letter *"Divino Afflante Spiritu"* (September 30, 1943), by Pope Pius XII, that this misunderstanding was finally cleared up for Roman Catholics. According to Pius XII, the intention of Trent was merely to affirm, in a juridical rather than a critical sense, the authenticity of the Vulgate because of its legitimate use in the Church for so many centuries.[50]

"It is imperative to recall," with Carl Peter, "that at times the real issue between Trent and the Reformers was the power of the Church to legislate in such a way as to bind in conscience."[51] So the basic issue was juridical in many of the Council's deliberations. "A particular canon," as Peter says, "might anathematize those rejecting a certain law or custom or practice and do so not to proclaim the latter as divinely established but rather to defend the authority of the Church in directing man to eternal life."[52] Hence it was possible, as Fransen has shown, for the Fathers of Trent to " 'define a dogma' while remaining perfectly conscious of the fact that the content of this *dogma* was not necessarily immutable."[53]

All twelve of the canons on marriage are embellished with the *anathema sit;* but, as Schillebeeckx points out, not all of them "contain as such a real doctrine on faith."[54] These propositions are concerned mainly with the jurisdictional power of the Church; and, in some of the canons, this is the exclusive concern. Canon twelve, for example, condemns anyone who says that "matrimonial lawsuits" do not come under the jurisdiction of ecclesiastical courts.[55] It would, indeed, be difficult to read into this concise legal statement anything more than a jurisdictional concern arising from the historical dispute with the Reformers and certain secular rulers—such as Philip of Hesse, for example. Must we assume *a priori*, without reference either to the complexities of the historical context or to the uncertain connotations of the terms used, that the Tridentine pronouncement on polygamy refers to so much more than this general dispute? The Reformers, we may recall, had argued that a secular ruler could, by his own authority, have more than one wife at the same time. Is it really evident, at all, that the Council Fathers here intended to deal with anything other than the immediate questions raised by the Reformers with reference to certain historically concrete marriage cases?

The opinion that Trent's brief comment on polygamy amounts to a comprehensive and definitive teaching becomes even less plausible when we see what the Council Fathers meant, and did not mean, when they spoke of "divine law." If this legal concept is ambiguous today, it was even more so then. In the tradition of the medieval canonists, little influenced as they were by the more reflective developments in scholastic theology and always anxiously defending ecclesiastical jurisdiction against the encroachments of the secular powers, the general tendency had been to confuse divine law with both natural law and ecclesiastical law.[56] Within the walls of ancient Christendom, some grounds for this confusion could, of course, be found in the New Testament: "He who hears you hears me" (Luke 10:16). With such a broad and amorphous notion of divine law, however, there had to be considerable flexibility in the areas of concrete application; and, as we shall presently see, some of this flexibility remains even in the modern canonical understanding of divine law.

So it is not surprising that, even at the time of Trent, the expression "divine law" was, as Louis Monden tells us, "often used for ecclesiastical and even for civil laws."[57] This vague usage is reflected in various conciliar discussions.[58] As used in Trent's canon on the necessity of confessing both the number and the species of all grave sins, the expression "divine law" seems to mean something more than a purely juridical obligation of merely ecclesiastical law, and something less than a divinely revealed obligation that is always binding upon all Catholics in every circumstance of historical time and place.[59] In this instance, "divine law" hardly refers to something that is absolutely unalterable and universally binding. Just as the Fathers of Trent had to recognize that "integral confession" had not always been required by the Church, so they surely would also have admitted that in the future there could develop forms of the sacramental rite which might not include "integral confession."[60] There is, to be sure, much more to be said about confession; but our purpose here is simply to indicate the need and the possibility of variously interpreting the Tridentine meaning of "divine law."

This matter of what is concretely forbidden by divine law —even as this law is understood in a more limited sense among modern Roman Catholic canonists and moralists—allows for considerable flexibility; and there is a large area of ambiguity, which calls for prudent human judgments in relation to the changing circumstances of different times and places. "The boundary between divine and human law is not unambiguously defined," writes Lukas Vischer, "and differences of opinion can arise over which has proper claim to a particular provision [of canon law]."[61] Even where there is agreement on the binding force of a particular provision of the divine law, there may still be wide differences of opinion when it comes to the actual application of the law in concrete historical situations. A Catholic, for example, may not marry a separated Christian ("heretic" or "schismatic"); and this, moreover, is forbidden by "divine law" if there is a danger that the faith or morals of the Catholic partner, or of the offspring, may be "perverted."[62] This condition, "if," means that in every concrete case the peculiar local circumstances must be considered and a prudent judgment made. This judgment, for all practical purposes, largely determines whether the particular "mixed-marriage" is, or is not, actually against the divine law. So, for many generations since the Reformation, and up until very recently in some countries, Roman Catholics were only rarely permitted to enter into such marriages.

Most canonists and theologians taught that, even when "mixed-marriages" were permitted the parents were obliged by divine law to effectively guarantee the Catholic education of their children. In more recent years, however, especially since Vatican II, there has been a notable shift in the official position which now, with a more prudent recognition of the human complexities involved, regards the divine-law obligation as extending simply to what is possible in the way of providing a Catholic education.[63] As Charles Curran points out, it is now officially recognized "in principle that sometimes another solution to the problem has to be tolerated."[64] In this example, anyway, we see that the divine law stands as an absolute norm of conduct; but the prohibitions of this law, in concrete reality, are always a matter of interpretation in the light of particular historico-cultural circumstances, which vary considerably from period to period, and from country to country. Something forbidden in one situation may be tolerable in another and vice versa. It was not always and everywhere appreciated by Christians that slavery is incompatible with the divine law of love. Nor is the Christian conscience today particularly sensitive to the divine-law implications of certain highway traffic regulations, behind which there would seem to be a universally normative divine law: "Thou shalt not kill."[65]

CONCLUSION

It would be unreasonable to suppose that the Council Fathers of Trent really intended to answer, once and for all, a question that they had never even considered. A look at the historical evidence tells us that they did not, in fact, consider the missionary and pastoral question of simultaneous polygamy as it arises in non-Western societies, where this form of marriage is held to be a traditional, normal, valid, licit, and even preferential, socio-economic institution. What the Council had in mind, rather, was the unusual and vulnerable position taken by the Reformers in a part of the world where simultaneous polygamy was generally held to be incompatible, not only with Christianity, but also with the traditional (even pre-Christian) ethico-cultural understanding of marriage. Nor are we compelled, because of Trent's use of *anathema sit* and "divine law," to suppose *a priori* that the canon on polygamy sets forth, as divinely revealed, a comprehensive and immutable dogma of the Christian faith.

It would, therefore, be a mistake to imagine that the second of Trent's canons on matrimony precludes, as far as Roman Catholic scholars are concerned, the possibility of searching further for an authentically Catholic—and thus more fully Christian —approach to the contemporary missionary and pastoral problem of customary plural marriage in Africa south of the Sahara. The way is open for further study.

NOTES

1. Petro Gasparri gives a list of references to statements of the ecclesiastical magisterium in relation to the prohibition of polygamy in Canon Law: cf. *Codex Iuris Canonici*, with preface, sources, notes and index by Petro Gasparri (Typis Polyglottis Vaticanis, 1933), Canon 1013, no. 2, n. 4, pp. 290–291. While none of these statements is in itself an answer to the polygamy question as it arises today, some of them have no noticeable bearing at all on the question.

2. Sometimes also, but less frequently, the Second Council of Lyons (1274) is cited. See Heinrich Denzinger, *The Sources of Catholic Dogma*, translated from Denzinger's *Enchiridion Symbolorum*, edition 30, by Roy J. Deferrari (St. Louis and London: B. Herder, 1957), no. 465, p. 185: "But concerning matrimony it [the Roman Church] holds that neither one man is permitted to have many wives nor one woman many husbands at the same time. But she [the Church] says that second and third marriages successively are permissible for one freed from legitimate marriage

through the death of the other party." This passing reference to polygamy certainly reflects the traditional position of Western Christendom; but it occurs in a document which was composed outside the Council, by Pope Clement IV and the Eastern Emperor Michael VIII Palaeologus in 1267; and which was intended and used mainly as an instrument of political, rather than theological and pastoral, interest. Moreover, it may perhaps be assumed from the historical intentions of the Council, to reconcile the Eastern and Western Churches, that the point of particular interest in the two relevant sentences of the document was not simultaneous polygamy as such, but the widespread belief among Eastern Christians—following their own magisterium and several prominent Greek Fathers—that successive plural marriage was somehow wrong even for widows and widowers. See Henry J. Schroeder, ed., *Disciplinary Decrees of the General Councils*, trans. H.J. Schroeder (St. Louis: B. Herder, 1937), p. 35, n. 78. See also Hans-Georg Beck, and others, *From the High Middle Ages to the Eve of the Reformation*, Vol. IV of *Handbook of Church History*, ed. Hubert Jedin and John Dolan, trans. Anselm Biggs (Freiburg: Herder; Montreal: Palm Publishers, 1970), pp. 124–125, 203–206.

3. Pius XI, *Acta Apostolicae Sedis* 22 (1930), p. 547; and Denzinger, *op. cit.*, no. 2231, p. 585; with particular reference to the Council of Trent, Denzinger, no. 969, p. 296. Some others, who cite Trent as the only conciliar source on this point, are Felice M. Cappello, *De Matrimonio*, Vol. III of *Tractatus canonico-moralis de sacramentis*, 4th ed. (Rome: Marietti, 1921–1939), p. 47; Hieronymus Noldin, *De Sacramentis*, Vol. III of *Summa Theologiae Moralis*, 26th ed. (Innsbruck: F. Rauch, 1940), p. 527; and Adolphe Tanquerey, *De Paenitentia, De Matrimonio et De Ordine*, Vol. I of *Synopsis Theologiae Moralis et Pastoralis*, 13th ed. (Paris: Desclée, 1947), p. 413; Jozef Aertnys and C.A. Damen, *Theologia Moralis Secundum Doctrinam S. Alfonsi de Ligorio*, 2 vols. (Turin: Marietti, 1947), II, no. 632, p. 471.

4. Denzinger, *op. cit.*, no. 972, p. 296. See also *Concilium Tridentinum: Diariorium, Actorum, Epistularum, Tractatuum Nova Collectio*, ed. Societas Goerresiana (Freiburg: Herder, 1901), Vol. IX, p. 286: "Si quis dixerit, licere Christianis plures simul habere uxores, et hoc nulla lege divina esse prohibitum: anathema sit." Subsequently this source will be designated CT.

5. Piet Fransen, "The Authority of the Councils," in *Problems of Authority*, ed. John M. Todd (Baltimore: Helicon, 1962), pp. 76–77.

6. Edward Schillebeeckx, *God the Future of Man*, trans. N.D. Smith (New York: Sheed and Ward, 1968), p. 19.

7. Fransen, "Authority of the Councils," p. 76. See also Jerome Mills,

234   POLYGAMY RECONSIDERED

"The Council of Trent on the Permanence of Marriage," *Resonance* 3 (1967) 35–47.

8. See Fransen, "Authority of the Councils" and "Divorce and Remarriage on the Ground of Adultery—the Council of Trent," trans. Theo Westow, in *The Future of Marriage as Institution,* ed. Franz Böckle, Concilium 55 (New York: Herder and Herder, 1970), pp. 89–100. See also Jordan Bishop, "Divorce and Remarriage," *New Blackfriars* 49 (August 1968) 591: "It now appears certain that the Council, both because of reluctance to condemn the doctrine of various Fathers of the Church and because of pressure from the Venetian ambassadors who had Greek subjects to rule, abstained from any condemnation of the Greek practice. Thus, while some post-Tridentine authors have attempted to find a dogmatic declaration in the statement of the Council, the Fathers of Trent seem to have limited themselves to a defence of Western practice, but without condemning the greatly different practice of the Eastern churches." For another recent study, which supports the view of Fransen and provides a comprehensive list of references, see Peter McEniery, "Divorce at the Council of Trent," *The Australasian Catholic Record* 167 (1970) 188–201.

9. Schillebeeckx, *God the Future of Man,* p. 19.

10. See Roger Aubert, "Church History as an Indispensable Key to Interpreting the Decisions of the Magisterium," trans. Paul Burns, in *Church History in Future Perspective,* ed. Roger Aubert, Concilium 57 (New York: Herder and Herder), p. 103: "Not only are the declarations of the magisterium fortuitous (produced by a contingent incident) and partial (made from a certain point of view, concerning one aspect that claimed attention at a certain moment), but they are also made within a determined cultural context." See also Avery Dulles, "Dogma as an Ecumenical Problem," *Theological Studies* 29 (1968), p. 406: "To the extent that traditional statements of the faith are conditioned by a cultural situation no longer our own, they must be reinterpreted. . . . Otherwise they will inevitably seem meaningless, incredible, or at least irrelevant."

11. Yves Congar, "Church History as a Branch of Theology," trans. Jonathan Cavanagh, in *Church History in Future Perspective,* ed. Roger Aubert, Concilium 57 (New York: Herder and Herder, 1970), p. 87: "We have become more aware of the historical conditioning of the documents of the magisterium itself—with regard to language, mental categories, a framework of concerns affecting the whole approach to certain questions. . . . We should need a philological, historical, and canonical commentary on *Denzinger.*"

12. Schillebeeckx, *God the Future of Man,* pp. 18–19.

13. See Roger Aubert, "Church History as an Indispensable Key," p.

105: "To understand exactly what it [the magisterium] is trying to say, one has to begin with a study of what the theologians of the day were thinking, what their method of approach was, and what their thought patterns were. . . . Trying to interpret encyclicals or conciliar texts without asking the historians who originated them (and what their aims were) is risking a fall into grievous error, as history—again—shows happening only too often for lack of sufficient historical sensitivity."

14. See CT, Vol. 6, pp. 93–95; Vol. 9, pp. 380, 412, 466.

15. P. Melanchthon, in *Corpus Reformatorum*, ed. C.G. Bretschneider (Halis Saxonum: C.A. Schwetschke et Filium, 1835; London and New York: Johnson Reprint Corporation, 1963), Vol. 2, col. 536. Subsequently *Corpus Reformation* will be designated CR.

16. See M. Luther and P. Melanchthon, in CR, Vol. 3, cols. 856–863.

17. *Ibid.*, col. 857. For more on this historical debate, see Adrian Hastings, *Christian Marriage in Africa* (London: S.P.C.K., 1973).

18. Luther, "On Marriage Matters," trans. F.C. Ahrens, in *Luther's Works*, ed. R.C. Schultz and H.T. Lehmann (Philadelphia: Fortress Press, 1967), Vol. 46, p. 291.

19. See Luther and Melanchthon, in CR, Vol. 3, col. 862.

20. *Ibid.*

21. See Dennis Doherty, *The Sexual Doctrine of Cardinal Cajetan* (Regensburg: F. Pustet, 1966), p. 200.

22. See William Durandus, in *IV Sent.*, d. 33, q. 1, a 2; as cited by Doherty, *op. cit.*, p. 203, n. 65.

23. See Antonius M. Mruk, "Singularis opinio Gerardi Odonis, O.F.M. circa naturam divortii in casu adulterii," *Gregorianum* 41 (1960), pp. 273–283.

24. In 1561 a book was published containing an index of what were alleged to be the errors of Cardinal Cajetan, including his views on polygamy: see Ioanne Eckio, *Enchiridion Locorum Communium Aduerfus Lutherium, et alios hostes Ecclesiae* (London: Apud Theobaldum Paganum, 1561), p. 446. Among the errors listed are these: "Nunquam iure divino prohibita fuit uxorum pluralitas. . . . Multi in primitiva Ecclesia habebant plures uxores, imitantes patres veteris testamenti. . . . Etiam jure naturae uxorum pluralitas nihil habebit indecentiae." It may therefore be assumed that the views of Cajetan on the question of polygamy were known to the theologians and the Fathers of Trent.

25. Augustine, "Contra Faustum," xxii, 22, c. 47, PL, 42, col. 428; English translation in *A Select Library of Nicene and Post-Nicene Fathers of the Christian Church*, ed. P. Schaff, and others (Grand Rapids, Michigan: Eerdmans, 1956), vol. IV, pp. 289–290. See also Augustine's discussion of this in "De doctrina Christiana," iii, c. 12, n. 20, PL, 34, col. 73; "De

civitate Dei," xvi, c. 38, PL, 41, col. 517; and "De bono conjugali," i, c. 7–21, PL, 40, cols. 378, 384–388.

26. Cajetan, Thomas de Vio, "In Genesis Caput XVI," v. 2; "In Leuitici Cap. XVIII," v. 18; *Omnia Opera Quotquot Sacrae Scripturae*, (Lyons, 1639), vol. I, pp. 71, 313. See also Doherty, *Sexual Doctrine of Cajetan*, p. 201; and note 24 above.

27. Cajetan, *Commentaria in S. Evangelia et Actus Apostolorum* (Paris: Ambrise Givault, 1536), on Mark 10:11, p. 90. See also Doherty, *Sexual Doctrine of Cajetan*, p. 205.

28. Cajetan, on 1 Tim. 3:2; on Titus 1:6; as cited in Doherty, *Sexual Doctrine of Cajetan*, p. 205, n. 78. See also note 24 above.

29. See Doherty, *Sexual Doctrine of Cajetan*, p. 233; and Ludwig F. von Pastor, *The History of the Popes* (London: 1929–1953), Vol. 10, p. 277, n. 2.

30. See Sir Gregory Casale's letter to Henry VIII, September 18, 1530, in *Letters and Papers, Foreign and Domestic, of the Reign of Henry VIII*, ed. J.S. Brewer (London: 1876), Vol. IV, Part III, No. 6627, p. 2987: "A few days since the Pope secretly proposed to me the following condition;—that your Majesty might be allowed to have two wives." See also the letter of Ghinucci to Henry VIII, September 1530, *ibid.*, Vol. IV, Part III, Appendix, No. 261, p. 3189: "[Ghinucci] reports another interview with his Holiness upon a Sunday, when the Pope said he could with less scandal give the King a dispensation for two wives, than grant what the writer asked;—but not knowing how this would suit his Majesty, [Ghinucci] thought it better to stick to the point. The Pope, however, continued to speak of the King's having two wives." And the letter of William Benet to Henry VIII, October 27, 1530, *ibid.*, Vol. IV, Part III, No. 6705, pp. 3023–3024. This letter from Benet is quoted directly by Pastor, *History of the Popes*, Vol. 10, p. 276: "I asked Clement VII if he were certain that such a dispensation [from the monogamy rule] was admissible, and he answered that it was not; but he added that a distinguished theologian had told him that in his opinion the Pope might in this case dispense in order to avert a greater evil; he intended, however, to go into the matter more fully with his council. And indeed the Pope has just now informed me that such a dispensation was not possible."

31. See Erwin Doernberg, *Henry VIII and Luther: An Account of Their Personal Relations* (Stanford, Calif.: Stanford University Press, 1961), p. 74.

32. Desiderius Erasmus, Letter to Wives, September 2, 1527, quoted by Doernberg, *Henry VIII and Luther*, p. 74.

33. See Benet's letter to Henry VIII, as quoted by Pastor, in note 30 above.

34. Innocent III, quotation from letter "Gaudemus in Domino" to the Bishop of Tiberius, in Denzinger, *Enchiridion Symbolorium*, no. 408, p. 159.

35. See Cajetan, *Commentaria in S. Evangelia et Actus Apostolorum*, on Matt. 19:8, p. 52: "Nam decretales pontificiae de hac materia non sunt definitivae fidei sed iudiciales facti. Profitentur autem ipsi pontifices . . . Romanos Pontifices aliquando in his iudiciis matrimoniorum errasse. . . . Adverte quod hinc Innocentius Tertius . . . accipit quod non licet habere plures uxores. Nam si liceret plures uxores, qui dimissa non fornicaria acciperet aliam non moecharetur sed conjungio cum secunda uteretur: in textu autem dicitur quod moechatur. Et nisi Marcus apposuisset in eam, scrupulo careret argumentum Innocentii." See comments on this, and additional references, in Doherty, *Sexual Doctrine of Cajetan*, pp. 202, 248–251.

36. Innocent III, as cited in note 34 above.

37. See CT, Vol. 9, pp. 415, 418.

38. Paul III, Constitution *Altitudo*, June 1, 1537, *Codicis Iuris Canonici Fontes*, ed. Petro Gasparri (Typis Polyglottis Vaticanis, 1926–1939), Vol. I, No. 81, pp. 140–141. (This document is discussed in Chapter One, section 2.)

39. See Carl Peter, "Auricular Confession and the Council of Trent," in *The Catholic Theological Society of America: Proceedings of 22nd Annual Convention* 22 (1967) 191.

40. Peter, *ibid.*, p. 196.

41. Hubert Jedin, *A History of the Council of Trent*, trans. Ernest Graf (London: Thomas Nelson and Sons, 1961), Vol. II, p. 391. See also Paolo Sarpi, *History of Benefices and Selections from History of the Council of Trent*, trans. Peter Burke (New York: Washington Square Press, 1967), p. 235.

42. Fransen, "The Authority of the Councils," p. 73.

43. Karl Rahner, ed., *The Teaching of the Catholic Church as Contained in Her Documents*, comp. Heinrich Roos and Joseph Neuner, trans. Geoffrey Stevens (Cork: Mercier Press, 1967), pp. 354–355.

44. See CT, Vol. 9, pp. 642, 644.

45. See John Enders, "The Council of Trent and Original Sin," in *The Catholic Theological Society of America: Proceedings of the 22nd Annual Convention* 22 (1967) 52.

46. See Charles E. Curran, *Contemporary Problems in Moral Theology* (Notre Dame: Fides, 1970), pp. 119–136, 228–229, 233–235, and also p. 177: "There is a realization today that the Scriptures cannot be used as proof texts to definitely indicate that one particular action is always wrong."

238 POLYGAMY RECONSIDERED

47. See Fransen, Enders, Peter, Schillebeeckx, Monden, Ullmann, and Curran, as cited in this chapter; and also Fransen, "Réflexions sur l'anathema au Concile de Trente," *Ephemerides Theologicae Lovanienses* 29 (1953) 657–672; Heinrich Lennerz, "Notulae Tridentinae, Primum Anathema in Concilio Tridentino," *Gregorianum* 27 (1946), pp. 136–142; F.X. Lawlor, "Heresy," in *New Catholic Encyclopedia* (New York: McGraw-Hill, 1967), Vol. VI, pp. 1062–1063; P. De Letter, "Anathema," in *New Catholic Encyclopedia*, Vol. I, p. 481.

48. See CT, Vol. V, pp. 90–91.

49. See E.F. Latko, "Trent and Auricular Confession," *Franciscan Studies* 14 (1954) 24; Hadriano Simon and J. Prado, *Propaedeutica Biblico* (Turin: Marietti, 1938), pp. 178–179.

50. Pius XII, *Acta Apostolicae Sedis* 35 (1943) 308–309.

51. Peter, "Auricular Confession," p. 191.

52. *Ibid.*

53. Fransen, "The Authority of the Councils," p. 74.

54. Edward Schillebeeckx, *Marriage: Secular Reality and Saving Mystery*, trans. N.D. Smith (London: Sheed and Ward, 1965), Vol. II, p. 170.

55. See CT, Vol. 9, p. 682: "12. Si quis dixerit, causas matrimoniales non spectare ad iudices ecclesiasticos: anathema sit." Also in Denzinger, *Enchiridion Symbolorum*, no. 982, p. 298.

56. See Walter Ullmann, *Medieval Papalism* (London: Methuen, 1949), pp. 42–47.

57. Louis Monden, *Sin, Liberty and Law* (New York: Sheed and Ward, 1965), p. 48.

58. See Peter, "Auricular Confession," p. 198; and also Sarpi, *History of the Benefices*, pp. 34–37, 91, 185–186, 211–217, 245, 254–255, 281, for evidence of the Tridentine use of "divine law" with reference to purely juridical issues like the duty to pay tithes and other taxes to ecclesiastical officials, to pay annates to popes, and the duty of bishops to reside in the dioceses from which they derive revenues.

59. See Peter, *ibid.*, pp. 198–199.

60. See Curran, *Contemporary Problems in Moral Theology*, pp. 62–67.

61. Lucas Vischer, "Reform of Canon Law—An Ecumenical Problem," *The Jurist* 26 (October 1966) 400; and also pp. 399–400: "The Roman Catholic Church makes the important distinction between *ius divinum* and *ius mere ecclesiasticum*. Thereby it indicates that the ecclesiastical law is not a rigid order, but that in principle it can undergo change within fixed limits. As the Church generally as a historical entity participates in historical development, so the ecclesiastical order also develops. While the *ius divinum* remains unchanged for all time and is always directly applicable, the *ius ecclesiasticum* can change." See also Franz Böckle,

Fundamental Concepts of Moral Theology, trans. William Jerman (New York: Paulist Press, 1968), pp. 46–67.

62. See *Codex Iuris Canonici,* Canon 1060.

63. See Congregation for the Doctrine of the Faith, Decree "Matrimonii Sacramentum, March 18, 1966, trans. ("Decree on Mixed Marriage") in *The Jurist* 26 (July 1966), pp. 361–366; Pope Paul VI, Apostolic Letter "Matrimonia Mixta, April 29, 1970, trans. ("Mixed Marriages") in *The Jurist* 30 (July 1970) 356–362; The National Council of Catholic Bishops of the United States, "Mixed Marriage Guidelines," November 10, 1970, *The American Ecclesiastical Review* 164 (January 1971) 56–67.

64. Charles E. Curran, *A New Look at Christian Morality* (Notre Dame: Fides, 1970), p. 109. See also Curran's *Christian Morality Today* (Notre Dame: Fides, 1966), pp. 93–105.

65. See Peter Huizing, " 'Gottliches Recht' und Kirchenverfassung," *Stimmen der Zeit* 183 (1969) 166.

BIBLIOGRAPHY

Ackroyd, P.R. and others, eds., *The Cambridge Bible Commentary*. London and New York: Cambridge University Press, 1966.

Ajayi, J.F. Ade. and Ayandele, E.A. "Writing African Church History." *The Church Crossing Frontiers: Essays on the Nature of Mission, in Honor of Bengt Sundkler*. Uppsala, Sweden: Boktryckeri Aktiebolag, 1969.

Apple, R.W. Jr. "No. 1 Topic in Tanzania." *New York Times*, October 9, 1969, p. 18.

Aquinas, St. Thomas. *Summa Theologiae*. 5 vols. Ottawa: Impensis Studii Generalis O.Pr., 1941–1945.

————. *Summa Theologica, Literally Translated by the Fathers of the English Dominican Province*. 3 vols., first complete American edition. New York: Benziger Bros., 1948.

Aubert, Roger. "Church History as an Indispensable Key to Interpreting the Decisions of the Magisteriun." Translated by Paul Burns. *Church History in Future Perspective*, Concilium 57. New York: Herder and Herder, 1970.

Ayandele, E.A. *The Missionary Impact on Modern Nigeria 1842–1914: A Political and Social Analysis*. London: Longmans, Green, 1966.

Bäeta, C.G., ed. *Christianity in Tropical Africa*. London: Oxford University Press, 1968.

Bailey, Derrick S. *The Man-Woman Relationship in Christian Thought*. Toronto: Longmans, 1959.

Baron, Salo Wittmayer. *A Social and Religious History of the Jews*. 14 vols. 2nd ed. revised and enlarged. New York and London: Columbia University Press, 1962.

Barnard, L.W. *Justin Martyr: His Life and Thought*. London and New York: Cambridge University Press, 1967.

Barrett, David B. "AD 2000: 350 Million Christians in Africa." *International Review of Mission* 59 (January 1970) 41–47.

————. "Church Growth and Independency as Organic Phenomena: An Analysis of Two Hundred African Tribes." *Christianity in Tropical Africa*. Edited by C.G. Baëta. London: Oxford University Press, 1968.

────. *Schism and Renewal in Africa.* Nairobi, Addis Ababa, Lusaka: Oxford University Press, 1968.

Barth, Karl. *Church Dogmatics.* Edited by G.W. Bromiley. Translated by G.T. Thompson and H. Knight. Edinburgh: T. & T. Clark, 1961.

Bartoccetti, Vittorio. "Polygamy." *Dictionary of Moral Theology.* Compiled and edited by Franceso Roberti and Pietro Palazzini. Translated by H.J. Yannone. 2nd ed. Westminster, Md.: Newman Press, 1962.

Bascom, William R. and Melville J. Herskovits, eds., *Continuity and Change in African Cultures.* Chicago: The University of Chicago Press, 1959.

Bassett, William W., ed. *The Bond of Marriage.* Notre Dame and London: University of Notre Dame Press, 1968.

Baum, Gregory. "Does Morality Need the Church?" *The Catholic Theological Society of America: Proceedings of the 25th Annual Convention* 25 (June 1970) 163 ff.

────. *Man Becoming: God in Secular Experience.* New York: Herder and Herder, 1970.

Beck, Hans-Georg, and others. *From the High Middle Ages to the Eve of the Reformation.* Volume IV of *Handbook of Church History.* Edited by Hubert Jedin and John Dolan. Translated by Anselm Biggs. Freiburg: Herder; Montreal: Palm Publishers, 1970.

Benedict, Ruth. *Patterns of Culture.* New York: New American Library, Mentor Books, 1958.

Berger, Peter. *A Rumor of Angels: Modern Society and the Rediscovery of the Supernatural.* Garden City, N.Y.: Doubleday Anchor Books, 1970.

Binet, Jacques. *Le mariage en Afrique noire.* Paris: Les Editions du Cerf, 1959.

Bishop, Jordan. "Divorce and Remarriage." *New Blackfriars* 49 (August 1968) 591 ff.

Blenkinsopp, Joseph. *Sexuality and the Christian Tradition.* Dayton: Pflaum Press, 1969.

Bohannan, Paul. *Africa and Africans.* Garden City, N.Y.: The Natural History Press, 1964.

Bonte, M. and van Balen, H. "Prolonged Lactation and Family Spacing in Rwanda." *Journal of Biosocial Science* 1 (April 1969) 97–100.

Böckle, Franz. *Fundamental Concepts of Moral Theology.* Translated by William Jerman. New York: Paulist Press, 1968.

──── ed. *The Future of Marriage as Institution.* New York: Herder and Herder, The New Concilium, May 1970.

────. "The Problem of Social Ethics." *American Ecclesiastical Review* 163 (November 1970).

Boer, Harry. "Polygamy." *Frontier* 1 (Spring 1969) 24.

Bouscaren, Timothy L. and Ellis, A.C. *Canon Law: A Text and Commentary*. Milwaukee: Bruce, 1957.

Bouyer, Louis. *Dictionary of Theology*. Translated by Charles U. Quinn. New York: Desclée, 1965.

Brass, William, ed. *The Demography of Tropical Africa*. Princeton, N.J.: Princeton University Press, 1968.

Bremen Mission. Church Rules. As cited by E. Grace, "Missionary Policies As Seen in the World of Missions with the Evangelical Presbyterian Church, Ghana." *Christianity in Tropical Africa*. London: Oxford University Press, 1968.

Bremer, J.S., ed. *Letters and Papers, Foreign and Domestic, of the Reign of Henry VIII*. London: 1876. Volume IV.

Brown, Raymond E., and others, eds. *The Jerome Biblical Commentary*. 2 vols. Englewood Cliff, N.J.: Prentice-Hall, 1968. Volume II.

Bryant, John. *Health and the Developing World*. Ithaca and London: Cornell University Press, 1969.

Buijs, Louis. "Polygamy." (A paper presented to a group of missionaries at Generalate of Verona Fathers in Rome, April 1967). Translated from Italian by R. Cefalo. Typewritten.

Bultmann, Rudolf. *Theology of the New Testament*. Translated by Kendrick Grobel. 2 vols. New York: Charles Scribner's Sons, 1951. Volume I.

Burce, Willard. "Polygamy and the Church." *Concordia Theological Monthly* 34 (1963) 224–228.

Bushayija, Stanislas. *Le mariage coutumier au Rwanda*. Brussels: Maison Ferdinand Larcier, 1966.

Buthelizi, Manas. "Polygyny in the Light of the New Testament." *Africa Theological Journal* 2 (February 1969) 58–70.

Butterfield, Herbert. *Christianity and History*. London and Glasgow: G. Bell and Sons, 1949. Collins, Fontana Books, 1957.

Cajetan, Cardinal. *Commentaria in S. Evangelia et Actus Apostolorum*. Paris: Ambrise Givault, 1536.

———. *Omnia Opera Quotquot Sacrae Scripturae*. Lyons, 1639. Volume I.

Caldwell, John C. and Okonjo Chukuka, eds. *The Population of Tropical Africa*. New York: Columbia University Press, 1968.

Carcopino, Jerome. *Daily Life in Ancient Rome*. Translated by E.O. Lorimer. New Haven: Yale University Press, 1940; Harmondsworth: Penguin Books, 1964.

Carter, Charles W. and others, eds. *The Wesleyan Bible Commentary*. 6 vols. Grand Rapids, Michigan: William B. Eerdmanns Publishing Co., 1965, Volume V.

Catholic Bishops of Eastern Africa. *Pastoral Perspectives in Eastern Africa after Vatican II.* AMECEA Study Conference Record. Nairobi, 1967.

Catholic Bishops of Tanzania. "Draft Statement." *Pastoral Orientation Service,* No. 8. Mwanza: Bukumbi Pastoral Institute, 1969.

Chaine, Joseph. *Le livre de la Genèse.* Paris: Editions du Cerf, 1948.

Charbonnier, G. *Conversations with Claude Levi-Strauss.* Translated by John and Doreen Weightman. London: Jonathan Cape, 1969.

Chenu, M.D. *Nature, Man, and Society in the Twelfth Century.* Translated and edited by J. Taylor and L.K. Little. Chicago and London: University of Chicago Press, 1968.

Clignet, Remi. *Many Wives, Many Powers: Authority and Power in Polygynous Families.* Evanston, Ill.: Northwestern University Press, 1970.

Cochin, Augustin. *The Results of Slavery.* Translated by M.L. Booth, Walker, Wise and Company, 1863.

Colenso, John W. *Remarks on the Proper Treatment of Cases of Polygamy as Found Existing in Converts from Heathenism.* Pietermaritzburg: May & Davis, 1855.

————. *Ten Weeks in Natal: A Journal of a First Visitation among the Colonists and the Zulu Kafirs of Natal.* Cambridge: Macmillan, 1855.

Collectanea S. Congregationis De Propaganda Fide (Rome 1907). Volume I.

Collingwood, R.G. *The Idea of History.* London, Oxford, New York: Clarendon Press, 1946.

"The Committee of Churches of Dar es Salaam on the Government's Proposals for a Uniform Law of Marriage." *Tanzania Standard,* November 28, 1969 pp. 4–9.

Congar, Yves. *A History of Theology.* Translated by Hunter Guthrie. New York: Doubleday 1968.

————. "Church History as a Branch of Theology." Translated by Jonathan Cavanaugh. *Church History in Future Perspective,* Concilium 57. New York: Herder and Herder, 1970.

————. "The Place of Poverty in Christian Life in an Affluent Society." *War, Poverty, Freedom: The Christian Response,* Concilium 15. New York: Paulist Press, 1966.

————. *This Church That I Love.* Translated by Lucien Delafuente. Denville, N.J.: Dimension Books, 1969.

Coser, Rose L., ed. *The Family: Its Structure and Functions.* New York: St. Martin's Press, 1964.

Cox, George W. *The Life of Bishop John W. Colenso.* London: W. Ridgway, 1888.

Crespy, George and others. *Marriage and Christian Tradition.* Translated by Agnes Cunningham. Techny, Ill.: Divine Word Publications, 1968.

Crowe, M.B. "Human Nature: Immutable or Mutable." *Irish Theological Quarterly* 30 (1963) 213–218.

Curran, Charles E. *A New Look at Christian Morality*. Notre Dame, Ind.: Fides, 1970.

——, ed. *Absolutes in Moral Theology?* Washington and Cleveland: Corpus Books, 1968.

——. *Christian Morality Today*. Notre Dame, Ind.: Fides, 1966.

——. *Contemporary Problems in Moral Theology*. Notre Dame, Ind.: Fides, 1970.

——. "Methodological and Ecclesiological Questions in Moral Theology." *Chicago Studies* 9 (1970) 60–62.

Currens, G.E. "A Policy of Baptizing Polygynists Evaluated." *Africa Theological Journal* 2 (February 1969) 71–83.

—— and Payne, R.J. "An Evaluation of the Policy of the Lutheran Church in Liberia on the Baptism of Polygamists." Monrovia, June 1965.

Currens, Harvey J. "Polygamy in the Church in Native Africa." Chicago: Lutheran Theological Seminary, January, 1950.

Curtin, P.D., ed. *Africa Remembered*. Madison, Milwaukee, London: The University of Wisconsin Press, 1969.

Daniélou, Jean and Marrou, Henry. *The First Six Hundred Years*. Translated by Vincent Cronin. London: Darton, Longman and Todd, 1964.

Daube, David. *The New Testament and Rabbinic Judaism*. London: Athlone Press, 1956.

Dawson, Christopher. *Progress and Religion*. Garden City, N.Y: Doubleday Image Books, 1960.

de Fraine, Jean. *Adam and the Family of Man*. Translated by Daniel Raible. Staten Island, N.Y.: Alba House, 1965.

De Letter, P. "Anathema." *New Catholic Encyclopedia*. New York: McGraw-Hill, 1967. Volume I.

de Reeper, John. *The Sacraments on the Missions*. Dublin: Browne and Nolan, 1957.

de Vaux, Roland. *Ancient Israel: Its Life and Institutions*. Translated by John McHugh. New York: McGraw-Hill, 1961.

De Vine, C.F. "The Sin of Onan." *Catholic Biblical Quarterly* 4 (1942) 340.

Demuth, Paul E. "The Nature and Origin of the Privilege of the Faith." *Resonance* 3 (Spring 1967) 60–73.

Denzinger, Heinrich, ed. *The Sources of the Catholic Faith*. Translated by Roy J. Deferrari from Denzinger's *Enchiridion Symbolorum*, 30th edition. St. Louis, Mo.: B. Herder, 1957.

Dickinson, Richard. "So Who Needs Liberation?" *The Christian Century* 88 (January 13, 1971) 43–46.

Diop, Alioune. "Colonization and the Christian Conscience." *Cross Currents* 3 (Summer 1953) 353–355.

Dodd, C.H. *Christ and the New Humanity.* Philadelphia: Fortress Press, 1965.

———. *Gospel and Law.* New York: Columbia University Press, 1951.

Dodge, Ralph E. *The Unpopular Misssionary.* Westwood, N.J.: Revell Co., 1964.

Doernberg, Erwin. *Henry VIII and Luther: An Account of Their Personal Relations.* Stanford, Calif.: Stanford University Press, 1961.

Doherty, Dennis. *The Sexual Doctrine of Cardinal Cajetan.* Regensburg: F. Pustet, 1966.

Dorjahn, Vernon R. "The Demographic Aspects of African Polygyny." Ph.D. dissertation, Northwestern University, 1954.

Dubos, René. *So Human an Animal.* New York: Charles Scribner's Sons, 1968.

Dulles, Avery. "Dogma as an Ecumenical Problem." *Theological Studies* 29 (1968) 406 ff.

Dumont, René. *False Start in Africa.* Translated by Phyllis N. Ott. New York: Praeger, 1966.

Dunston, Gordon R. "Hard Sayings—V." *Theology* 66 (December 1963) 491–492.

Eckio, Ioanne. *Enchiridion Locorum Communium Aduerfus Lutherium, et alios hostes Ecclesiae.* London: Apud Theobaldum Paganum, 1561.

Edwards, Adrian. "Marriage and Mysterion: Reflections of a Bush Theologian." *New Blackfriars* 51 (August 1970) 382–383.

Ekka, Philip. "Anthropology and the Idea of a Universal Moral Law for Society." *Light on the Natural Law.* Edited by Illtud Evans. London: Burns and Oates, 1965.

Enders, John. "The Council of Trent and Original Sin." *The Catholic Theological Society of America: Proceedings of the 22nd Annual Convention* 22 (1967) 52.

Fay, Charles. "Human Evolution: A Challenge to Thomistic Ethics." *International Philosophical Quarterly* 2 (1962) 50–80.

Falk, Ze'ev W. *Jewish Matrimonial Law in the Middle Ages.* London: Oxford University Press, 1966.

Feucht, Oscar E., ed. *Sex and the Church: A Sociological, Historical and Theological Investigation of Sex Attitudes.* St. Louis: Concordia Publishing House, 1961.

Firth, Raymond. *Elements of Social Organization.* Boston: Beacon Press, 1963.

———. *Human Types: An Introduction to Social Anthropology.* New York: New American Library, 1958.

Fitzpatrick, Joseph P. "Faith, Freedom and Cultural Difference: Cuernavaca and Christian Mission." *International Review of Mission* 59 (July 1970) 333–340.

Fox, Robin, *Kinship and Marriage.* Harmondsworth, Baltimore, Victoria: Penguin Books, 1967.

Francis, E.K. "The Nature of the Ethnic Group," *American Journal of Sociology* 52 (March 1947).

Fransen, Piet. "The Authority of the Councils." *Problems of Authority.* Edited by John M. Todd. Baltimore: Helicon, 1962.

———. "Divorce and Remarriage on the Ground of Adultery—The Council of Trent." Translated by Theo Westow. *The Future of Marriage as Institution,* Concilium 55. New York: Herder and Herder, 1970.

———. "Réflexions sur l'anathema au Concile de Trente." *Ephemerides Theologicae Lovanienses* 29 (1953) 657–672.

French, David. "Does the U.S. Exploit the Developing Nations?" *Commonweal,* May 19, 1967, pp. 257–259.

Fuchs, Josef. "The Absoluteness of Moral Terms." *Gregorianum* 52 (1971) 437–438.

———. *Human Values and Christian Morality.* Translated by M.H. Heelan and others. Dublin: Gill and Macmillan, 1970.

———. "Is There a Specifically Christian Morality?" *Theology Digest* 19 (Spring 1971) 44.

Gasparri, Petro, ed. *Codex Iuris Canonici.* Typis Polyglottis Vaticanis, 1933.

———, ed. *Codicis Iuris Canonici Fontes.* Typis Polyglottis Vaticanis, 1926–1939. Volume I.

George, Poikail John. "Racist Assumptions of the 19th Century Missionary Movement." *International Review of Mission* 59 (July 1970) 271–284.

Gibbs, James L., ed. *Peoples of Africa.* New York, Toronto, London: Holt, Rinehart and Winston, 1965.

Glass, D.V. and Eversley, D.E.C., eds. *Population in History: Essays in Historical Demography.* Chicago: Aldine, and Edward Arnold Ltd., 1965.

Goerresiana Societas, ed. *Concilium Tridentinum: Diariorium, Actorum, Epistularum, Tractatum Nova Collectio.* Freiburg: Herder, 1901. Volume IX.

Gordon, Milton M. *Assimilation in American Life: The Role of Race, Religion and National Origins.* New York: Oxford University Press, 1964.

Gray, Robert F. *The Sonjo of Tanganyika.* London: Oxford University Press, 1963.

—— and Gulliver, P.H. *The Family Estate in Africa: Studies in the Role of Property in Family Structure and Lineage Continuity.* London: Routledge and Kegan Paul, 1964.

Grelot, Pierre. "The Institution of Marriage: Its Evolution in the Old Testament." Translated by Lancelot Sheppard. *The Future of Marriage as Institution,* Concilium 55, New York: Herder and Herder, 1970.

——. *Man and Wife in Scripture.* Translated by Rosaleen Brennan. London: Burns & Oates, 1964.

Häring, Bernard. "Magisterium and Natural Law." *The American Journal of Jurisprudence* 14 (1969) 95.

——. *Marriage in the Modern World.* Westminster, Md.: Newman Press, 1965.

——. *A Theology of Protest.* New York: Farrar, Straus, and Giroux, 1970.

Harries, Lyndon. "Christian Marriage in African Society." *Survey of African Marriage and Family Life.* Edited by Arthur Phillips. London: Oxford University Press, 1953.

Hastings, Adrian. *Christian Marriage in Africa.* London: S.P.C.K., 1973.

Henin, R.A. "Marriage Patterns and Trends in the Nomadic and Settled Populations of the Sudan." *Africa* 39 (July 1969) 239.

Herrell, P.E. *Divorce and Re-Marriage in the Early Church.* Austin, Texas: R.B. Sweet Co., 1967.

Herskovits, Melville J. *The Human Factor in Changing Africa.* New York: Knopf, 1962.

Hillman, Eugene. "The Development of Christian Marriage Structures." *The Future of Marriage as Institution,* Concilium 55. New York: Herder and Herder, 1970.

——. "Polygyny Reconsidered." *Renewal of Preaching,* Concilium 33 New York: Paulist Press, 1968.

——. *The Wider Ecumenism.* New York and London: Herder and Herder, Burns and Oates, 1968.

Holst, Robert. "Polygamy and the Bible." *International Review of Mission* 56 (April 1967) 205–213.

Howells, William. *Back of History.* Revised edition. Garden City, N.Y.: Doubleday Anchor Books, and the American Museum of Natural History, 1963.

Hughes, Robert and others. "The American Family: Future Uncertain." *Time,* December 28, 1970, pp. 41–42.

Huizing, Peter. "'Gottliches Recht' and Kirchenverfassung." *Stimmen der Zeit* 183 (1969) 166 ff.

Hunter, Guy. *The New Societies of Tropical Africa*. London: Oxford University Press, 1962.

Idowu, Bolaji. *Towards an Indigenous Church*. Oxford University Press, 1965.

International African Institute (London). *Social Implications of Industrialization in Africa South of the Sahara*. Paris: UNESCO, 1965.

James, E. O. *The Beginnings of Religion*. London: Hutchinson's University Library, n.d.
———. *Marriage Customs Through the Ages*. New York: Macmillan, Collier Books Edition, 1965.

Janssen, R.M. "Religious Encounter and the *Jamaa*.'" *Heythrop Journal* 8 (April 1967) 141.

Jedin, Hubert. *A History of the Council of Trent*. Translated by Ernest Graf. London: Thomas Nelson and Sons, 1961. Volume II.

Jeffery, R.M.C. "Marriage and Baptism Regulations." Report ME/SR/4. Church of England. London: no date, c. 1966 (mimeographed).

Jeremias, Joachim. *Jerusalem in the Time of Jesus*. Translated by F.H. and C.H. Cave. London: SCM Press, 1969.

Joyce, George Hayward. *Christian Marriage: An Historical and Doctrinal Study*. London and New York: Sheed and Ward, 1933, 1948.

Jones, Alexander and others, editors and translators. *The Jerusalem Bible*. London: Darton, Longman and Todd, 1966.

Kale, S.I. "Polygamy and the Church in Africa." *International Review of Mission* 31 (April 1942) 222–223.

Katoke, Israel K. "Encounter of the Gospel and Cultures." *Lutheran World* 19 (1972) 24–41.

Kautsky, Karl. *Foundations of Christianity*. Translated by Henry F. Mins. New York: Russell and Russell, 1953.

Kenya Government. *Report of the Commission on the Law of Marriage and Divorce*. Nairobi: Government Printer, 1968.

Kenya News Agency. Report in *Daily Nation*, Nairobi, September 14, 1967, p. 4.

Kenyatta, Jomo. *Facing Mount Kenya: The Tribal Life of the Gikuyu*. London: Secker and Warburg, 1938.

Kerns, Joseph E. *The Theology of Marriage*. New York: Sheed and Ward, 1964.

Kibira, Josiah. "The Church in Buhaya: Crossing Frontiers." *The Church Crossing Frontiers: Essays on the Nature of Mission, in Honor of Bengt Sundkler*. Uppsala, Sweden: Boktryckeri Aktiebolag, 1969.

King, Noel Q. *Religions of Africa*. New York, London, Evanston: Harper & Row, 1970.

Kipengele, N.P. "Marriage Celebrations Among Wamatumbi." *Studia Missionalia, Ethnologie Religieuse*, 14 (1964) 84.

Kittel, Rudolf, ed. *Biblia Hebraica*. Stuttgart: Privilegierte Wurtternbergische Bibelanstalt, 1929.

Kosnik, Anthony. "The Pastoral Care of Those in Canonically Invalid Marriages." *The Jurist* 30 (January 1970) 36.

Kowovele, Judah B.M. "Polygamy as a Problem to the Church in Africa." *Africa Theological Journal* 2 (February 1969) 7–26.

Kraemer, Hendrik. *The Bible and Social Ethics*. Philadelphia: Fortress Press, Facet Books, 1965.

Kuper, Hilda, ed. *Urbanization and Migration in West Africa*. Berkeley and Los Angeles: The University of California Press, 1965; London: The University of Cambridge Press, 1965.

The Lambeth Conference, 1968: Resolutions and Reports. London and New York: S.P.C.K. and Seabury Press, 1968.

Lang, Andrew. *The Making of Religion*. London, 1898.

Latko, E.F. "Trent and Auricular Confession." *Franciscan Studies* 14 (1954) 24.

Latourette, Kenneth Scott. *A History of the Expansion of Christianity*. New York: Harper, 1937.

Lawlor, F.X. "Heresy." *New Catholic Encyclopedia*. New York: McGraw-Hill, 1967. Volume VI.

Lawson, W. Michael. "Roman Law: A Source of Canonical Marriage Legislation." *Resonance* 3 (Spring 1967) 9.

Lebreton, Jules and others. *The History of the Primitive Church*. Translated by Ernest C. Messenger. 4 vols. New York and London: Macmillan, 1942–1947. Volume I.

Leclercq, Jacques. *Marriage and the Family: A Study in Social Philosophy*. Translated by Thomas R. Hanley. New York and Cincinnati: Pustet, 1949.

Leguerrier, René. "Recent Practice of the Holy See in Regard to the Dissolution of Marriages Between Non-Baptized Persons Without Conversion." *The Jurist* 25 (1965) 453–465.

Legum, Colin, ed. *Africa: A Handbook to the Continent*. New York and Washington: Praeger, 1966.

Lennerz, Heinrich. "Notulae Tridentinae, Primum Anathema in Concilio Tridentino." *Gregorianum* 27 (1946) 136–142.

Lepp, Ignace. *The Psychology of Loving*. Translated by Bernard G. Gilligan. Baltimore: Helicon Press, 1963.

Leslie, Gerald R. *The Family in Social Context*. New York and Toronto: Oxford University Press, 1967.

Levi-Strauss, Claude. *The Scope of Anthropology*. Translated by S.O. Paul and R.A. Paul. London: Jonathan Cape, 1967.

———. *Structural Anthropology*. Translated by Claire Jacobson and B.G. Schoepf. Garden City, N.Y.: Doubleday Anchor Books, 1967.

Levis, R.J. "Marriage (Theology of): The Ends of Marriage." *New Catholic Encyclopedia*. New York : McGraw-Hill, 1967. Vol. IX, p. 270.

Little, Kenneth. "Some Urban Patterns of Marriage and Domesticity in West Africa." *Sociological Review* 21 (July 1959) 65–82.

Lonergan, Bernard. *Insight: A Study of Human Understanding*. New York: Philosophical Library; London: Longmans, 1957.

———. *Method in Theology*. New York: Herder and Herder, 1972.

———. "Revolution in Catholic Theology." *The Catholic Theological Society of America: Proceedings of the 27th Annual Convention* 27 (1972).

Lowie, Robert H. *Primitive Man*. New York: Boni and Liveright, 1920.

Lowy, S. "The Extent of Jewish Polygamy in Talmudic Times." *The Journal of Jewish Studies* 9, Nos. 3 and 4 (1958) 130–134.

Luther, Martin. "On Marriage Matters." Translated by F.C. Ahrens. *Luther's Works*. Edited by R.C. Schultz and H.T. Lehmann. Philadelphia: Fortress Press, 1967. Vol. XLVI.

Macquarrie, John. *Three Issues in Ethics*. New York, London, Evanston: Harper and Row, 1970.

Magubane, Bernard. "A Critical Look at the Indices Used in the Study of Social Change in Colonial Africa." *Current Anthropology* 12 (October–December 1971) 431.

Maguire, Daniel. *Moral Absolutes and the Magisterium*. Washington and Cleveland: Corpus Papers, 1970.

Malina, Bruce. "Does *Porneia* Mean Fornication?" *Novum Testamentum* 14 (1972) 10–17.

Malinowski, Bronislaw. *A Scientific Theory of Culture and Other Essays*. New York: Oxford University Press, 1960.

Marie-André du Sacré-Coeur. *The Household Stands Firm: Family Life in West Africa*. Milwaukee: Bruce, 1962.

Marrou, Irenée. "The Church and Greek and Roman Civilization." Translated by John Griffiths. *Church History in Future Perspective*, Concilium 57. New York: Herder and Herder, 1970.

Mayr, Ernst. *Animal Species and Evolution*. Cambridge: Harvard University Press, 1966.

Mbiti, John. *African Religions and Philosophy*. New York and Washington: Praeger, 1969.

Mboya, Tom. *Freedom and After*. London: Andre Deutsch, 1963.

McCormick, Richard. "Notes on Moral Theology: Specificity of Christian Morality." *Theological Studies* 42 (1970) 71–78.

McDonagh, Enda. "Towards a Christian Theology of Morality." *Irish Theological Quarterly* 37 (July 1970) 188–189.

McEniery, Peter. "Divorce at the Council of Trent." *The Australasian Catholic Record* 167 (1970) 188–201.

McGavran, Donald A., ed. "Polygamy and Church Growth." *Church Growth Bulletin* 5 (March 1969) 59–60, 66–68.

McHugh, James T., ed. *Marriage in the Light of Vatican II*. Washington: Family Life Bureau, U.S.C.C., 1968.

McKenzie, John L. *Dictionary of the Bible*. Milwaukee: Bruce, 1965.

———. *The Power and the Wisdom*. Milwaukee: Bruce, 1965.

———. "Q.E.D." *The Critic* 29 (November–December 1970) 95.

Melanchton, P. *Corpus Reformatorum*. Edited by C.G. Bretschneider. Halis Saxonum: C.A. Schwetschke et Filium, 1835; London and New York: Johnson Reprint Corporation, 1963. Volume II.

Mendelsohn, I. "The Family in the Ancient Near East." *The Biblical Archeologist* 11 (February 1948) 25.

Messmer, Sebastian G., ed. *The Works of John England*. 5 vols. Cleveland: Arthur H. Clark Co., 1908. Volume V.

Metz, Johannes B. "Religion and Society in the Light of Political Theology." *Harvard Theological Review* 61 (October 1968).

Migne, J.P., ed. *Patrologia Graeca*. Paris, 1857–1866.

———, ed. *Patrologia Latina*. Paris, 1844.

Milhaven, John Giles. *Towards a New Catholic Morality*. Garden City, N.Y.: Doubleday, 1970.

Mills, Jerome. "The Council of Trent on the Permanence of Marriage." *Resonance* 3 (Spring 1967) 35–47.

Molinski, Waldemar. "Marriage: Institution and Sacrament." *Sacramentum Mundi: An Encyclopedia of Theology*. Edited by Karl Rahner and others. New York: Herder and Herder, 1969.

Monden, Louis. *Sin, Liberty and Law*. New York: Sheed and Ward, 1965.

Montagu, Ashley. *Man's Most Dangerous Myth: The Fallacy of Race*. New York and Cleveland: World Publishing Co., 1964.

Morris, Philip D., ed. *Metropolis: Christian Presence and Responsibility*. Notre Dame, Ind.: Fides, 1970.

Mruk, Antonius M. "Singularis opinio Gerardi Odonis, O.F.M. circa naturam divortii in casu adulterii." *Gregorianum* 41 (1960) 273–283.

Murdock, George P. *Africa: Its Peoples and Their Cultures*. New York, Toronto, London: McGraw-Hill, 1959.

———. *Social Structure*. London: Collier-Macmillan, 1949; New York: The Free Press, 1965.

Needd, Moya. "Many Favor Polygamy." *Daily Nation* (Nairobi), December 1, 1967, p. 1.

Neill, Stephen. *Call to Mission.* Philadelphia: Fortress Press, 1970.

———. *Christian Faith and Other Faiths: The Christian Dialogue with Other Religions.* 2nd edition. London: Oxford University Press, 1970.

———. *A History of Christian Missions.* Harmondsworth: Penguin Books, 1964.

Newbigin, Lesslie. *The Finality of Christ.* Richmond, Va.: John Knox Press; London: SCM Press, 1969.

———. *Honest Religion for Secular Man.* London: SCM Press, 1966.

Newing, Edward G. "The Baptism of Polygamous Families: Theory and Practice in an East African Church." *Journal of Religion in Africa* 2 (1970) 130–141.

Niebuhr, Reinhold. *Moral Man and Immoral Society.* New York: Charles Scribner's Sons, 1959.

———. *The Structure of Nations and Empires.* New York: Charles Scribner's Sons, 1959.

Niebuhr, H. Richard. *The Social Sources of Denominationalism.* Cleveland and New York: World Publishing Co., 1957.

Nimkoff, M.F. *Comparative Family Systems.* Boston: Houghton Mifflin, 1965.

Noonan, John T. Jr. *Contraception: A History of Its Treatment by the Catholic Theologians and Canonists.* Cambridge: Harvard University Press, 1965.

———. "Freedom, Experimentation, and Permanence in the Canon Law of Marriage." *Law for Liberty: The Role of Law in the Church Today.* Edited by James E. Biechler. Baltimore: Helicon, 1967.

———. "Indissolubility of Marriage and Natural Law." *The American Journal of Jurisprudence* 14 (1969) 92–94.

———. "Making One's Own Act Another's." *The Catholic Theological Society of America: Proceedings of the 27th Annual Convention,* 27 (1972) 33 ff.

Nyerere, Julius. *Hotuba ya Rais wa Jamhuri katika Baraza Kuu la Taifa, Tarihe 10 Desemba, 1962.* Dar es Salaam: Tanzania Government Printer, 1962.

O'Callaghan, Denis. "Theology and Divorce." *The Irish Theological Quarterly* 37 (July 1970) 217.

Okpaku, Joseph O. "Let's Dare to be African." *Africa Report* 13 (October 1968) 13 ff.

Oosthuizen, G.C. *Post-Christianity in Africa: A Theological and Anthropological Study.* London: C. Hurst and Co., 1968.

Oraison, Marc. *Learning to Love.* Translated by Andre Humbert. New York: Hawthorn Books, 1955.

O'Shea, W.T. "Marriage and Divorce: The Biblical Evidence." *The Australasian Catholic Record* 167 (1970) 90.

Otterbein, Keith F. "Marquesan Polyandry." *Marriage, Family, and Residence.* Edited by Paul Bohannan and John Middleton. Garden City, N.Y.: The Natural History Press, 1968.

Parrinder, E.G. *The Bible and Polygamy.* London: S.P.C.K., 1950.

Paul VI. "Africae Terrarum." *Acta Apostolicae Sedis* 59 (1967) 1073–1097. English translation in *African Ecclesiastical Review* 10 (January 1968).

Paulme, Denise, ed. *Women in Tropical Africa.* Translated by H.M. Wright. London: Routledge and Kegan Paul, 1963.

Perbal, Albert. "L'Ethnologie et les missionaires." *Rythmes du Monde* 5 (1950) 3–4.

Peter, Carl. "Auricular Confession and the Council of Trent." *The Catholic Theological Society of America: Proceedings of 22nd Annual Convention* 22 (1967) 191.

Philipps, Arthur, ed. *Survey of African Marriage and Family Life.* London and New York: Oxford University Press for the International African Institute, 1953.

Phillips, John. *Agriculture and Ecology in Africa: A Study of Actual and Potential Development in Africa South of the Sahara.* London: Faber and Faber, 1959.

Piper, Otto. *The Biblical View of Sex and Marriage.* New York: Charles Scribner's Sons, 1960.

Pius XI. "Casti Connubii." *Acta Apostolicae Sedis* 22 (1930) 547.

Pius XII. "Divino Afflante Spiritus." *Acta Apostolicae Sedis* 35 (1943) 325–397.

———. "Allocutiones" (to Italian midwives). *Acta Apostolicae Sedis*, 43 (1951) 835–854.

———. "Sacra Virginitas." *Acta Apostolicae Sedis* 46 (1954) 161–191.

———. "Summi Pontificatus." *Acta Apostolicae Sedis* 31 (1939) 413–453.

Plautz, Werner. "Monogamie und Polygynie in Alten Testamenti." *Zeitschrift für die Altestamentliche Wissenschaft* 75 (new vol. 34, 1963) 1–27.

Poikail, John George. "Racist Assumptions of the 19th Century Missionary," *International Review of Mission* 59 (July 1970) 271–284.

Radcliffe-Brown, A.R. and Forde, Daryll, eds. *African Systems of Kinship and Marriage.* London, New York, Toronto: Oxford University Press, 1950.

Rahner, Karl. "Evolution and Original Sin." Translated by Theodore L. Westow *The Evolving World and Theology*, Concilium 26. New York: Paulist Press, 1967.

———, ed. *The Teaching of the Catholic Church as Contained in Her Documents*. Compiled by Heinrich Roos and Joseph Neuner. Translated by Geoffrey Stevens. Cork: Mercier Press, 1967.

——— and Vorgrimler, Herbert. *Theological Dictionary*. Edited by Cornelius Ernst. Translated by Richard Strachar. New York: Herder and Herder, 1965.

———. *God, Christ, Mary and Grace*. Theological Investigations, Volume I. Translated by Cornelius Ernst. London: Darton, Longman and Todd, 1966.

Ramaroson, Leonard. "Une nouvelle interpretation de la 'clausule' du Mt. 19:9." *Science et Esprit* 23 (May–September 1971) 247–251.

Ramsey, Paul. *Fabricated Man: The Ethics of Genetic Control*. New Haven and London: Yale University Press, 1970.

Renckens, Henricus. *Israel's Conception of the Beginnings*. Translated by Charles Napier. New York: Herder and Herder, 1964.

Reyburn, William D. "Polygamy, Economy and Christianity in Eastern Cameroun." *Practical Anthropology* 6 (1959) 1–19; reprinted in *Readings in Missionary Anthropology*. Edited by William A. Smalley. Tarrytown, N.Y.: Practical Anthropology, 1967.

Ringeling, Hermann. "Die biblische Begrundung der Monogamie." *Zeitschrift für Evangelische Ethik*, 10 (January 1966), 81–102.

Ritzer, Korbinian. "Secular Law and the Western Church's Concept of Marriage," in *The Future of Marriage as Institution*. Edited by Franz Böckle. Concilium 55, New York: Herder and Herder, 1970, pp. 69–75.

Robinson, H. Wheeler. *Corporate Personality in Ancient Israel*. Philadelphia: Fortress Press, 1964.

Romaniuk, A. "Infertility in Tropical Africa." In *The Population of Tropical Africa*," edited by John C. Caldwell and Chukuku Okonjo. New York: Columbia University Press, 1968.

Rommen, Heinrich A. *The Natural Law: A Study in Legal and Social History and Philosophy*. Translated by Thomas R. Hanley. St. Louis and London: B. Herder, 1948.

Ryan, Liam. "The Indissolubility of Marriage in Natural Law." *Irish Theological Quarterly* 30 (1963), 293–310; 31 (1964) 62–77.

Sabourin, Leopold. "Notes and Views: The Divorce Clauses" *Biblical Theology Bulletin* 2 (February 1972) 80–86.

Salacuse, J.F. "Developments in African Law." *Africa Report* 13 (March 1968), 39–42.

Santin, Carlos. "The Law of the Kings: A Study of Deuteronomy XVII: 14–20." Master's Thesis, Baptist Theological Seminary, Ruschlikon-Zurich, April 1969.

Sarpi, Paolo. *History of Benefices and Selections from History of the Council of Trent.* Edited and translated by Peter Burke. New York: Washington Square Press, 1967.

Sarpong, Peter. As quoted by Desmond O'Grady, "The Church in Africa: Coming into Its Own." *U.S. Catholic* 38 (February 1973) 32.

Schaff, P. and others, eds. *A Selected Library of Nicene and Post-Nicene Fathers of the Christian Church.* 1st series, 14 volumes. Grand Rapids, Mich.: William B. Eerdmans, 1956. Volume XIII.

———. *A Selected Library of Nicene and Post-Nicene Fathers of the Christian Church.* 2nd series, 14 volumes. Oxford, 1890–1900. Volume VI.

Schaumberger, Johannes B. "Propter quale peccatum morte punitus sit Onan?" *Biblica* 8 (1927) 212.

Schillebeeckx, Edward. *God the Future of Man.* Translated by N.D. Smith. New York: Sheed and Ward, 1968.

———. *Marriage: Secular Reality and Saving Mystery.* Translated by N.D. Smith. London: Sheed and Ward, 1965.

Schleck, Charles A. *The Sacrament of Matrimony: A Dogmatic Study.* Milwaukee: Bruce, 1964.

Schnackenburg, Rudolf. *The Moral Teaching of the New Testament.* Translated by J. Holland-Smith and W.J. O'Hara. New York and London: Herder and Herder, Burns and Oates, 1965.

Schoonenberg, Piet. *God's World in the Making.* Translated by Walter van de Putte. Pittsburgh: Duquesne University Press, 1964.

Schroeder, Henry J., ed. *Disciplinary Decrees of the General Councils.* Translated by H.J. Schroeder. St. Louis: B. Herder, 1937.

Schüller, Bruno. "What Ethical Principles Are Universally Valid?" *Theology Digest* 19 (Spring 1971), 25–26.

Schuyler, J.B. "Conceptions of Christianity in the Context of Tropical Africa: Nigerian Reactions to Its Advent." *Christianity in Tropical Africa.* Edited by C.G. Bäeta. London: Oxford University Press, 1968.

Schwab, William B. "Urbanism Corporate Groups and Culture Change in Africa below the Sahara." *Anthropological Quarterly* 43 (July 1970) 187–214.

Senghor, L.S. "What is Negritude?" As quoted by Joseph Gremillion. *The Other Dialogue.* Garden City, N.Y.: Doubleday, 1965.

Shaner, Donald W. *A Christian View of Divorce.* Leiden: E.J. Brill, 1969.

Sherrard, Philip. "The Sexual Relationship in Christian Thought." *Studies in Comparative Religion* 5 (Summer 1971) 153–161.

Simon, R. "Spécificité de l'éthique Chrétienne." *Le Supplément de la Vie Spirituelle* 23 (February 1970).

Skinner, Elliot. "Christianity and Islam among the Mossi." *American Anthropologist* 60 (December 1958) 1002–1119.

Snoek, Jaime. "Marriage and the Institutionalization of Sexual Relations." Translated by Paul Burns. *The Future of Marriage as Institution.* Concilium 55. New York: Herder and Herder, 1970.

Southall, Aidan, ed. *Social Change in Modern Africa.* London, New York, Toronto: Oxford University Press, 1961.

Spencer, Paul. *The Samburu.* London: Routledge and Kegan Paul, 1965.

Stendahl, Krister. *The Bible and the Role of Women.* Translated by Emilie T. Sander. Philadelphia: Fortress Press, 1966.

Tacitus. "Germania," 18. *Tacitus on Britain and Germany.* Translated by H. Mattingly. Harmondsworth: Penguin Books, 1948.

Talbot, C.H., ed. and trans. *The Anglo-Saxon Missionaries in Germany.* London and New York: Sheed and Ward, 1954.

Tanner, Ralph E.S. *Transition in African Beliefs.* Maryknoll, N.Y.: Maryknoll Publications, 1967.

"Tanzania Debates Polygamy." *Christian Science Monitor*, October 27, 1969, p. 2.

Tanzania Government. *Mapendekezo ya Serikali juu ya Sheria ya Ndoa.* Dar es Salaam: Government Printer, September 1, 1969.

———. *Preliminary Results of the Population Census Taken in August 1967.* Dar es Salaam: Government Printer, 1967.

Tasker, R.V.G. *The Gospel according to St. Matthew: An Introduction and Commentary.* Grand Rapids, Mich.: Eerdmans, 1961.

Taylor, John V. *The Primal Vision.* London: SCM Press, 1963.

Taylor, Vincent. *The Gospel according to St. Mark.* 2nd edition. London: Macmillan; New York: St. Martin's Press, 1966.

Thiel, Josef Franz. "The Institution of Marriage: An Anthropological Perspective." Translated by John Griffiths. *The Future of Marriage as Institution*, Concilium 55. New York: Herder and Herder, 1970.

Thielicke, Helmut. *The Ethics of Sex.* Translated by John W. Doberstein. New York: Harper and Row, 1964.

Tillich, Paul. *Theology of Culture.* New York: Oxford University Press, 1964.

Tippett, Alan. "Polygamy as a Missionary Problem: The Anthropological Issues." *Church Growth Bulletin* 5 (March 1969) 60–63.

Troeltsch, Ernst. *Christian Thought.* London: Unversity of London Press, 1923.

Turner, Harold W. "Monogamy: A Mark of the Church?" *International Review of Mission* 55 (July 1966) 313–321.

Ullmann, Walter. *Medieval Papalism*. London: Methuen, 1949.

United Nations Economic Commission for Africa. "Polygamy, the Family and Urban Phenomenon." *Workshop on Urban Problems: The Role of Women in Urban Development*. United Nations Document, mimeographed, E/CN,14/URB/6,25 (July 1963).

van Iersel, Bas. "The Normative Anthropology of the Gospel." Translated by David Smith. *Man in a New Society*, Concilium 75. New York: Herder and Herder, 1972.

Van Wing, J. "Polygamy in the Belgian Congo." *Africa* 17 (April 1947).

von Allmen, J.J., ed. *A Companion to the Bible*. Translated by P.J. Allcock and others. New York: Oxford University Press, 1958.

Vass, George. "Divorce and Remarriage in the Light of Recent Publications." *Heythrop Journal* 11 (1970) 259–260.

Vatican II. "Decree on Ecumenism." "Decree on the Missionary Activity of the Church." "Dogmatic Constitution on the Church." "Pastoral Constitution on the Church in the Modern World." *Documents of Vatican II*. Edited by Walter M. Abbott and Joseph Gallagher. New York: Guild Press, America Press, Association Press, 1966.

Vawter, Bruce. *The Four Gospels*. Garden City, N.Y.: Doubleday, 1967.

Vischer, Lucas. "Reform of Canon Law—An Ecumenical Problem." *The Jurist* 26 (October 1966) 400 ff.

Vollebregt, G.N. *The Bible and Marriage*. Translated by R.A. Downie. London: Sheed and Ward, 1965.

von Pastor, Ludwig F. *The History of the Popes*. London: 1929–1953. Volume X.

von Rad, Gerhard. *Genesis: A Commentary*. Translated by John H. Marks. London: SCM Press; Philadelphia: Westminster Press, 1961.

Vorgrimler, H. "Polygamie." *Lexicon für Theologie und Kirche*. Edited by Michael Buchberger and others. 10 volumes. Freiburg: Herder, 1957–1965.

Watson, Gerard. "Pagan Philosophy and Christian Ethics." *Morals, Law and Authority*. Edited by J.P. Mackey. Dublin: Gill and Macmillan, 1969.

Weber, Leonhard M. *On Marriage, Sex and Virginity*. Translated by R. Brennan. Freiburg: Herder, 1966.

Wellbourn, F.W. *East African Rebels: A Study of Some Independent Churches*. London: SCM Press, 1961.

Wellman, Carl. "The Ethical Implications of Cultural Relativity." *The Journal of Philosophy* 60 (March 28, 1963) 169–184.

Westermann, Claus. *The Genesis Accounts of Creation*. Translated by Norman E. Wagner. Philadelphia: Fortress Press, 1964.

Westermarck, Edward. *The History of Human Marriage.* 3 volumes. New York: Allerton Book Co., 1922.

Williamson, S.G. *Akan Religion and the Christian Faith.* Accra: Ghana University Press, 1965.

Wilson, Monica. *Good Company: A Study of Nyakyusa Age-Villages.* London, New York, Toronto: Oxford University Press, 1951.

Wright, J.S. and Thompson J.T. "Marriage." *The New Bible Dictionary.* Edited by J.D. Douglas. London: The Inter-Varsity Fellowship, 1962.

Yadin, Yigael. "L'attitude essénienne envers la polygamie et le divorce." *Revue Biblique* 79 (January 1972) 98–100.

INDEX

Abraham: 221
Adam: 147
Adultery: 124, 125, 139, 143, 146, 158, 159, 162, 183, 193, 194, 219, 223, 225
Aeschylus: 186
Ajayi, A.J. Ade.: 56
Akan: 95
Alexander III (Pope): 19
Altitudo: 27, 28
Anathema: 227, 228, 229
Anthropology: 7, 10, 25, 31, 51, 57, 62, 70, 192
Apologetics: 187, 196
Aquinas, Thomas (Saint): 9, 24, 31, 48, 73, 180–182, 184, 196, 197, 203, 204
Arnobius: 71
Athenagoras: 71
Augustine (Saint): 17, 21, 22, 24, 25, 180, 196, 223
Augustine of Canterbury (Saint): 23, 25
Ayandale, E.A.: 56

Bantu: 117
Baptism: viii, 7, 31, 32, 33, 34, 35, 192, 193, 198, 199, 200, 204, 205, 206
Barrett, David B.: 87
Barth, Karl: 139, 179, 198–199
Batem: 91, 92
Bartoccetti, Vittorio: 186
Belloc, Hilaire: 52
Benedict, Ruth: 59
Berger, Peter: 48, 62
Bethrothal: 92

Bible: 8, 139; interpreted literally, 11, 254, 260, 267, 296
Blenkinsopp, Joseph: 141–142
Bohannan, Paul: 120, 121–122, 123, 125–126
Boniface (Saint): 23
Bremen Mission: 33
Bucer, Martin: 220–221
Buijs, Professor Louis: 199–200
Buthelezi, Manas: 188

Cain: 143
Cajetan, Cardinal: 166, 223–225
Calvin: 182, 226
Canon. *See* Law.
Cash: 95
Catholic (Roman Church): 4, 27, 30, 182, 199, 217, 228, 230–231, 232
Catholicity: 3, 4, 30, 69, 207
Celibates: vii, 21, 164, 220
Cephas: 4
Christ: vii, 36–37, 73, 139, 140, 141, 149, 155, 168, 203
Christian: attitudes toward slavery, 28, 48, 184–185, 196; conscience, 75; conversion, 195; early, Church, 67; evangelized polygamist as quasi-, 205; leaven in the Western world, 196, 222; methodology, 69; norm as independent of the Western Church, 207; obtuseness in missionary activity, 50–54; people facing poverty as a moral issue, 191; solutions to moral problems, 9, 16; tensions

Dar es Salaam Committee of Churches: 36
Damascus Document of Qumran: 143
David: 221
De Nobili, Robert: 54
de Vaux, Roland: 144
de Vio, Thomas. See Cajetan, Cardinal.
Dialogue with Typho: 20
Diocletian: 21
Dispensation: 182
Dissolution: 28–29
Divorce: and the law of Moses, 160; as social shock, viii; authorized, 29; Bible and, viii; categorized with polygamy, 56; correlation between social change and rate of, 124; Council of Trent's canon on, 218–219; grounds for, 218–219; increasing frequency of, in the West, 113; Jesus' teaching on, 156; justification of, 157–158; legally possible under fixed conditions, 122; polygyny and, 145; problem of, 68; rabbinic argument against, 150; repudiation of, 139, 162; simultaneous polygamy as an alternative to, and remarriage, 223; tendency toward, 183
Dodd, C.H.: 67
Dorjahn: 91
Dubos, René: 64
Dunstan, Gordon R.: 153
Durandus, William: 222

Eastern Church: vii
Ecumenical outlook: 70
Eliot, T.S.: 109
Elkanah; 146, 187
England, Bishop John: 185
Epistula ad Diognetem: 20, 69
Erasmus, Desiderius: 224
Esau: 161
Ethics: 8, 53, 70, 71, 72, 195, 199

in relation to culture, 48–49, 66–67, 68; understanding of marriage, 26; universalism, 69; witness, 75
Chrysostom (Saint): 166
Circumcision: debates in early Christian Church, 51; in Pauline theology, 165
Clement VII (Pope): 224
Colenso, Bishop John of Natal: 31–32
Community: 112
Concubinage: 11, 21, 28, 101, 124, 194
Congar, Yves: 8, 219
Constantine: 71
Constitutio Piana: 29
Contract: 197
Conversion (to Christianity): 195
Council of Florence: viii
Council of Toledo: 28
Council of Trent: 24–25, 217–220, 226–232
Covenant: vii, viii, 143, 147, 153, 168–169
Crossan, Dominic: 162–163
Culture: as conditioner, 59; as human achievement, 58; as humanizer of individuals, 58; Christianity and, 4, 49; concept of progress in, 64–66; definition of, 57; differences in, 60–66; diversity of, 48; divorce in context of, viii, 60; evolution of, 61–62; marriage values dependent upon, 188–189; obtuseness of, 50–57; patterns of, 58; relationships sanctioned by tribal, 194; sensitivity to and learning from an alien, 55, 60; study of, 7; taken seriously, 49, 51; Western arrogance regarding, 52, 56, 207
Curran, Charles E.: 197, 231
Custom: plurality of wives as a, 223; sins against, according to Augustine, 180
Cyprian (Saint): 71

Ethnocentrism: 7, 31, 49–50, 52, 182, 186
Etiological: 154
Exegesis: 7, 142, 149, 156, 157, 179
Ezekiel: 147

Faith: vii, 204, 205, 222, 229, 232
Family: 110–11i, 114–119, 121, 122, 123, 144–145
Faustus: 223
Fertility: 123–125, 145
Fidelity: vii, 203
First Vatican Council: 227
Firth, Raymond: 66
Flexibility: 23, 229, 230
Fox, Robin: 110
Fransen, Piet: 218–219, 226, 228
Fuchs, Josef: 6, 8, 9, 27, 73–74, 183–184, 201, 202, 206,, 208

Genesis: 150, 152, 155, 158
Gikuyu: 91, 116, 118
God: vii, viii, ix, 73, 193, 203, 204
Goethe: 186
Gospel: viii, ix, 141, 192, 198, 204, 205
Grace: 73, 204
Greco-Roman: attitudes, 19, 25; culture, 21, 30, 67, 141; law and tradition, 21, 166; world, 20, 25, 167
Greco-Teutonic mythology: 186
Gregory the Great (Pope Saint): 23, 25–26
Gregory II (Pope); 21–22
Gregory XIII (Pope): 29
Greece: culture of ancient, 65, 219
Grelot, Pierre: 155

Hanin, R.E.: 90
Hannah: 146, 187
Häring, Bernard: 6, 51, 53, 163–164, 183, 187, 195
Hausa: 100
Henry VIII (king of England): 24, 221, 224
Hillel: 157, 158, 160

Hillman, Eugene: ix
Homosexuality: 125, 140
Human: 63–66, 202–203, 230. See also Nature (human).
Hunter, Guy: 101

Idowu, Professor Bolaji: 52
Illegitimate children: 91–92
Incarnation: principle of, 67, 74
Indissolubility of marriage: vii, 139, 141, 146, 154, 155, 156–157, 158, 160, 161, 162, 181–182, 192, 220
Individuality: 112, 113, 187
Intercourse. See Sex.
Innocent III (Pope): 7, 24, 26, 182, 225–226
Isaac: 180

Jacob: 146, 161, 180, 187
Janssen, R.M..: 117
Jedin, Hubert: 226
Jeremiah: 147, 169
Jerome (Saint): 166
Jews: and polygamy, 20–21, 140, 163, 165, 166; and their culture, 67–68; and their view of marriage, 161–162, 163, 165; tensions between Christians and, 28; who became Christians, 166, 167
Josephus: 20
Justin Martyr: 20

Kaka: 120
Kenyatta, Jomo: 50, 51, 56, 91, 113, 116
Kerns, Joseph: 26
Kibira, Bishop Josiah: 37
Kinship: and polygamy, 124; marriage and, 109–114, 145, 152, 153, 154, 189
Koko: 96
Kosnik, Anthony: 156

Laban: 161
Lambeth Conference: 32–33

Language: 59–60
Law: canon, 8, 9, 20, 182, 217,
    223–224, 226–227, 228–229, 232;
    divine, 199, 221, 223, 227,
    229–231, 232; natural, 24, 47–48,
    180–185, 197–198, 199, 202–203,
    207–208, 223, 227; Mosaic, 145,
    146, 157, 160, 161, 162, 163, 164,
    165, 222; Roman, 19, 20, 30, 68
Legalism: x, 192, 198, 200
Legislation regarding polygamy:
    98–99
Lepp, Igance: 186
Leslie, Gerald: 21, 92
Levirate: 121, 163, 164
Levi-Strauss, Claude: 59, 62, 123
Lex Antoniana de Civitate: 20
London, Bishop of: 184
Lonergan, Bernard: 112, 116, 207
Love: as an end of marriage, 181;
    priority of the law of, 199, 231;
    psychology of, 186–189; roman-
    tic, 125
Lowie, Robert: 61
Lust as motivation for polygamy:
    180, 223
Luther, Martin: 24, 220, 221–222,
    223, 224, 226

Maguire, Daniel: 9, 25
Mali: 100
Malinowski, Bronislaw: 11, 58
Marriage: according to Genesis in-
    terpretations, 149–155; and cul-
    tural accommodation, 6, 18,
    167, 188–189, 202–203, 207–208,
    232; and family stability, viii; as
    belonging to Western culture,
    6–7, 113, 206; as sacrament, 26,
    203; as social instrument,
    144–145; Christian and pagan,
    in the early Church, 19, 20, 25,
    68, 225; contractual basis of, 11,
    22; Council of Trent's canons
    on, 218–219, 228–229; current
    Western understanding of, 113;

ethics and, 6; group, 11; in con-
    nection with the legitimacy of
    children, 11; kinship and,
    113–114, 117–118; love and,
    125–126, 186–189; New Testa-
    ment teaching on, 30, 139–140,
    158, 168, 179, 192, 229; Old Tes-
    tament teaching on, 140,
    143–149, 168; permanence in a
    polygamous, 122; plural, 9, 11,
    19–20, 232; problem of what
    constitutes a valid, 19, 22, 180,
    181; purpose of, 19, 26, 141,
    180, 181, 183, 188–189; regula-
    tions for dissolution of, 28
Masai: 92, 94, 112, 117, 119
Masturbation: 164
Maximian: 21
Mayr, Ernest: 151, 152
Mbiti, John: 56, 109, 118–119, 127
Mboya, Tom: 47, 51
McKenzie, John L.: 7, 139, 152
Melanchthon, Philip: 24, 217,
    221–222, 224, 226
Mellitus: 23
Middle Ages: 7, 8, 184
Milhaven, John Giles: 29, 72
Minucius: 71
Monden, Louis: 230
Montagu, Ashley: 82
Morality: 8–9, 65, 70, 72, 73, 185,
    197, 202, 206
Morgenroth, Anton: 203
Mortality rates: 89–90, 115–116,
    189
Moses. See Law, Mosaic.

Nature (human): 9, 207. See also
    Law, natural.
Nazism: 73
Neill, Stephen: 51
Newbigin, Lesslie: 47, 195–196
Nicholas I (Pope): 19
Niebuhr, Reinhold: 184
Noonan, John T., Jr.: 29
Nuer: 121

Nyakyusa: 91, 119
Nyerere, Julius: 51

O'Callaghan, Denis: 187, 202, 206
Odonis, Gerard: 223
Okpaku, Joseph: 56
Onan: 164
Oraison, Marc: 186
Origen: 71
O'Shea, W.T.: 141

Pastoral Constitution on the Church in the Modern World: 55
Paul (Saint): 4, 18, 54, 67, 141, 164–169, 196
Paul III (Pope): 27, 28, 226
Paul VI (Pope): 87
Pauline privilege: 27
Paulme, Denise: 126–127
Perbal, Albert: 4
Peter: 204
Peter, Carl: 226, 228
Pharisaism: 194, 200
Pharisees: 141, 156, 157, 160, 161, 162
Philip of Hesse: 24, 221, 226, 229
Piper, Otto: 141, 187
Pius XI (Pope): 217
Pius V (Pope): 28
Pius XII (Pope): 4, 26, 29, 228
Plato; 186
Plautz, Werner: 148–149
Pluralism: in societies and cultures, 99, 201; of expression, vii
Plurality of God's people: 148, 168, 203
Polyandry: 10–11, 139, 180–181, 186
Polygamy: definition of, 10, 11
Polygenesis: 151–152
Polygyny: definition of, 10, 11
Populis: 29
Primitive (as description of culture): 60, 61–62
Privilege (of the faith): 27–28, 29, 30, 226

Prostitution: 21, 89, 124, 140, 167

Qumran. See Damascus Document of Qumran.

Rachel: 147, 187
Radcliffe-Brown, A.R.: 114, 125
Rahner, Karl: 151, 226
Ramaroson, Leonard: 158–159
Ramsey, Paul: 63
Ranke, Leopold von: 62
Rationalization (in moral theologizing): 12
Reformation: 182, 221, 222, 226–227, 229, 231
Relativity: moral, 48, 202; of thought, 47, 181
Revelation: 74, 182, 225
Ricci, Matteo: 54
Ring (as sign of betrothal and contract): 19
Ringeling, Hermann: 148, 155
Roman: authority, 165, 167; custom, 19, 25–26, 28; law, 19, 30, 68; rite, 19, 146–147
Romani Pontificis: 28
Ryan, Liam: 48

Sadducees: 164
Santin, Carlos: 145
Sarpong, Peter; 37–38
Scandal: 192–195, 199
Schillebeeckx, Edward: 20, 22, 24, 26, 139, 140, 146, 152–153, 160, 166, 218–219, 229
Schism: 4
Schnackenburg, Rudolf: 156
Scholasticism: 7, 26, 182
Schoonenberg, Piet: 149
Schopenauer, Arthur: 186
Second Vatican Council: 3, 4, 5, 6, 10, 55, 69, 208, 231
Senghor, L.S.; 52
Sex: psychology of, 186–188; purpose of, 25–27, 122, 145; regulation of, 70–71, 91, 122–123
Shammai: 157, 160, 162

Slavery: 48, 65, 69, 75, 180–181, 184–185, 192, 196–197, 231
Snoek, C.J.: 110
Social: structure as necessary for human existence, 111; structures of African society, 113, 116; structures of Western society, 113–114
Sociological conjecture regarding polygamy: 190–191
Southall, Aidan: 101
Springer, Robert; 142
Stoicism: 68
Stoic view of sex: 25
Synod of Elvira: 20

Tertullian: 71
Theodoret of Cyr: 166
Theodosius: 21, 221
Theological interpretations of polygamy: viii, 7, 24, 25, 26, 27, 141, 142, 179–208
Thielicke, Helmut: 186, 198
Tiberius, Bishop of; 225
Troeltsch, Ernst: 52–53

Universal: nature of the Church, 5, 69; norms, 188, 202, 207
Urban areas of Africa: 96–97, 99–100, 191

Valentinus (Emperor): 221
Valid. See Marriage.
van de Walle, Etienne: 93
Vass, George: 161
Vawter, Bruce: 158
Venn, Henry: 32
Vischer, Lukas: 230
von Allmen, Jean Jacques: 141, 168
von Rad, Gerhard: 154

Wealth: 92–93, 119
Weber, Leonhard: 190
Westermann, Claus: 142
Western: Christianity, 3, 26, 169, 201; culture and orientations of

life, ix, xi, 26, 61, 124, 142, 169, 185–186, 187, 189, 190, 201, 207, 208
Wilson, Monica: 119, 125
Womanhood: African attitudes toward, 30, 189; historico-cultural attitudes toward, 25, 186, 197

Yahweh: viii, 143, 147, 168–169
Yoruba: 100, 124

Zulu: 121